DATE DUE

DEMCO, INC. 38-2931

Economic

Institutions and

Human Welfare

John Maurice Clark

COLUMBIA UNIVERSITY

Economic

Institutions and

Human Welfare

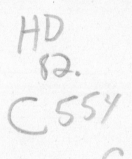

Alfred A. Knopf

NEW YORK   1957

L. C. catalog card number: 57–5796

© *John Maurice Clark, 1957*

THIS IS A BORZOI BOOK,
PUBLISHED BY ALFRED A. KNOPF, INC.

FIRST EDITION

Preface

This collection of essays deals not with economics in the technical sense, but with some of the human and community factors that underlie it. The subject matter of technical economics consists of the operations of what we call, for short, "the market." But the market operates in a community setting; and these essays deal with some of the elements that go to make up this setting. These include enabling attitudes, institutions, and mechanisms, without which the things we call economic laws or principles would not work; and the standards of value or conceptions of welfare, and the motivations and ethical standards that work toward making these conceptions of welfare effective. Without these, it would be very nearly a matter of chance whether the operations of the market were serviceable or destructive in their net effect on the values by which a community lives.

One section of the essays attempts to define a concept of welfare which the author hopes would command assent; and to come to grips with the question whether modern

types of welfare policies are in conflict with the necessary conditions for a healthy and adequate sphere of economic freedom. The conclusion reached is that there are
problems, perhaps dangers, but no irreconcilable conflict.
The result is conceived as a "balanced economy." The balance between social and private forces is not fixed, but is
conceived as an evolutionary process of creative adaptation,
operating in the area intermediate between total *laissez
faire,* in which the "market" takes charge of what should
be community values, and total collectivism, in which market concepts are reduced to accounting devices, manipulated by the government for its own ends, which in such a
system appear destined to be undemocratic. The author's
contention is that, for a humane and democratically conceived society, all tolerable economic systems lie in this intermediate area.

The essays here reprinted or adapted were written during the period from 1940 through 1955, but the major portion belongs to the last few years of this period, and the
final chapter, while utilizing fragments of published material, is virtually a fresh composition. The essays were ad-
dressed to various audiences. Two were prepared for religious bodies studying social and economic questions. Two
deal with educational questions, one for a general work and
one for a committee of the American Economic Association. Two were based on lectures on Economic Ethics, de-
livered for the Kazanjian Foundation to university audiences not limited to economists. Had this subject not been
specified by the Foundation, the author might not have
had the hardihood to write specifically on it. His paper for
the Columbia University Bicentennial Conference No. III
is here divided into three chapters. In general, the essays
presuppose in the reader some knowledge of economics, but
they are not written exclusively for the specialist.

In editing the selections for republication, problems

were presented by statements referring in the present tense to happenings now past, and more serious problems where changing conditions have altered the aspect or emphasis of a problem—the outstanding example being the changing aspect of the problem of high-level economic activity and employment from 1940 to the period just before the Korean War, and again to the period of the early fifties. This shifting perspective adds force to the suggestion that all economic treatises should be dated in their titles. After venturing, in Chapter 12, into the relevance of Western or American experience and theory for the struggle between free and Communist systems for the minds of the uncommitted portions of the world, the author sees added force in the further idea of geographical and cultural identification of economic writings. In adapting these essays to changes wrought by time, the author has followed no one method; sometimes leaving the original unchanged and reminding the reader of its date in a footnote, sometimes altering a phrase and sometimes rewriting more extensively. The section on competition, in Chapter 7, has been shortened, being disproportionately long in the original, and covering ground that the author hopes to treat more fully in a future volume.

In the title of Chapter 10, originally published as "The Interplay of Politics and Economics," the author has restored his original word, "Interpenetration," feeling that, at a cost of three extra syllables, it more accurately expresses the way in which these disciplines reach into one another's structure. Finally, no attempt has been made to eliminate all overlapping between the various selections, though a few cross references have been inserted.

Thanks are due to the publishers who have kindly given permission for the use of the materials, some of which are now out of print and unavailable. To the many writers whose thinking has contributed to the shaping of the ideas here expressed, no really adequate acknowledgment is possible. The author merely expresses in general terms an indebtedness which is immeasurable.

JOHN MAURICE CLARK

Westport, Connecticut
July, 1956

Contents

Economic

Institutions and

Human Welfare

CHAPTER ONE

Economics and Education for Citizenship: Problems of an Era of Transition

Economic systems and economic policy are in an era of transition, and the discipline of economics is in a corresponding transitional state. As a result, the problem what to attempt in teaching the subject is one of peculiar difficulty. What is here undertaken is limited to outlining the nature of the situation in which this discipline finds itself and making some provisional suggestions as to the more general objectives. The traditional "economic laws" are not wholly obsolete, but they can no longer be presented as representing the dominant tendencies of the actual economic system now existing. And new materials are pressing for a place in the recognized canon of the subject, but have not yet been digested, seasoned and tested sufficiently to warrant presenting them as definitively established truths. To these conditions the teaching of economics must somehow adapt itself,

Adapted by permission from "The Role of Economics" in *Education for Citizenship Responsibilities,* Franklin S. Burdette, ed. (Princeton, N.J.: Princeton University Press, 1942), pp. 31–8.

even at those levels that have to deal with the adolescent mind.

Very broadly speaking, the economic system used to be presented as a scheme of unplanned co-operation in which "economic laws" automatically convert the self-seeking efforts of individuals into an efficient organization and distribution of the resources of the community. Growing recognition of the shortcomings of the system and of the need for growing measures of public intervention have for some time changed the character of this picture until, in some forms of presentation, the emphasis seems to have become unduly negative and critical, the criticism bearing largely on a system of free and irresponsible self-seeking which is already past or passing and affording too little positive guidance to the constructive responsibilities in which all individuals and groups must share if the economic community of the future is to be built on a healthy basis.

In this period of criticism massed economic power was perhaps typically thought of as residing wholly or mainly in organized "big business," and the emphasis was perhaps too exclusively on reliance on government to redress the balance and to protect the interests of other groups, by measures some of which would have been rejected by an earlier generation as "class legislation." At present, mass economic power has been extended to include organized labor and agriculture; and many groups now have power of this sort, which may be used not only to protect their own interests, but, if their action is not tempered by wise responsibility, to protect them at the expense of the larger interest of the community.

The forces embodied in earlier "economic laws" still set limits on what groups can successfully do in their own interest—and even stricter limits on what can successfully be done in the interest of a just and efficient organization of the economic system. To express their importance in this new setting requires reformulations which have not yet been made, which will not be easy to make, and which probably cannot be made in very precise terms. Pending future progress in the working-out of such standards, it is possible that education can do little more than point to the existence of such limitations and the corresponding responsibility of all groups not to push self-seeking demands to destructive or damaging lengths. There may nowadays be few economic certainties that can be taught with confidence, but one is that a spirit of live-and-let-live between groups has become an absolute necessity if the economic system is to go on working without a breakdown.

The same basic truth may be expressed in a different way. The tendency to rely on government to cure all ills is a part of a tendency to think in terms of economic interests without corresponding duties, and to regard citizenship, with its duties, as primarily or exclusively a political affair. What I have been saying is, in effect, that one's economic dealings are matters of vital community interest and that the obligations of good citizenship apply to them directly and not merely through the medium of the obligation to vote right on political issues in which economic interests are involved. If there is a tendency to dismiss this as "impractical idealism" and to insist that as realists all we can expect is that any individuals or groups will conduct their economic dealings in the spirit of getting as much and giving as little as possible, then there is need to consider what I believe to be a well-nigh demonstrable fact, that that way lies the death of liberty—and not only economic liberty, but also those liberties of thought, expression and criticism which, in a society of democratic ideals, have a more unquestioned standing.

The life of this nation has been lived in a period of great advances in industrial efficiency, liberty, democracy and humanitarianism. We had come to regard these as assured possessions, only to awake to find the first threatened by de-

pression and the last three fighting for their lives against totalitarianism. These advances were made under a system of
free collaboration. Neither the freedom nor the collaboration were at any time perfect, but the system worked. And I
believe that free collaboration expresses the most basic essential of the way of life this country is defending and the
thing which most distinguishes it from the rival systems by
which it is threatened.

During the present generation the conditions and attitudes necessary to the successful co-operation of essentially
free men have undergone one of those shifts of emphasis
which are so far-reaching as to call for a basically changed
attitude and altered philosophy. The nineteenth century had
a philosophy that corresponded with nineteenth-century
conditions imperfectly, but workably. Under that philosophy
co-operation was consistent with freedom by virtue of the
restraints that competitive individualism imposed on individual self-seeking. Beyond a rather elementary common
honesty, and refraining from monopoly, these restraints
were external and objective rather than personal and moral;
and even fairly irresponsible self-seeking received a qualified sort of tolerance.

Now that the restraints of competitive individualism are
increasingly imperfect and inadequate, free collaboration
and irresponsible self-seeking are no longer compatible. If
we are to have collaboration by free men, it must be on the
basis of a spirit of teamwork and a recognized obligation to
co-operate. If irresponsible self-seeking remains the dominant mood, we can have freedom without co-operation—
which means chaos and breakdown—or we can have co-
operation without freedom—which means totalitarianism
in some form. We cannot have both.

I am trusting the reader to recognize that the above
statements are consciously oversimplified and to supply his
own elaborations and qualifications. I have elsewhere stren-

uously contended that freedom is not one thing, but many, and that it may be subjected to many varieties and degrees of control without being destroyed. It is even arguable that we might have a system in which production would be completely collective and there would be no free business enterprise, while the individual remained free in other respects and the system therefore could remain democratic. But there is, I believe, a stronger case for the contrary position: that if every individual were a state employee and every employer an agency of the state, soon the state would no longer have independent citizens, and democracy would thus be fatally undermined. Democracy depends on some independence of status among the citizens, and there is strong reason to believe that this includes some kind and degree of economic independence, not only for the mass of hired workers but for the organizations that employ them.

The essential point is not that we know the answers to this and similar questions, but precisely that we do not know them. Therefore it is not safe to act as if we did, either in legislating on economic questions or in instructing the young. We need to know more than we do about the relations that exist between the various forms of economic liberty and those other kinds of liberty which are more truly personal. The prima facie presumption is that such connections do exist and that economic liberty cannot be abolished without affecting liberties of other sorts. All this brings us back to the importance of maintaining a system under which free men work together and, to that end, of establishing the basic human attitudes of responsibility and teamwork which have in our generation become indispensable necessities if such a system is to maintain itself.

In terms of education for citizenship, these basic attitudes are vastly more important than the particular specific content of factual information or theoretical proposition which may be covered in the courses. These attitudes need to be developed, not by preaching them, as I have perforce been doing in this brief discussion, but by presenting the facts, relationships and processes of the economic system in such fashion as to exhibit the specific ways in which we are dependent on these attitudes to make a free system work. There is no greater present danger than the "realistic" view that freedom means irresponsible self-seeking and nothing else. A behaves responsibly according to his lights. To B, A's behavior *seems* irresponsible because B can see certain interests that A's conduct disregards. What is probably the fatal step comes when B concludes (on insufficient grounds) that the rules of the game are completely unmoral and thereupon deliberately adopts completely unmoral rules for his own future conduct. Successful education for economic citizenship depends on developing citizens who will be forewarned and forearmed against taking this fatal step.

So far I have said nothing of the more specific content of which the body of academic courses must necessarily consist. The body of available material is so vast that the problem becomes one of selection, and of the setting and perspective in which the selected material is to be presented. There are some things every student should learn, but much of the specific content of courses must be optional; and in this area there will, necessarily and properly, be a great deal of experimentation. One of the most general requirements will be a clear distinction between a number of different kinds of material.

First, perhaps come a limited number of general propositions that are true without qualification, or without major qualification, of the actual economic system. Here belong, for example, the "laws of supply and demand," conceived not as statements that demand and supply must inevitably be equal in fact and under all circumstances, but as statements of the character of the dependence of the amount that can be sold on the price charged, plus conditions making for elasticity and for inelasticity, and of the dependence of amounts produced on volume of orders at a price. Here belong also some of the simpler mathematical relations between spending and the resulting flow of incomes, and between total fund of capital and annual rate of capital formation.

Another body of general statements includes those traditional "laws of equilibrium" which are strictly true only under simplified conditions, seldom or never found or closely approximated in fact. These "laws" are still useful, but not as unqualified statements of what actually tends to happen, and this limitation needs to be carefully recognized. The remaining usefulness of such propositions is twofold. They afford help in judging what is likely to happen in actual situations, largely by the process of comparing actual conditions with the simplified ones that are necessary to the "ideal" or "theoretical" result, and in judging the character and importance of the departures to be expected in practice. They also afford an instrument that can be of considerable aid in analyzing actual results into the complex of causes which have combined to produce them.

There is also organized statistical observation and analysis of current processes. Here there is need for some attention to the conditions that are necessary if these processes are to repeat themselves in the future. These limitations can perhaps best be driven home by the help of a setting of historical material, some of which will also be statistical, which warns the student of the omnipresence of change and of the combination of old and new elements of which every historical situation consists. Every crisis affords fresh instances in which new factors can be seen operating to prevent history from repeating itself precisely.

Finally, while the vast variety of concrete situations can by no possibility be covered, there would seem to be an extremely important place for studying some concrete situation in a way that exhibits as much as possible of its complexity and detail. Or perhaps several such situations from different fields could be so treated. One type that should probably be included is a situation in which competition, though "imperfect," still exerts some real force. Another would be some attempt at public control, so treated as to show the complexities and difficulties, the unexpected results and reactions, and the way in which the original problem develops and ramifies. Some attention needs to be paid to the imperfections of the governmental machinery by which controls are necessarily carried out: all serving as a warning against expecting perfect results merely from "passing a law" or setting up a commission.

The type of economics here roughly sketched will not be easy to formulate, or to teach. It will be one in which, while there are fewer certainties than we used to try to inculcate, there still remain some underlying principles. Indoctrination will presumably not disappear, but it will find its soundest basis in the lessons carried by facts. If successful, it will present a system, not all of whose laws can be learned out of books, but in which books afford a starting point and background for a process of progressive understanding that should last a lifetime and for a process of creative contribution to community development in which each genuine citizen should play some part and in which the contribution of each is needed.

Such a program requires, among other things, really wise teachers, and since not all teachers are really wise, many imperfections are to be expected. It will be harder for the teacher than bookish indoctrination—while the student is in the classroom. But if the teacher is thinking of the results after the student leaves the classroom, enduring effects will be easier to secure if the student is not exposed to the experience of finding that the facts he later faces do not agree with the books he has studied, thereby being led to the conclusion that the books were nonsense. It is unsafe to conclude that the modern student, even while he is in the classroom, does not possess some factual background, and a skeptical disposition, that may tend to the discrediting of inapplicable theories. Insofar as the teacher undertakes to present the "unseen" relations as well as the "seen"—and he must do this—the "unseen" needs to be presented in such a way that it does not also appear unreal.

CHAPTER TWO

Economic Means—
To What Ends? A Problem in
the Teaching of Economics

What do students want? Judging by the numbers who flock into courses in economics, there must be either great expectations of what they are going to get out of the courses, or at least a great felt need for something they have some reasonable hope of getting. Something has happened to the "deadly dull science." It seems evident that students expect to gain something important, and some of them find the subject vital and appealing. This presents a tremendous stimulus and responsibility to those who teach, or prepare materials for teaching, to do the utmost humanly possible to meet the need and to fulfill all reasonable expectations, within the limits set by the enormously difficult material we have to deal with.

What do intelligent students hope to get from a course in economics? Presumably a number of things, serving ends in which personal success, disinterested understanding, and

Adapted by permission from *American Economic Review Supplement,* Vol. XL, No. 5, Pt. 2, pp. 34–51.

ambition for human betterment are variously combined. What should a wise educational statesman wish to offer the students? To those interested in personal success he would presumably offer only the kind of help that comes from objective understanding of the environment to which the individual has to adapt himself: the same kind of objective understanding, in fact, which the zealous reformer would need, if his reforms are to have a fair chance to be effective. As between the self-seeker and the reformer, each probably needs about equally to understand the other, and his place in the scheme of things.

We have moved a long way since the days of Adam Smith. In his original conception economic laws were the decrees of a divinely appointed and beneficent nature, "seeking always the good of the species," wiser in man's behalf than man was on his own account, and turning his selfish strivings to the common good. If men were free to pursue their several ends, they need not concern themselves about the common good; nature, via economic law, would attend to that. Nevertheless, Smith's mature examination of the facts of economic life brought out numerous exceptions or qualifications, and they have been multiplying since his time. Later generations, following Bentham, came to view the economy, not as decreed by nature, but as a human mechanism: an instrument, to be judged by its results and to be guided to whatever ends men might collectively choose to pursue by a wisely devised system of incentives, including both rewards and penalties. Nowadays, a good many economists realize that an economic system is a good deal more than a mechanism; it has its own tendencies and its own ways of resisting simple and naïve attempts to steer it, frequently bringing them to unexpected and unintended results. But this does not lead us to give up the attempt. For better or worse, modern man is committed to trying to shape his economic destiny.

This is bound to find its reflection in classroom economics, in one way or another, even for the student whose father is a member of the Chamber of Commerce and who wishes his professor were not so eagerly interested in the ideas of the much-abused "welfare state." What is, and what is wanted, each has to find its place; and the method of articulating them is full of problems. On this matter, some hints may be got from two types of analysis which command particularly keen and widespread interest at present: the analysis (following lines mapped by the late Lord Keynes and others) of the factors determining the total flow of income, production, and employment; and the field of "welfare economics."

Bridging the Gap Between Causal Analysis and Value Judgment

What is the source of the great appeal of the "Keynesian" economics? One obvious answer is that it takes hold of the problem which the interwar experience drove home deep in the feelings of mankind as the major sickness of Western economic society, and it does so with an analysis that commands standing as objectively scientific, centering in a formula of the way in which the economic mechanism operates, the analysis being translatable into statistically observable quantities. In short, it makes this analysis exciting by bringing it into working relation with one of the chief things people want their economic system to give them and which it has failed to give—dependable job opportunities for all who want them and are qualified. This economics purports to explain why a system that multiplies mink coats and countless inane and frivolous gratifications neglects something so much more important.

Turning to "welfare economics," we find the same theme in a different form. It is an exploration of the ways in which the economic system serves or disserves the people's welfare; and the modern type lays especial stress on employing standards that can claim to be scientific and not to represent the writer's own "value judgments," which may be mere matters of traditional convention or personal taste or prejudice. This pursuit of scientific standards generally comes down to taking people's desires as they are, from the basest impulses to the highest ideals, and examining how well the system is adapted to facilitate their attainment. Without at present expressing judgment on how successful this attempt at scientific treatment of value judgments is, one may point out that it evinces a deep desire both to make welfare judgments and to put the authority of "science" and objective inquiry behind them. The welfare judgments want the support of objective evidence and analysis; the objective inquiry wants a link to social and moral purposes.

To generalize still further: there are two worlds, the world of impersonal investigation of cause and effect, and the world of desires, ideals, and value judgments. The natural sciences deal with the first; ethics deals with the second. In these terms, the peculiarity of economics is that it is called upon to bridge this gap. It is a science—or tries to be—and its subject matter consists of desires and values. If "science is measurement," the measures that give economics its claim on that score are of the sort in which things are measured, not in terms of their weight or any physical quality, but in terms of their "value" or their cost. Economics simply cannot report those relations between phenomena which are most characteristic of it without translating physical quantities into terms of value or cost.

The nearest thing to an exception that occurs to me is the law of diminishing return, in physical terms, to increasing amounts of one physically defined factor of production, used in connection with constant amounts of other physically defined factors. "Diminishing return" is understood to mean that total product increases, but by a smaller proportion than the increase in the variable factor, so that product per unit of this factor diminishes. But, on examination, one finds that there is no physical law requiring that return shall behave in this way under all circumstances. At different stages return may increase more than in proportion to the increase of the variable factor, proportionately, less than in proportion, not at all, or it may even decrease: that is, it is physically possible to use so much of one factor that added amounts are worse than useless. But this is not economical behavior. The "law" is that, when factors of production cost something, it is economical to use them in the stage just defined as "diminishing return," and not beyond that stage. Thus the nearest thing in economics to a purely physical principle turns out on analysis to be a principle of economical choice in terms of cost.

The national income is a sum of tons of coal and steel, gallons of gasoline, movies and concerts attended, surgical operations performed, overfeeding, undernourishment, and ignorant malnutrition—an endless variety of things, good, bad, and indifferent, all somehow reduced to a common measure in terms of their market "value." An economist can hardly escape asking what this value means and what lies behind it, or whether the market yardstick is a safe and dependable guide to the organization of a country's resources. Does it lead us to produce the right things in the right amounts, or not? Could any other system, or any modification of this one, do better?

The questions thus raised can be handled in a variety of ways; they can hardly be ignored. In these terms, the attitudes of the people themselves toward their economic system show a deal of variety and a deal of tendency to change. Corresponding to this, there is room for a deal of experimenting with different ways of handling these questions in the classroom; and one can expect that teachers will be trying different methods. Some of them may be deliberately experimenting, but it is likely that a good many will not think of what they are doing as experimentation; they will have proved to themselves that the particular method they have espoused is the one truly scientific method and they will follow it out with all the zeal and certainty that such a conviction inspires.

Opinions range, or have ranged, from the view that economics has nothing to do with ethics, to the view that it must formulate explicitly the ethical standards that furnish its setting and give its analysis meaning. Some would describe and appraise in the same breath; others would insist that description and appraisal are two completely separate acts; still others regard them as distinct, but see a need to establish a working relation between them. Some feel that scientific economics, as such, is obliged to accept the valuations individuals make in markets as final.[1] Others reject this strict disciplinary boundary line.

At this point it would be easy to become involved in methodological arguments, tending to become abstruse and perhaps convincing no one who was not convinced before. But the final verdict does not rest with such abstract debates; the test of a method lies in the results it can yield in use. Naturally it is not possible in this chapter to try out all possible methods of handling these questions, but we can get a rough idea of what some of them would look like in action.

[1] See Lionel Robbins, *Essay on the Nature and Significance of Economic Science* (New York: The Macmillan Co., 1935), especially 2nd ed., pp. 136–43. Here Robbins is not setting standards for policy judgments, merely defining the limits of economics.

Possible Methods: Specific Survey of Wants, Needs, and Products

One of the most obvious and simple approaches, and not the least promising, is to ask the direct questions: What do we want of our economic system? What are we getting from it? To the extent that it succeeds or fails in giving us what we want, how and why does it succeed or fail?

We want a large and growing supply of goods and services of the kinds that individuals buy. This we get in measure that appears well-nigh miraculous when one traces the story back a hundred or more years. This is what the system is best adapted to produce. We want these goods to be of kinds that serve our most essential needs—or do we? The question is premature, using a term that implies grading of values before we have settled on our standards of value. For the present we must be more specific, naming values without trying to grade them.

We want health. On this score Americans do quite well, though many sections of the country have far fewer doctors and hospital facilities than we have come to consider necessary for satisfactory care. The span of life has increased wonderfully, and many diseases have lost the terrors they had for our fathers. On examination, the most significant thing here is that health is not, in the main, in the hands of business institutions but of a group of professions. The most definitely commercial branch of health service—the proprietary medicine industry—is the least satisfactory sector. It is used to their harm by many who feel, with or without sufficient reason, that they cannot afford the cost of regular medical service. Preventive medicine has vast unused possibilities for improving the health of the population, partly in ways that require enforced controls like quarantine and compulsory immunization, partly through systematic arrangements for personal check-ups and early diagnosis and treatment. Without going into the controversial question of socialized medicine, it is clear that health is a national asset, and that the undisputed judgment of the people is that it is worth conserving, more or less regardless of whether it could be done on purely commercial principles.

People want various kinds of "security." Consider, first, safety from physical injury; and consider one of the most everyday sources of danger, the automobile. To start with, the makers turn out remarkably dependable mechanisms, subjecting them to punishing tests. Their interest in the matter is related both to competition plus large-scale production, making expensive tests practicable; and to the fact that the units of each make are structurally uniform, so that a failure of one impairs the reputation of the maker's whole output, and repeated failures would soon cost him his competitive market. The writer had a near-accident, which narrowly escaped being serious, caused by a structural feature of his car that could be dangerous in rare cases, and which was corrected in subsequent models. But there are also publicly enforced safety standards and inspections. Safety depends also on improved highway construction, on signs, and on traffic rules and policing. In short, we depend on a combination of private incentives and public controls. It is interesting to compare this with safety of residential construction; where there are many more builders, the product is much less standardized and reliance is much heavier on public standards of safe construction. The pure-food-and-drugs act affords another instructive comparison. In all three cases the ordinary individual purchaser is not in a sufficiently good position to judge the quality of what he is getting with respect to the hidden features that spell safety or danger.

Security of economic income raises a different set of questions. It requires, for one thing, that hiring and firing, at least in large industries, should not be arbitrary or dependent on one's political or religious views or on other considerations irrelevant to the service one is prepared to render on the job. This kind of job security is inconsistent with old-fashioned, irresponsible individualism on the part of employers or employer organizations, but it is a matter in which the employer's interest in efficient production tends to set limits on any tendencies he may have to wholesale arbitrary action. Unions can set up further safeguards, though with no automatic assurance that they will not encroach on the employer's legitimate interest in selecting his workers. Equity is called for and it is not automatically guaranteed by market forces.

Security of income in case of accident, illness, old age, or loss of job is an obvious need, and minimum protection is provided by the nonbusiness method of social security. To this collective bargaining is adding private pension plans, the economic effects of which raise further problems, especially as to occupational mobility. But unemployment benefits are an inferior substitute for an adequate and stable supply of job opportunities, and this the system of private enterprise has not shown itself adapted to furnish on a dependable basis.[2] If it is to be done by methods other than direct public furnishing of jobs and control of the worker's choice of occupation, it will be a task of creative experimentation in which government, industry, and unions will all have their parts to play.

[2] The above was written in 1950. While it remains literally true at the time of republication, in 1956, the intervening years have afforded a record of sustained high-level employment, with fluctuations kept within limits that have been easily assimilated. The causes include large expenditures for defense and foreign aid, "built-in" mitigators of fluctuations due to progressive taxation and social security, and also, apparently, some stabilization of private capital outlays due to advance scheduling by large business firms, based on long-range trends of economic growth. The relative importance of these different factors is uncertain, and their dependability under stress remains to be tested, but the current situation justifies cautious optimism.

It is presumably a foregone conclusion that a system of modified private enterprise, with whatever governmental and other action may be consistent with its essential conditions and requirements, cannot furnish as high a degree of stability as a collectivistic system would be able to do, assuming as one may fairly do that the collective system would make this one of its primary objectives. The freedom, flexibility, and progress which mark the private system may be worth some added instability, but how much? In particular, most American trade unions may feel that they are freer under a system of private enterprise than they would be likely to be under a collectivist system, even if, or especially if, it were in the hands of a labor government. Aside from this, they would have to change over their ideology, which has been built up around a contest over the earnings of the business with a profit-taking employer. Reluctance to incur the need of such a change-over is an imponderable factor, probably of considerable weight, though hardly possible to measure. Another is the superior influence in union councils of the workers who have seniority rights and therefore have less personal reason to fear a moderate reduction in employment. All these are elements tending to make the complex social-political entity we call "organized labor" willing to stand by the complex "mixed system" we call "private enterprise," even if it has to pay a moderate price in higher unemployment.

But how high a price would it be willing to pay before it would revise this decision and decide to espouse collectivism? No one knows the answer. What may be more likely is that the result would come about without conscious decision, partly by an increase in the size of the collectivized sector of a mixed system, partly by laying burdens on the remaining private sector, increasing tax loads as the private sector narrows, and demanding more rigorous standards of performance than private enterprise can meet and still remain private. This adds another question to which no one knows the answer: how far can this kind of process go before private enterprise reaches the limit of its capacity to adjust? For our present purpose the point of outlining this network of questions is that it represents a crucial framework within which existing values will be weighed and out of which modified valuations will emerge, valuations that will be of decisive importance for the destiny of our society. And—last but not least—these are values which the market is simply not adapted to measure. They are, perhaps, sociological or political values. But are they any more sociological than the value of a home on the right side of the tracks? The chief difference would seem to be that the market measures the one kind of value and not the others.

Another of the most important products of an economic system consists of human relations on the job which are consistent with the individuality, worth, and dignity of the worker as a human being. And this, once more, is not a commodity or service to be bought or sold and so given a monetary measure. But it is a more important product than many or most of the multiplicity of gadgets which the increasing productivity of modern manufacturing brings into being by those same processes of mass production which, if left to their unguided, natural tendencies, run risks of seriously impairing the human quality of the job. They do not always do so; and it may be that they need never do so, if properly handled. The point is that whether they impair human conditions or not hinges on something different from so-called "economic motives," meaning generally the employer's pursuit of profit, as determined by competition or monopoly under conditions set by monetary demand and monetary cost. To report that a given employer seeks maximum profits, as so determined, may miss the most important things about his conduct of his business.

The pursuit of profits may be consistent with maintaining good human conditions on the job, but it is not by itself a guarantee. It has in the past led to sweatshop conditions and other abuses. Mechanical industry breaks down many old-time craftsman's standards and needs to contrive some human equivalent or substitute, perhaps of a very different sort. The pursuit of profits promotes the adoption of machines; the resulting task of creative social adjustment calls for a broader combination of motives. It depends less on the pursuit of gain than on the degree of enlightenment with which it is pursued by all the groups concerned. This degree of enlightenment may decide whether the outcome will be good or not.

When one says this, one is of course expressing a tentative judgment on the relative importance of dollar values and costs on the one side and, on the other, of human conditions as gauged by some other standard. But what standard? We shall not ignore that question but for the present we may postpone it. The standards by which men act are pervasive, and in time of rapid change they may be all the better for not being too explicitly formulated. Certainly one should avoid the kind of formulation which rates all values of one kind as superior to all of another kind. It is wrong to rate the verdict of profits as always superior to any other way of rating human values, but it would be about equally wrong to hold the reverse always true. The economist's business is, in the first instance, with the facts. And he has some reason to feel that, if the facts are fairly reported, a right-minded person's judgment of the relative values involved will not go far wrong—and not as far wrong as the unmodified guidance of dollar values in the market might lead the system in practice, if it were left to them alone.

Scales of Importance Outside and Inside the Classroom

If a number of thoughtful persons were removed from
all suggestion of the conventions of the discipline and tradition of economics and asked "What is the most important
product of a country's structure of industry?" there is little
doubt that the prevailing answer would be, not "material"
goods and services, or objective or marketable gratifications, but people: healthy and well-energized people with
strong and kindly characters and well-rounded development
of mental and physical capacities; people who experience
and value freedom because they understand and assume the
burdens of achieving it, maintaining it, and using, not abusing it; people with roots in the past, maintaining continuity
between the past and the changing future; people who belong
to a community and are well-adjusted and co-operating
members of it. More precisely, the most important product
of industry would be identified as its total effect on the people concerned, including both favorable and unfavorable
factors, judged by the general kind of criteria indicated.

Now put these same thoughtful observers in a class in
economics. They find themselves in a different and restricted
world. Here the final word on values is what individuals or
businesses (or other economic entities, including government) are willing to pay for them in markets; and costs are
also measured marketwise, though in less unambiguous
fashion. It is not that the student is expected to change his
former beliefs about what is most important; he is merely
told that those beliefs are out of place in an economics classroom, and *as an economist* he is expected to measure the
total value of chewing gum, patent medicines, and erotic
perfumes as greater than that of boy-scout camps or classic
literature, if people pay more for them. In some classes
nothing as specific as chewing gum may appear, only ab-

stract sums of gratification-bought-at-a-price. The broader
questions are alleged to be the business of sociology or ethics, or both. And at the same time the student may find that
the existing ethical judgments are often discredited as not
being based on sound and adequate economic analysis. Yet
when he comes as a student who has made some ethical
judgments on economic matters and wants to check them in
the light of economic analysis, he finds that this analysis ex-
cludes the most important evidence. It would seem that the
connection between ethics and economics has somehow
fallen between stools.

In some classes the student may find ethical judgments
stigmatized as "prejudices." Thus one who judges a certain
patent medicine harmful on the basis of medical evidence
would be expressing a "prejudice"; while a purchase of the
same remedy brought about merely by the persuasive tone
of the radio advertiser's voice is not only an economic
"fact," as distinct from a "prejudice," but a fact having due
weight as evidence of "welfare," medical evidence to the
contrary notwithstanding. Surely, there is some confusion
here.

There might be less concern about this if the sole use to
which economics was put was to indicate what makes things
come to pass in markets. But these same findings are constantly used to gauge social efficiency and afford guides for
community policy, sometimes with the caveat that this
judgment is made on economic grounds only and is open to
modification on other grounds. All of which is tantalizing,
as indicating a possible conflict between values of different
sorts but affording no hint as to how this conflict may be
resolved or rationally handled.

What I have suggested so far is simply that one way of
making the descriptive work more enlightening is not to confine it to abstract utilities and disutilities (or indifferent rates
of "substitution"), but to give representative examples of

the different kinds of human values involved in purchases of goods and in the doing of a day's work. That would at least make the description run in the same general kind of terms in which appraisals and judgments of policy are going to be made and this, as far as it went, would be a gain as compared to a treatment consisting exclusively of abstract curves on paper.

Examination of Different Available Agencies

This, however, is only one of several alternative ways in which the matter might be approached. It might well be introduced by some little account of human nature, not limited to a picture of "rational" weighing of utilities or other alternatives but going far enough to afford some basis for a concept of the main basic needs of human beings, as well as their desires, purposes, capacities, and impulses. An alternative method of approach is to start with some such picture of desires and needs, and then ask: What kinds of agencies are available for meeting them? And what are the strong and weak points of the different agencies? What kinds of desires or needs is one type of agency best adapted to serve and what kinds does it tend to neglect? The market is one such agency, but only one. The main alternative agency—but not the only one—is political government. Co-operatives, private organizations for educational, research, or civic purposes, all are significant variants, having their strong and weak points and their characteristic biases and particular kinds of service to which they are best suited.

It is both interesting and enlightening to compare market mechanisms with governmental, describing each in the terms we use for the other. The market has its nominating machinery, its campaign propaganda, its balloting—by customers with their dollars; the corporation and the union have their internal political organization, with its problems of representation, of discipline and its enforcement, and of bureaucracy. The union in particular has its foreign relations (with employers and other unions), its negotiations, treaties, and cold wars. Incidentally, the important process of economic bargaining and negotiation is something that traditional economic analysis pushes off stage. Its economic theory waits to be constructed out of inductive generalizations, plus material from Neumann and Morgenstern's *Theory of Games*. Then it may parallel the theory of international negotiation; the two might well develop together.

From the other side, government has its problems of choosing product-offerings to attract the customers, of truth in advertising, of monopolistic competition, of fulfillment of contracts. In short, these are not two worlds, as the classroom tends to treat them, but simply alternative ways of organizing for the fulfillment of desires and needs. Reform or progress consists of entrusting some function, or part of a function, to a different kind of agency. The hope is to strengthen the weak points of the old agency with the strong points of the new; and the thing to remember is that the old agency had its strong points also and that when you accept the new agency you must take its weak points along with the strong.

The Method of "Strategic Decisions"

Still another way of approaching this problem is one with which I experimented in my recent small volume entitled *Guideposts in Time of Change:* [3] that of asking a class to imagine themselves called on to make the strategic decisions involved in setting up an economic constitution for a society. For example, what things would they entrust to

[3] New York, Harper & Brothers, 1949.

"consumer sovereignty," under what limitations, and why? Whatever answers different members might make—and they could differ considerably—one outcome is inevitable; they will give consumers' choices a large place, not because these are unquestionable judgments, nor always right, nor always better than other sorts of judgments, nor because no scientific evidence can be adduced for modifying them, but because they are good enough for many purposes, because freedom in these matters is universally and strongly wanted, and because complete regimentation is both intolerable and impracticable. Secondly, they will overrule free consumers' choices in a wide variety of cases, for a wide variety of good and sufficient reasons. They will have been forced to weigh the kinds of values and valuations the market records against other kinds and to make some kind of adjustment between them. After such a process the traditional apparatus of utility curves or indifference curves can hardly be taken as seriously as pure theory takes them. Clearly, their precision is fictitious; they do not tell the whole story nor furnish the final verdict.

It seems, then, that there is a variety of methods with which teaching can experiment. One objection to all of them is that they take time and would crowd out some of the theoretical material which courses are regularly supposed to cover. Granted; the question is one of the relative importance of the insights secured as against the materials crowded out. Further, in the light of the insights gained, some of the detailed elaborations of customary theoretical concepts may appear as expendable refinements; the concepts may appear as what they are—rough first approximations, covering some, but not all, of the things we need to know. Finally, the student will have been put in contact with things that should command his interest in the soundest way because they are clearly important to human life and its problems. Then if he goes on to look at the curves in the diagrams, he should be more likely to remember what human facts they purport to represent—something he does not always remember when they are presented in abstract fashion—and that is an invaluable safeguard against wrong conclusions.

Should Science Be "Value-Free"?

There remains the objection that science should be *wert-frei,* should deal with facts, not values. Economics has one thing in common with ethics or morals: it deals, among other things, with the relative values of qualitatively different ends. Its distinguishing feature is that it deals with people's actual valuations, not with what these valuations ought to be. This we may accept, without accepting the conclusion often drawn from it: that economics must accept the verdict of the market, or verdicts of the market type, as final for its purposes.

Market valuations are not the only actual ones; and if the goal is an unbiased attitude, the market has well-known and demonstrable biases. They are, by and large, better than various other biases, and that fact is one of its strong points. A dictatorship may direct a country's resources to military ends, to cultivating hate and suspicion toward other peoples, to undermining their governments, to obstructing and sabotaging postwar recovery. These can become the actual ruling values of the society, those implicit in what it actually does. We call these political ends, not economic; but most ends, as ends, are noneconomic. Economics is concerned with means and with relative ratings of ends. Such a dictatorship can have an economics of means to its kind of ends, moving tons of steel, laborers, scientists, artists, and propagandists into a pattern aimed at getting the most out of them in terms of the ruling ends.

To us, economic objectives mean something different because our ratings of ends are different. We want resources
put at the service of the wants and needs of the members of
society, who are free to say what they want. They have collective wants as well as individual ones, but the collective
wants are a composite picture, not a pattern unified by a dictatorship. In this picture minority values have their place.
They may have to be overruled, but this is an element of cost
or sacrifice to be taken into the reckoning. A value of vital
importance to a minority may deserve to outweigh a less important majority value. But in what scale? The best I know
is that suggested by Justice Holmes: the settled judgment of
the people. One might add that this judgment is pertinent
only to the extent that it is informed on the nature of the alternatives at issue and that it may be expressed either
through the regular political channels or through any others that may be available. In these terms, I suspect that, as I
have elsewhere suggested, Justice Holmes has come nearer
than the formulators of indifference curves to an acceptable
standard of value.[4]

There are still questions. Justice Holmes, as a judge, felt
an obligation to accept the actual prevailing judgment,
whether or not he agreed with it; and an economist, as a
value-neutral scientist, is under the same obligation. But
there are at least three grades of standard possible.[5] One is
the currently effective standard: the valuation expressed in
the conditions that society maintains. Another is the known
and expressed community judgment, which may be unfavorable to some features of these actually prevailing conditions though it may not as yet have been able to change
them. And a third is a more ultimate ethical standard, by

[4] See "Varieties of Economic Law and Their Limiting Factors,"
Proceedings of American Philosophical Society, Vol. 92, No. 2 (April,
1950), pp. 121, 124.
[5] A slightly fuller exposition of these three standards is given below, pp. 44–5.

which the prevailing community judgment may be judged right or wrong. Parallel to these, and confusing the issues, are the inertia of sheer custom and tradition and the rationalizations of personal and group interest. These standards all impinge on one another in subtle and complex ways and the disharmonies between them are a source of much tension and perplexity for people who try to rise above the simpler and more immediate dictates of particularistic interests. They are all, in their various ways, actual values. What is a value-neutral economist to do about them?

One of the simplest and often most effective things is to report the facts about the currently effective standard. The classic studies of Booth and Rowntree on nineteenth-century English poverty were reporting of this sort, and they were also the most effective means of bringing about change. They were conveying information about the currently effective standard to a public whose known prevailing standard was higher. For this purpose, it would not have been particularly helpful merely to draw an indifference map to show how the poor choose between different commodities. But suppose an economist wants to go further and express an ethical judgment, perhaps appealing to a standard different from that actually prevailing? I suggest that his responsibilities as a scientist can be met if, when he applies an ethical standard, he defines the standard he is using and tells enough about the facts to make clear the kind of judgment that necessarily follows. The ethical standard could be one he accepts or one he rejects; the process could, at least in theory and barring natural human limitations, be equally objective in either case. It would leave the readers of his book or the students in his class equally free and forewarned to accept or reject his conclusion, according as they accept or reject his standard.

Economics has several inescapable links with ethics. First, as science, it has one dominant ethical imperative: the imperative to find in accordance with the evidence. Second, the economic life which it studies is built upon a basic ethical requirement: the ethics of voluntary co-operation. Any economic system rests on law and law rests on acceptance. In our kind of system, which economizes coercion, there is all the more need of voluntary acceptance of the ethical standards necessary to co-operation, going beyond what law can possibly embody in its formal requirements. This is especially true in the modern economy of organized groups, which are freed in various degrees from the impersonal compulsions of unmitigated competition and given various degrees of power and of discretion in its exercise. As I have said more than once, if the system is to go on working, it must be either on a basis of compulsion or of voluntary assumption of responsibility for the exercise of these degrees of power and discretion which organized groups possess. In this enlarged sense ethical conduct has become, more actively than ever before, an absolute necessity to the continued operation of a voluntary economic mechanism. And in that same sense ethics and economics can no longer be thought of—if they ever could—as separate worlds; the one is part of the working mechanism of the other.

In concluding, one may ask: what is the most dangerous thing in the appallingly dangerous world we live in? One answer is "thought," which has given us "ideologies" that break away from custom-tested mores and chart new and untried courses, ruthlessly directed toward intellectually conceived goals; and has armed these ideologies with the resources of scientific knowledge of ways to attain their ends. Another answer, representing another facet of the same devastating set of forces, is "power at the service of a sinister purpose." And a close second to this is "power without purpose, or without adequately defined and well-grounded purpose," because it leaves the house swept and garnished for the entrance of the seven devils of sinister purpose, who will not neglect the opportunity.

From the standpoint of these questions, what is economics? In the first place, it is thought. In the second place, it is thought about means, neutral as between ends, ready to be put at the service of whatever ends the people may have: in short, power without defined purpose. As such, it qualifies as one of the most dangerous things in the world. It is all the more dangerous because its main instrument—the market—is not a passive instrument but a social institution that acts as if it had a life and purpose of its own, independent of those of the people who operate it and doing things to them that none of them planned or desired. It will be our master, not our servant, subjecting us to its purposes, not serving ours, unless we are very clear what our purposes are and work hard at the problem of making them effective wherever the market does not automatically do so.

Does the Task Fall on the Humanities?

Dean J. Douglas Brown, of Princeton, an economist, is reported as commenting on an increase in enrollment in the humanities in these words: "This indicates that young men realize that the answers to many of the problems facing the world today lie in the humanities, where they may gain an understanding of the age-old values which have been the strength of Western civilization. Students are seeking to understand the values inherent in our religious and humanistic heritage so that they may accept them as a guide to action. Knowledge in the fields of science and social science, standing alone, may be turned to purposes that are disastrous to our way of life." [6] This estimate of the importance

[6] *The New York Times,* Jannuary 15, 1950.

of the humanities is unquestionably just, as is also the warning of the liability of physical science to misuse. This warning may apply equally, or even more, to economics, if economics is handled so as to be effectively insulated from the values found in the humanities. But need it be so handled?

This theory of the insulated treatment of economics seems to rest on the idea that an economic system is a neutral instrument, furnishing people means of realizing their values whatever these may be; so that if the system does not produce humanely satisfying results, this can only be because the individuals operating it did not have the right values. The misleading character of this can be brought out by carrying it one step further to the implication that if the system is inhumane, the thing to do is to educate and reform the values of the individuals who compose it but not to change the system; an inhumane or a humane people would find the same system equally serviceable to their quite different ends. This last is clearly false. If the system is to serve a changed scheme of values, the system must change: as, for instance, by the growth of labor unions or social insurance. The system is not a neutral instrument—this will bear reiteration. While the humanities are speaking from the classroom with the somewhat muffled voices of books and of the past, the values of the market place—good, bad, and indifferent— are speaking with the urgent voice of present expediency and necessity, with no tender regard for the heritage of the past and often with no visible connection, no formative cultural roots.

Nevertheless, there is a positive cultural value in the ethics of voluntary co-operation, and the study of economics should deepen one's understanding of it, as well as of its effect on other cultural values and why it has the effects it does. What do the humanities do with this very real cultural value? As represented by current literature, they strongly suggest that, far from capturing the economic system for humane values, or at least waging a positive campaign toward that end, the victory has gone in the other direction and it is current literature, or major sections of it, that has been uprooted and torn loose from its cultural base by the impact of the material world of the present. Toward the economic system, current literature seems starkly and dangerously negative, presenting it as an arid waste of sordidly selfish and otherwise purposeless striving. Unsparing criticism is essential to a free system, but this somehow lacks sufficient two-sided understanding to be constructive in effect, and instead impresses one as the kind of criticism that is either impotent or likely to throw the baby out with the bath. I realize that current literature has many sides that are strong and positive. I am not indicting it as a whole, merely registering what seems a widespread and dangerous tendency in its representation of things economic. American politics is no better than it is, partly because so many good Americans look down on politicians. Are they coming to look down in somewhat the same way on business men and, if so, what effect will this have on the quality of a civilization in which statesmanlike business leadership is becoming more important than ever before?

In the field of religion the prevailing attitude is, naturally, more positive and more responsible; and in this field much important formative thinking is being done on economic problems. The difficulty here is twofold. Religion starts with values so pure that they are likely to seem inapplicable in any economic and political life except one for which an earthy humanity is not yet ready. And if one tries to carry out some of these values in the world of politics, business, or trade unions, one faces the necessity of marginal adjustments between values of different sorts. But because these values have been presented as absolutes, not subject to compromise, the individual finds himself convicted of inevitable sin, no matter how selfless his motives and how clear his understanding, because, forsooth, he is acting like an economic man and weighing marginal increments of different kinds of values against one another.

In spite of these difficulties, religious sources are furnishing a large and growing body of material, treating economic problems with technical competence and in the light of religious standards. The great papal encyclicals on these subjects are well known; the National Council of Churches has issued studies of a high order, well suited to use as classroom material.[7] On the international level the Amsterdam Conference was significant, but more in terms of general attitudes than of specific issues. In this and some other recent pronouncements the attitude toward an ill-defined entity called "capitalism" appears to an American more a reflection of the struggle against communism than a realistic picture of actual alternative tendencies.

An Age with a Split Personality

All this is evidence that our age has a badly split personality. Religion, art, and literature, economic life and economic analysis are too little integrated with one another, to put it mildly. The handling of economics as a discipline insulated from the content of human values is not solely responsible for this state of affairs, but it bears its share of responsibility and lies under a corresponding duty to present its material as an integral part of a working scheme of social values. As I have tried to indicate, this does not require the economist to sacrifice his scientific objectivity; rather, the shoe is on the other foot. Such handling of economics will not by itself be enough to heal the split personality of our

[7] The Federal Council of Churches issued excellent studies in pamphlet form; and its successor, the National Council, is bringing out a series of volumes. Chapter 3 of the present volume is a selection from the first volume of this series.

time, but it should represent the contribution that economics is in a position to make toward that unification, and it might be a fairly important contribution.

Not that we need a uniform and unanimously held scheme of values: that is not what freedom and democracy mean. The highest values in our scheme must be those that permit difference without disruption, and contention without disintegrating conflict. The common purposes, of which we stand in deep need, must be such as bind together widely diverse particular purposes, rather than extinguishing them in a blank uniformity. It is differences that develop the electric potentials that have power to get things done, and we need that kind of difference, stopping short of shattering potentials. This kind of unity in variety we need to achieve, before we find uniformity imposed on us under some totalitarian compulsion because we have been unable to compose our differences voluntarily.

The modern student needs to get a sense of the situation his country is in, which is inseparable from a sense of the situation the world is in. He needs a sense of the values that are at stake in internal conflicts and in conflicts with the values of other countries. This would define for him that sense of purpose, lack of which is the weakest point of a free individualistic-utilitarian society in contrast to totalitarian cultures. He needs a sense of historical movement, balanced by a sense of enduring elements persisting through evolutionary change. He needs a sense of shifting relations between community and individual, between ruler and citizen or subject. And he needs a sense of unsolved problems, in a world that is not finished but becoming. Student and teacher are probably about equally at fault in demanding finality where it does not exist. It takes more than economics to give all these forms of awareness, but economics has its contribution to make, if it is willing to make it.

In conclusion, while I have argued strongly against the

attempt to exclude values from economics or to recognize only market ratings, I have recommended no one way of dealing with them. Instead, I have indicated a number of different ways with which it might be fruitful to experiment. Any one of them might help to restore more effective liaison between economics—a science of values—and the values which are its natural subject matter, thus improving, rather than impairing, the value-neutral quality of the treatment.

CHAPTER THREE

Aims of Economic Life as
Seen by Economists

Introduction

PREVIEW OF THE PROBLEM

Ask an economist what the goal or aim of the economic
system is in a free society such as ours, and he will probably
reply that the system, as a system, has no specific aims; the
service it renders is to give its members a maximum of means
and opportunity to pursue their several aims, whatever they
may be. The system is conceived as neutral, ready to serve
any and all kinds of wants; the responsibility of directing it
to good wants, rather than bad, lies with those to whom the
service is rendered. For the economist, people's wants are
facts; those expressed in markets are economic facts; and
his task as a scientist is to study facts, not to approve or dis-
approve them.

Adapted by permission from *Goals of Economic Life*, A. Dudley
Ward, ed. (New York: Harper & Brothers, 1953), the first volume of a
series of studies on Ethics and Economic Life, produced by a Study
Committee of the National Council of Churches, under the Chairman-
ship of Charles P. Taft. These studies are not official statements of the
Council.

If that were all, this chapter might end here, having defined the attitude of economists toward the aims of economic life. But that is not all; the system is not as neutral as this definition suggests. No doubt its proper place is at the service of whatever ends the society may have. But the market naturally gives a preferred position to wants for marketable products. And it is taking generations of struggle to make slow progress in recognizing and making provision for other wants, some of which are far more important than an individualistic age has permitted itself to understand. To make goods cheaper and more plentiful, technical improvement has driven forward, from Adam Smith's pin factory to modern mass production; and only after we are committed to this irreversible movement do we arrive at the disturbing realization that something not fully understood has happened to conditions of work, to human relations on the job, and to the impact of work on the personality of the worker. Are we developing the kinds of personalities modern society needs, if it is to hold together and keep working, while maintaining freedom? If we fail in eternal vigilance in such matters, economic techniques could become our masters, precisely through our failure to realize that they are anything but docile servants.[1]

Up to a point, economists realize that the market is not neutral, and they express this realization in their policies, if not in their theories. But as to the more far-reaching human and social imponderables, even those who realize their importance are hardly equipped to deal with them. Economics is a quantitative discipline, and it does not know how to handle such qualitative material. Its most unqualified criteria of economic progress are more goods to consume and,

---

[1] The writer has developed this theme in "The Empire of Machines," *Yale Review,* October, 1922, reprinted in *Essays in Contemporary Civilization,* C. W. Thomas, ed. (New York, The Macmillan Co., 1931), pp. 146–57. Karl Polanyi's thesis of the absorption of the society by the economy seems to be a different way of putting essentially the same idea.

on the side of conditions of production itself, a shorter work week and more leisure.

If you catch an economist in an expansive mood, he may define the goal as "the good things of life for the many, as widely distributed as practicable, in an ever-increasing flow." This adds several elements, and raises more questions than it settles. How wide a distribution is "practicable"? And who is to be the judge of what things are good? If the many are free to choose, they are free to choose wrong as well as right—that is what freedom means. We recognize this by practicing a limited censorship in the interest of health, safety, and, to a dwindling extent, morals. But outside these limits, economists traditionally think that the things people want for themselves and their families are likely to be less harmful than the goals that self-appointed mentors or rulers set for them. This question of the wisdom of wants economists prevailingly regard as somebody else's business, and they have satisfied themselves that quantitative economic gains are good as far as they go.

Our system stresses the self-interested (or family-interested) side of human nature as a prime mover in the business of producing and distributing goods and services, and undertakes to harness it to the economic requirements of the community by the most nearly voluntary methods, involving the least interference with its natural expression. Traditionally, the harness has been viewed as a rather simple matter of legal rights of person and property, plus competition as a game in which, to serve oneself, one must serve others. Ethical motives were thought of mainly as entering into the spending of incomes; they were good but not necessary to the working of the system, and pretensions to moral motivations in business were actually suspect.

In fact, the traditional harness depends on a general underlying sense of right, which is necessary to respect for property rights and faithfulness to contracts. This moral sense is also built into the legal machinery for interpreting and enforcing these rights. And as group power is less precisely limited by competitive checks, the sense of right becomes an increasingly active feature of economic life, and social responsibility in the use of group power has become an absolute necessity if the industrial system is to go on working on a basis containing enough freedom to be fairly characterized as voluntary. The tradition of utilizing self-interest has made us slow to realize this necessity, and thus the tradition is a source of weakness as well as of strength.

Furthermore, whatever responsibility for social ends there may be in our system needs to become explicit and conscious. It is not enough that the system be serviceable; serviceability must appear to flow naturally from its inherent character. Otherwise it concedes a dangerous propaganda advantage to rival systems. Our system must be animated by awareness of its obligation to be directed to serviceable ends, not merely tricked by an "invisible hand" into pursuing such ends in spite of the fact that the main preoccupation of its members is with self-interested motives.

In addition to self-interest, human nature has another and sharply contrasting side: the impulse to identify oneself with something bigger than oneself or one's family, to merge oneself in it, and to find there support, an inner sense of security and of sharing in a larger realization than an unattached individual could attain, supplying a sense of meaning that smaller objectives fail to convey. This self-identifying, self-merging, or self-dedicating impulse appears in many guises—in fraternal orders, in trade unions, in political parties, in any service that has a strong *esprit de corps,* and most profoundly in religions and in totalitarian systems. The last two have this in common, despite being poles apart in their objects of loyalty; and this is presumably the most deeply rooted reason for the attraction the Soviet system has had for many Western Christians, who set a high value on self-dedication and are repelled by the degree to which our economic system neglects this side of man's nature. While Soviet strength rests also on fear and ruthless coercion, it is a dangerous error to suppose that they are its sole source.

This system now threatens our own, in what amounts to an antireligious holy war; and the requirements of defense against this threat will probably be the greatest single force determining the character of the changes our system will experience in the foreseeable future. Liberals are already warning us that we might win the contest and lose the thing we are fighting for. So we need not only to arm for defense, but to rediscover and redefine the qualities of our system that make it worth defending, the weaknesses of which it needs to be pruned, and the points at which the pruning may or may not involve risks to the essentials. Every generation needs such a rediscovery. Ours faces the need in the heat and confusion of conflict. It will make its decisions, with or without a clear eye to the values they affect and the valuations they imply.

SOME BASIC CONCEPTS

If the term "goal" implies a final terminus, it had better be translated "aspirations"; since we look to endless change and can hardly hope to resolve all the conflicts between different aspirations and organize them into a single unified goal. For economists, "goals" will remain plural, made up of wants of different sorts. In general, economists are most keenly alive to personal wants for personal use. They are tolerant of altruistic wants, so long as these do not assume too much power to interfere in the affairs of others, for they continue to hold that people are on the whole better judges of their own needs than of the needs of others. Wants as to the kind of community one wishes to live in they tend to relegate to the realms of the noneconomic. They accept the necessity for group decisions on collective matters, such as national defense, though they are alive to the defects of such decisions. And as to wants purporting to emanate from some superindividual entity, such as abstract "right"—which generally turns out to be customary—or the glory or prestige of the state as such, they are profoundly distrustful, suspecting a camouflaged sacrifice of the interests or welfare of the actual members of the society to some idea or interest that would not stand scrutiny in terms of democratic tests of welfare.

Problems of policy are always conflicts of values; and in making recommendations on them, economists reveal their working standards more dependably, if less explicitly, than in their theories. For such judgments between rival values, no ready-made yardsticks are available. Methods used in ethics and in law are suggestive, but not transferable just as they stand, if economists are to make the contribution which their background peculiarly qualifies them to make. They do not arrange generic values in an order of priority (e.g., health is, or is not, more important than freedom) and they would consider such a scale misleading. Their problems are always more specific. Should disease carriers be denied freedom to handle food in public restaurants? Should physiologically harmful use of tobacco be prohibited by law? Nearly everyone would decide the first question in favor of protecting the health value, and the second against the proposed method of protection. Such policy decisions deal with marginal increments; and, at some point, every generic class of values has to be limited in the interest of others.

Among value criteria, several grades may be distinguished. First comes the currently effective standard, expressed in the conditions society maintains or permits. This includes things approved as desirable, but it includes also many recognized abuses which society has merely not found effective ways of removing. The existing verdict of the market on the worth of different economic activities is a standard of this sort. It has the inertia of custom behind it, and this is entitled to some weight, but to limited weight only. Some economists regard their job, *qua* economists, as ending with this standard.

Second comes the known and expressed community judgment of what is desirable—where such a judgment exists. It implies a consensus prevalent enough to be regarded as representative—complete unanimity would be an unreasonable requirement. By this standard many existing practices and conditions may be judged unsatisfactory, as evidenced by efforts to improve them. The persistence of the unsatisfactory condition means merely that these efforts have not been able to succeed completely, within the limits of means we are prepared to use and disturbance we are prepared to incur. This is presumably the kind of standard to which Justice Holmes appealed as the settled judgment of the people, which a judge should follow, even against his personal predilections. The present writer contends that economists can and should appeal from the first standard to the second, this being required in order to fulfill the ideal of neutrality between actual ends. In the process they may modify existing standards by developing their unrealized implications; or as Booth and Rowntree did, a half century and more ago, by reporting the facts of British urban poverty.

Third, there is the search for more ultimate ethical standards by which the prevailing community judgment might be held right or wrong. This is outside the economist's special field. But his training prepares him, when he encounters claims of right, to look into their consequences and to scrutinize the standards themselves to see if they contain rationalizations of group interests or traditional and inherited preconceptions that should be freshly scrutinized, or both. In this area he can contribute a healthy skepticism which is the beginning of wisdom.

Historical Evolution of Economists' Attitudes

1. THE MEDIEVAL PERIOD

Current attitudes of economists are explainable partly in terms of their roots in the past development of their tradition. In sketching some high points of this development we may take medieval thought as a point of departure. Here social and ethical goals were frankly set for economic activity, under the leadership of the church, which had sufficient authority and power to give its standards a considerable degree of effect. It accepted the customary class structure of society, and sanctioned the income suitable to one's station in life, as against unlimited arbitrary exploitation or unlimited business acquisition. Wealth was a trust, charity a duty, usury forbidden, and exchange subject to the (elastic) doctrine of the "just price."

In the large, this thinking was suited to a nearly static handicraft system, set in a strong frame of custom and obedience to authority, temporal and ecclesiastical. Its defects and abuses were many. Its strongest point was its insistence that men were members of one body, with mutual duties. This doctrine, largely submerged by early modern individualism, is having to be slowly and painfully recreated in different forms and in a less hospitable environment.

2. MERCANTILIST-NATIONALIST ATTITUDES

With the end of the fifteenth century a dynamic, nationalistic commercialism broke the bonds of medieval customary authority and ecclesiastical control. The goals of the new nationalistic states were dynastic and militaristic, with growing influence exercised by the mercantile class, who were making the first large modern accumulations of capital. A large population was a national asset. Colonial empires were sought, and managed, with a view to allowing the mother country to do the manufacturing, which would support a dense population, while the colonies sent home raw materials and took manufactured products in exchange.

One prominent aim was a favorable balance of trade, sometimes fortified by disapproval of imported luxuries. But liberal expenditure by the rich was generally approved, as giving employment to the poor, while for the mass of workers low wages were generally sought, in order that they might be under pressure to work hard for the benefit of the more fortunate classes.[2] And a working class was coming into existence, free of both the trammels and the protections of medieval status and dependent on employment in what seems to have been a buyers' oftener than a sellers' market.

The mercantilists understood one thing which later economists ignored, and which still later economists have had to rediscover: namely, the importance of spending as conditioning the level of economic activity. They represent the earliest and crudest phase of the kind of economic thinking that seeks methods of increasing the "wealth of nations" (as they conceived it) by utilizing and channeling the "free" activities of private traders.

3. THE PHYSIOCRATS

The physiocrats (whose name signifies "the rule of nature") made a rather remarkable attempt, under the circumstances, to rescue the sick economy of France from the abuses of the decaying Bourbon monarchy. Quesnay, court physician to king and economy alike, urged that taxes should be paid by the landed aristocracy, instead of falling with hampering or crushing weight on peasant cultivators and on trade and industry. The great landowners should also plow back capital into the land, to restore and maintain the pro-

---

[2] This aspect is well brought out in E. S. Furniss, *The Position of the Laborer in a System of Nationalism* (Boston: Houghton Mifflin Co., 1920), especially Chapter VI.

ductiveness of agriculture. This idea of direct taxation was a permanent contribution to economic thinking, though nowadays we do not confine it to land taxes. It is linked to the idea of the "natural order" of laissez faire, since direct taxes do not distort and hamper economic activity as indirect taxes do.

The physiocrats were probably sincere in believing that the resulting increase in productiveness would more than repay the landed nobility and enrich the king. One need not take too seriously any implication that in the physiocrats' minds this was the purpose of it all. Nobles and king were the powers who had to be persuaded, and Quesnay exhibited the wisdom of the serpent in devising ways of lubricating the insertion of his ideas into the mind of Louis XV. Moreover, the limits of free speech were narrow: the Abbé Galiani defined eloquence as the art of saying everything without going to the Bastille. Ideas of burden-sharing by the aristocracy could not safely have been presented in a less sugar-coated capsule.

4. ADAM SMITH

Adam Smith was a pioneer of the conception that the proper goal of economic policy was primarily the increase of goods for consumption by the common man, sold at the lowest prices the producers could afford and still have adequate incentive for vigorous production. His consumer standpoint was an antithesis to the sponsorship of producer interests by the mercantilists, who were his main object of attack. But for a quantitative concept he was forced to fall back on the total exchange value of the nation's products, though he had already concluded that the exchange values of goods are not in proportion to their use values. Another criterion was a selection of occupations under which a given capital would set a maximum amount of productive labor in motion—but natural liberty would bring this about.

Smith evidenced solicitude for those with low incomes. Increased wealth does not bring proportional increase in happiness. People who gain substantial wealth, hoping to gain happiness thereby, are disappointed; but in the process they improve productive methods, and this brings a modest gain in real income to the masses, which does count in the scale of happiness. It tends to be eaten away by a consequent increase of population; but with continuing progress wages can be kept above a bare subsistence, and this is desirable. It is well that those who feed and clothe the rest of society should be themselves tolerably well fed and clothed. Hardly startling, but a notable advance over the mercantilist attitude.

A position of personal independence is a desideratum. Laws in favor of workers are always just, since they must run the gauntlet of a Parliament that represents the other classes. At one point Smith excoriated the deadening effect on workers' minds and characters of the monotonous jobs that the subdivision of labor was creating. His suggested countermeasure was education. He approved of the effect of small religious sects because, among other things, they gave more people a chance to count for something in the life of a group.

On the ground that "defense is more important than opulence," he justified some deviations from "natural liberty"; but, in the conditions of the time, a few minor exceptions were sufficient. Perhaps his greatest departure was his approval of the navigation acts, which had ruined the carrying trade of Britain's rival, Holland. His many-sided thinking included some mercantilist elements. He did not question the "natural right" of landowner and capitalist-employer to their shares of the product at their "natural levels," which in the case of capitalist-employers meant the necessary supply price of capital and enterprise. But his arguments for individualism were not applied to joint-stock companies.

As the physiocrats spoke for a sick economy in which agriculture was basic, and the mercantilists spoke for trade and protected manufactures, Smith spoke, in the infancy of the industrial revolution, for a freely balanced economy in which manufacturing was the most dynamic element, needing no leading strings. The problems and tasks of a more developed industrialism came later.

5. BENTHAM

Bentham rejected intuitive concepts of natural right as a standard of appraisal and insisted that institutions should justify themselves by a rational scrutiny of their results. These were to be measured by maximum happiness, conceived as an algebraic sum on a scale of pleasure and pain, which in turn are the things people actually seek or avoid. The task of the legal framework of economic life is, by rules of general application, to prevent people from pursuing their interests to the injury of others, leaving them free to pursue them in any other way. Since each is supposed to pursue his own interest more faithfully than others can be trusted to do it for him, this system leads to the maximum result. Thus Bentham laid the basis for a more rationalistic and doctrinaire system of *laissez faire* than did Smith. But it was built of elements that could lead, equally rationally, to quite different results; partly because law could not perform, or closely approximate, the miracle which the Benthamite system required.

In the Benthamite social sum of happiness every person counted as one; and Bentham assumed that the pleasures of different persons could be compared and added. He felt that this, while not strictly accurate, came nearer to the truth than any other practicable assumption; furthermore, without it his whole social mechanics of happiness became impossible. It afforded a strong case for distribution according to need; but he rejected this on the ground that it was more important to promote a progressive increase in the total income, through the stimulus afforded by the assurance that the person investing capital and assuming risk would reap the rewards that might come from ownership of the results. Nowadays, of course, we practice many methods of striking an intermediate balance.

Bentham laid the basis for economics as a science of subjective feelings. And his optimistic confidence in the possibility of devising institutions as mechanisms to produce calculated results has been irresistibly attractive, despite difficulties and disappointments. This view of institutions has refused to stop with *laissez faire,* and has moved on to new deals and collectivist utopias. The Benthamite idea of the negative function of law—the "policeman state" (not to be confused with the totalitarian "police state")—has been buried under the growth of more positive state activities.

6. MALTHUS

Malthus's *Essay on Population* gave currency to the idea that limiting population was a prerequisite to any large and lasting raising of the standard of living of the masses, together with considerable skepticism as to the feasibility of such large improvements. With this went a hardening of poor-law policy. In a more general way he may be said to have established, as a characteristic of the economic profession, the principle of hard-headed exclusion from economic goals of anything seen not to be feasible. (But some of the things that economists proved impracticable have subsequently come to pass.)

After Napoleon's blockade Malthus wanted England to be less dependent on imported food, and to that end he favored moderate agricultural protection. He also had the hardihood to suggest the need for a due balance between saving and consumption, and the possibility that saving might go too far. It is ironic that his heresy on this point has increased his stature in the eyes of the present generation, while his law of population, acclaimed in his day as basic orthodoxy, has been inoperative in the industrially developed part of the world. But for a majority of the world's population it is still to be reckoned with.

7. RICARDO

From our present standpoint, perhaps, Ricardo's chief impact was to reinforce the classical tendency to hold that ambitions for social betterment are narrowly limited by economic laws, which are independent of human institutions and which society transgresses at its peril. He emphasized national net income—surplus above subsistence—as an objective measuring a country's power to pay taxes and to support a war. Cheap food would increase this margin, resulting in lower money wages without reducing real wages; and on this ground he opposed agricultural protection. But his recommendations on policy are frequently bare of explanation of the criteria that underlie them.

8. JOHN STUART MILL

John Stuart Mill represented a transition from Benthamite-Ricardian orthodoxy to broader conceptions of human values, of institutions, of what is feasible, and of what government can and should undertake to do. Raising of real wages by trade-union action would be desirable if possible, but it is impossible (wages being limited by the ratio between the working population and the wages fund). In other ways, however, working with and not against economic law, gains may be made; and some of these may be substantial enough to become embodied in the standards of living which people will protect by restricting their birthrate, and may thus be perpetuated, in the face of the Malthusian law of population.

Mill sought to escape from the fatalism of economic

laws independent of human institution, searching for an area of laws that were matters of human institution and therefore modifiable. His charter of justified functions of government accepts private activity as the general rule. But Bentham, in the act of defining the logical basis of *laissez faire,* had also provided Mill with opportunity and grounds for a list of exceptions, which we can now see to be pregnant with possibilities of almost indefinite expansion under changed conditions or changed attitudes.[3] His specific suggestions were modest, and his chief restriction was that only highly important values justify the compulsory variety of governmental interference. But with Mill, as with Smith, the presumption in favor of *laissez faire* did not apply to joint-stock companies.

Mill discusses collectivism tolerantly, and suggests that the decisive consideration might be which system affords the greater freedom, indicating that this does not automatically settle the issue in favor of private enterprise. Another criterion is a healthy balance between the public and private spheres, in terms of the levels of ability they are able to enlist, and the scope for its exercise. In addition to the gratification of wants Mill appeared to be deeply concerned that individuals should exercise and develop their capacities in caring by their own efforts for the things that are important to them.

9. OTHER IDEAS OF THE CLASSICAL PERIOD

The thought of the early nineteenth century included forerunners of the historical school, institutionalists, aesthetic critics of early industrialism, early socialists, and other reformers. Sismondi noted that the Middle Ages afforded the security of belonging to a place in the community, a security which participants in the modern struggle lacked. The

[3] See his *Principles of Political Economy,* Book V, Chapters I, X, XI.

Middle Ages built enduringly, as modern builders did not. He was ahead of his time in viewing depressions as an inherent illness of the system. Fourier revolted against the waste and chicanery he saw in business. Robert Owen, successful industrialist, pioneered in welfare work and dissipated his fortune in collectivist experiments. Historical students envisioned social evolution, not bound by Benthamite specifications. Carlyle called economics the "dismal science" and blamed it for accepting poverty too calmly. But he had no sympathy for plodding utilitarianism or for "democratic" rule by the drab values of industrialized masses. He would not make them kings. Ruskin, as against economists' abstractions, insisted that "there is no wealth but life."

The dissents influenced somewhat the attitudes of regular economists, without radically diverting their current of thought. To Marx, the actual goal of the existing system was exploitation of the workers; and the Marxian goal was the workers' seizure of the economy, without detailed attention to the ends to which they would subsequently put it.

10. EARLY MARGINAL THEORY, 1871–1900

With the aid of Ricardo's great tool, the marginal method, an answer was found to the difficulty that had baffled the classicists—the apparent lack of correspondence between use value and exchange value. The solution hinged on the use value (or utility) dependent on the presence or absence of a little more or less of a commodity—a "marginal unit." Bentham's pleasure-pain mechanics could now be fulfilled in an economics of subjective values or utilities. Individuals' comparisons of utilities were accepted as meaningful, though the relative utilities of things to different individuals remained a problem, the more cautious theorists insisting that nothing can be known, scientifically, about it. (But when it comes to policy, most economists believe—scientifically or not—in reducing the inequalities of wealth and income which an unmitigated laissez-faire system would create.)

In the matter of incomes, the marginal-productivity theory—companion of marginal utility—rounded out a system in which, under competition, factors of production were allocated where they would be most productive, and their owners, including laborers, received the worth of their marginal contribution to the joint product. And this is not without an ethical element, though few would claim that it settles all ethical problems. It is the ethics of the parable of the talents, not that of the workers in the vineyard.

Under this theory, the bulk of the gain from improvements was seen as filtering rather quickly through to the workers (manual and directive) while business kept as profits no more than the minimum needed to attract capital and afford enterprise the necessary incentive to take the risks of pioneering. The industrial revolution in the Western world had progressed to the point of emancipating this area from the pressure of population as an insuperable barrier to prospects of progressive raising of the level of living of the masses. This and many related values were lifted out of the limbo of the unattainable, and became accepted goals of endeavor. Thus the tone of the period was optimistic.

The individual worker had the responsibility, as well as the opportunity, of finding employment and keeping it by satisfactory performance in a competitive struggle with others. It was assumed that he could always find some job, at some rate of pay. It was only later that this view was progressively altered by the impact of cycles of mass unemployment, arising from causes largely inherent in the business system and beyond the power of individual workers to remove.

The marginal economists were, however, moving in the direction of a moderate interventionism. They prevailingly viewed the system of private enterprise as basically sound,

though with particular defects. These should be remediable
by piecemeal methods, which would not alter the fundamental character of the system. Like John Stuart Mill, they
found exceptions to the laissez-faire theory, or necessary
conditions unfulfilled; and the exceptions multiplied. Nevertheless, a good deal—though not all—of the public intervention which was approved could be characterized as trying to make the actual system work more nearly like the
ideal model of free and fluid competition. With limitations,
this was accepted as the most pertinent economic objective
for a society made up mostly of everyday human beings,
neither saints, geniuses, nor criminals; ready to give value
for value received but not to make a charity of business; people with many and important generous impulses, but people
to whom the most dependable stimuli to daily toil were stimuli of self-interest.

So much for the antecedents of current ideas as to the
goals of economic life. The story reflects the liberation of
great productive forces by an individualism, not wholly un-
disciplined, but often ignorantly disruptive of the values of
the society it replaced. Then came belated recognition that
something more was needed, and attempts to rectify defects
and abuses. As we go on into the twentieth century, this
movement gathers momentum, until ways of thinking are
surprisingly transformed.

The Current Century: Moving Toward a New Balance Between Individual, Group, and Community

INSTITUTIONAL THEORY

While piecemeal exceptions to *laissez faire* multiplied in
the realm of policy, so also did divergent heterodoxies in the
realm of theory. The term "institutionalism" has been applied to a number of such theories, some of them having

little in common except departure from "marginalist" orthodoxy.

Charles H. Cooley performed the great service of showing that the mechanism of the market, which dominates the values that purport to be economic, is not a mere mechanism for neutral recording of people's preferences, but a social institution with biases of its own, different from the biases of the institutions that purport to record, for example, aesthetic or ethical valuations. Policy-wise, his theories looked largely in the direction of making the market responsive to a more representative selection of the values actually prevalent in the society.

By way of contrast, Thorstein Veblen combined a merciless deflation of the pretensions of the business system with an Olympian detachment from questions of what to do about it. His critique had much more of Marxian thought in it than Veblen himself would have willingly recognized, and it centered largely on failures in serviceability to the "material" interests of the common man. He appears to have taken democratic values as seriously as he took anything; but his final suggestion of a "soviet of technicians"—the germ of "technocracy"—was hardly a democratic proposal. His whole bent was against making purposive recommendations.

John R. Commons was at the opposite pole from the detachment of Veblen. A practical crusader, his thought was frankly purposive, and he defined institutions as "collective action in control of individual action." His dominant purpose was to make the business system serviceable enough to deserve to survive; though he was not certain this effort would succeed. His main emphasis was on labor conditions, including the maintenance of employment. In the field of theory he wanted "to give to collective action, in all its varieties, its due place throughout economic theory"—a place which would be something more than a list of specific abuses or exceptions to *laissez faire*.[4] With this in view he broadened the concept of a "transaction" to include social action, and added the conceptions of a "going concern" and its "working rules"—similarly broadened to include both private and social forms.

What these very different thinkers had in common was a refusal to accept the market as an adequate vehicle for expressing the importance of things to society. They looked beyond it in varying ways, according to their differing personalities.

WELFARE ECONOMICS

The reason for a separate subdiscipline labeled "welfare economics" arises as economics becomes growingly self-conscious in its attempt to separate its analysis of what actually is, from judgments of what is desirable. A. C. Pigou, in his *Wealth and Welfare*, published in 1912, proceeded on the basis of an "unverified probability" that welfare would be increased by an increase in the size of the national dividend, by a more equal distribution (unless it resulted in too great a reduction in the total), and by greater steadiness. But the use the poor make of relief funds should be supervised, or else the funds will be largely wasted. He justified, in principle, policies that would increase and regularize employment, but he had only cautious and limited suggestions to offer.

One sector of his analysis was a form of social accounting, aiming to identify cases in which a given added use of resources would add either more or less to the national dividend than to the income of the person making the outlay. He also justified some forms of negative eugenics, and raised the question whether some economic policies aiming at wel-

[4] *Institutional Economics* (New York: The Macmillan Co., 1934), p. 5.

fare might not have their effects canceled by a resulting deterioration of the biological stock of the population.

Two years later John A. Hobson brought out a welfare study of a very different kind, stemming from Ruskin's theme, "There is no wealth but life." [5] Hobson did not try, as Pigou did, to isolate *economic* welfare, but asked simply, "What is welfare, and how is it affected by existing methods of producing and circulating wealth?" His answer held that welfare is an organic whole, not an arithmetic sum of marginal units of gratification; and his particular contribution lay in giving primary emphasis to the effect of the character of work on the worker. Much earlier he had ventured an underconsumption theory of depressions. Thus he put his finger on the two biggest blind spots in conventional economics. But economists were not impressed, regarding his treatment as nonscientific.

If Hobson's welfare economics left the scientific economics out, the form of theory which now bears the name can without real unfairness be described as welfare economics with the welfare left out, in a remarkably resolute attempt to meet the real or supposed requirements of economic science. Rejecting "interpersonal comparisons," this body of theory seems to end in rather complete agnosticism, aside from policies that increase the national dividend without making anyone worse off. But the existence of a single disadvantaged person acts as a veto on scientific approval of any policy—one cannot be scientifically certain that his loss does not outweigh the gains of many. Such a theory cannot recommend that we install tax-supported poor relief or a progressive income tax; but equally it could not recommend that they be not established. It seems clear that this theory has not reached satisfactory final form.

[5] J. A. Hobson, *Work and Wealth* (New York: The Macmillan Co., 1914), pp. 10–12.

Meanwhile, no one has disproved the hypothesis that society cannot afford to let its less fortunate members starve, or that many highly important effects of industrialism are nonmarketable by-products, so that it appears almost a matter of chance whether they are beneficial or the opposite— almost, but not quite, since men, even in economic life, have not wholly lost their moral sense, and are not completely indifferent to the diffused good or harm they do. State action is no automatic panacea. Extensions of state power have unintended by-products also. And unmoral politics, like unmoral business, can fail to be directed to socially valid ends. Further, no one has disproved that if the moral fiber of the people deteriorates, and if the ethics of voluntary co-operation is submerged in self-seeking struggles, the material national dividend will suffer.

CURRENT THEORIES OF LIMITED COMPETITION

Competitive theory is probably in a transitional state, tending to set objectives too precise for realization, and therefore to underrate the effectiveness of actual ("imperfect") competition, while policy does not follow theory with any consistency. Briefly, theory has stressed the effect of competition in bringing prices and costs into equilibrium at levels that minimize profits and promote an economical scale of operation in a given state of techniques. This is a static problem for which price theory can produce precise answers. At least equally important is dynamic improvement of methods and products, but formal theory cannot reduce this to precision, especially in the diagrammatic forms of which it is so fond.

As one result, current theory tends to regard quality differentiation as a defect of competition, rather than a means of progress in quality and an essential additional service which can be thoroughly competitive, although, like all services, it may take defective forms. Scarcely less important, perhaps, is the fact that these dynamic forms of competition do not require such large numbers of competitors as "perfect" competition does, and they allow some producers to make profits while others are making losses. And actual competition takes many important forms besides those "obvious and simple" enough to be embodied in formal theory.

ATTITUDES TOWARD COMPETITION IN GENERAL

"Competition," as commonly used, refers to competition of business units in the production and sale of their products. In this sense, American economists support competition more consistently than prevailing policy does. For example, they generally oppose resale-price maintenance under the "fair-trade" laws. But it would be a rare economist who would hold that everything—employment, wages, agricultural production, and farm prices—should be settled by an unrestricted competitive struggle. Economists have accepted the idea that neither workers nor farmers should be exposed to the full rigors of competition in the sale of their labor or their products.

This country's legal enactment that "labor is not a commodity" took its meaning from Karl Marx's assertion that under capitalism labor *is* a commodity, "constantly exposed to all the vicissitudes of competition, to all the fluctuations of the market." [6] This particular statute freed unions from the antitrust laws; but as an expression of general policy the phrase had wider implications. Economists approved unions at first as an offset to the superior bargaining power of employers. The nearest practicable approach to equality of bargaining position, and one which economists of a generation ago typically set as an ideal, would be a situation in which, while bargaining is collective, neither side can control the supply of the thing it has to sell, or maintain its price regardless of an excess supply. This leaves unanswered such

[6] *Communist Manifesto*, 1847; authorized English translation, p. 15.

questions as that of industry-wide versus company-wide bargaining, and the conditions under which an employer should be protected in filling the places of striking workers. Equity seems to lie somewhere between an absolute right of the striker to hold his job vacant and the older practice of hiring strikebreakers.

Collective bargaining has not stopped with any such vague balance, and by degrees economists have found themselves tolerating bargaining methods which would unquestionably be classed as monopolistic if employed by business in the sale of its products. This became ominous with the increasing number of vital services which can be cut off by a strike, giving numerous minorities coercive power over the public. So far, in this perplexing dilemma, economists have prevailingly approved of efforts to get settlements by mediation and arbitration without power; and have acquiesced in moderate injury to the public interest from stoppages of service pending settlement, chiefly because these are questions on which only a settlement voluntarily reached, or at least acquiesced in without outright compulsion, can provide a basis for healthy employment relations afterward.

A genuine attempt to break unions is unthinkable. Economists today probably discount union power to raise the general level of real wages as being overrated, and judge that their greatest value lies in protecting workers' human rights on the job.

As to agriculture, there is general agreement that it is naturally subject to undue competitive pressure as compared with industry, and that this disparity needs to be remedied somehow; disagreements are mostly as to method. Other problem areas include bituminous coal, crude oil, rail-truck competition, and noncompetitive practices in the field of small trade.

To sum up, while current theory implies that competition can be too weak, but never too strong, attitudes on policy imply that it can be too severe, as well as not severe enough, even in business and still more in other fields. Economists are perhaps readier than others to recognize that it may not be strong enough unless it is sufficiently severe to be called "destructive" or "cutthroat" by some of those exposed to it. This is largely because one of its important services is to weed out inefficient enterprises more rigorously than a human judge or jury would have the hardihood to do. The assumption is that individuals bankrupted out of a business are merely forced to fall back on some second-choice livelihood. The chief exception occurs in the small trades, which unemployed workers may enter in order to have some kind of job, even though it pays less than standard wages.

THEORY OF BUSINESS FLUCTUATIONS AND UNEMPLOYMENT

Statistics of business cycles have gone far to dispel the once-prevalent idea that "everyone can get a job" if he tries hard enough. The great depression of the thirties found government committed to assuming responsibility. This period also produced suggestions of effective remedies in the Keynesian theory. For the younger generation of economists, such remedies became the primary frontier objective of economic policy. New force has also been lent to older objectives, especially to widely diffused income as a necessity for the prosperity of a mass-production economy which sells most of its product at home, as ours does. When employment is short of a satisfactory level, increased consumption is less important as an ultimate end than as a means to more jobs—always provided its effect is not canceled by reduction of capital outlays.

However, American economists have not generally adopted the theory, espoused by various economists speaking for organized labor, that a general wage increase regularly stimulates employment and can help avert a threatened depression (as was urged in 1945–46). Neither have American economists adopted the theory of recovery via wage reduction. A representative view would probably be that wages can be too low for maximum employment, but are not likely to be, the strength of organized labor being what it is; and that if wages are too high, the result may be either inflation or unemployment, according as employers are or are not able to pass on added costs in higher prices and still market an ample output.

WAR, OVEREMPLOYMENT, AND INFLATION

War reverses the problem of depression and upsets many of the ratings in our ordinary scheme of values. Increased consumer gratification is temporarily subordinated, so far as practicable. As to the basic personal liberties, against our present adversary, the paramount fact is that if we lose, these values have no future, and temporary and limited restriction is better than permanent blackout. But since they are what we are fighting to defend, we must do our utmost to minimize any encroachments upon them. Their postwar restoration is safer in proportion as a large measure of them have been preserved during the struggle.

In major war, economic controls become indispensable; but they have to make terms with the fact that the country's war objective does not automatically wipe out habits of self-interested action. Since controls require a measure of voluntary compliance, compromise with ordinary incentives is necessary. But an uncompromising determination on the part of powerful groups that "whoever has to endure a shrunken real income, it won't be us"—this can be disastrous. It spells inflation, the most inequitable way of sharing shortages.

PRICE STABILITY AND PRICE FLEXIBILITY

The question has been raised whether, over the long future, if we succeed in maintaining employment at a satisfactorily high level, the result will be a progressive inflationary trend of prices, due not to shortages but to ample buying power, sustaining and inviting a bidding up of money costs of production. Economists would agree that, beyond some very moderate limit—the present writer suggests a long-run trend averaging 2 per cent per year—inflation is a serious evil. So also is any policy that results in such a harmful degree of inflation.

While approximate stability of the general level of prices has long been one of the objectives of economists, they have laid even greater stress on the need for sufficient flexibility of particular prices to keep them in a healthy relation to changing costs. As to whether they should fluctuate still more actively, responding to every shift of demand, or of supply of productive factors, opinions are divided. The majority probably holds that general price movements in response to changes in over-all demand can do little or nothing to restore stability of operation and employment that could not be done in other ways with less disturbing consequences.

THE SOCIAL MINIMUM

Social insurance is now accepted, exclusive reliance on individualistic and voluntary methods in these matters having been gradually eroded away by time, statistics, and the impact of depressions. While unemployment benefits are in part a substitute for steady employment, they have some stabilizing effect on jobs by mitigating the fluctuations of purchasing power through which depressions spread and cumulate. And the Beveridge Report of 1942 linked the two objectives with the proposition that really adequate "cradle-to-grave" social security was financially feasible only if unemployment was kept within rather modest limits.

Free public education has been extended to include the school bus and school lunches, going a short distance with the principle that effective freedom, or opportunity, includes

command over the material means necessary to make adequate use of it.[7] This principle is one approach to a social
minimum. But it has a long way to go before reaching the
position of some liberal socialists, that everyone's income
should include a social dividend based on need, plus a further payment for individual effort and productive contribution. This may be an ideal, ultimately attainable by an economy even richer than ours is at present, with a population in
less need of differential incentives than Americans now are.
It is not an immediate issue.

Opportunity is the most characteristic part of the social
minimum in the free type of society. Economists generally
recognize that literal "equality of opportunity" is a fiction—
an inaccurate slogan if you prefer—so long as the private
family exists. A. B. Wolfe has suggested "equity of opportunity," including larger opportunities to those who earn
them by the use they make of those they start with—for example, academic scholarships. It might be considered equitable that successful parents should be able to give their children, in some degree, a better start in life than the basic
minimum that is open to all. Some combination of these
ideas seems to represent the prevalent standard.

It seems that, while theory has not been able to reach an
uncontested decision as to the relative individual utility of
goods to richer and poorer individuals, democratic judgments have sustained the social minimum largely on different grounds—as a means to individuals' appropriate par-
ticipation in the common life. Their needs, from this
standpoint, are a basis of claims of "rights," which are less
elusive than their relative capacities for enjoyment and
furnish a more solid ground for policy.

[7] This principle will be discussed below, pp. 81–3, 125.

SOME ALLIED CONCEPTS

The social minimum overlaps other matters. Safety and health, for example, include not only medical service but safety-appliance laws, quarantine, and compulsory vaccination; and the reasons for including these often have nothing to do with inability of the beneficiary to pay. Prohibition of harmful food ingredients, and truthful labeling, are both involved. And much useful information for consumers is available from private nonprofit agencies. On the whole, purchasers of goods are in a better position than voters to know what they are getting. Economists favor such agencies, just as they have long favored co-operative agencies competing with private business and furnishing an added check on the imperfections of business competition.

A MODERN SUBSTITUTE FOR STATUS

When private contracts set up enduring personal relations, these have a tendency to become standardized, often in the interest of the stronger party. Thus labor relations, in particular, acquire some of the features of "status," though entered by contract, not fixed by birth. This characteristic may give rise to a public interest in safeguarding conditions by minimum standards which contracts must meet. In this fashion there has evolved a sector of jurisprudence not confined to rules which are the same for all, but setting up differentiated requirements adapted to the different functions the parties perform. This extends to the construing of collective bargains, the best of which have a constitution-making character, establishing the rights of the parties in the employment relationship.

THE INTERESTS OF POSTERITY

In principle, economists recognize that the profit motive may promote the interests of posterity in some respects and

sacrifice them in others. They have long supported a growing number of policies coming under the general head of
"conservation." They presumably do not accept business
methods for calculating the value which public policy should
set on conserving irreplaceable assets for the use of our de-
scendants, but they have no equally definite standard to put
in the place of business methods. In such a case they do discount the future, but chiefly on the grounds of the uncertainty as to what new resources may be discovered, and especially what substitutes may be found for nonreproducible
resources that are now essential.

MAINTAINING ESSENTIAL FREEDOMS

Economists have obviously departed far from the attitude, prevalent a generation ago, which condemned any encroachment on the customary range of things that individuals were supposed to do for themselves, as contrary to the
principles of our system. C. H. Cooley long ago disposed of
the idea that the way to develop effective capacity for deci-
sion-making is to impose on everyone complete responsibility for all the decisions that affect his interests. It is no service to the principle of freedom and individual responsibility
to overload the individual with more decisions than he can
give proper attention to, or with decisions of a character
with which he cannot hope to cope successfully. The pertinent question, from this standpoint, is whether he has a sufficient range of responsibilities, of kinds that he has a reasonable chance of dealing with. To this end, since decision
is an effort unpleasant to many, and retreat from freedom
an attractive refuge, we probably need to be confronted
with more and heavier "challenges" than most of us would
voluntarily invite. Hence limits need to be set on the tendency to give the individual all the securities he is likely to
seek.

There are some freedoms everyone needs to exercise,

and others that are enormously important for their results to society, though only a few individuals have the rare combination of capacity and luck required to exercise them successfully. Such are the freedoms of leadership, including freedom to carve out new occupations or to introduce new products or new ideas. Business freedom is in this class, in differing degrees. The small self-employed enterprise is sometimes, though rarely, a source of pioneering improvements, and more often a refuge from unemployment. Corporate enterprise, on the other hand, makes possible mass production, using applied science, on a private basis; and this most economists continue to support. They do so only partly on grounds of efficiency and in spite of a bad past record of unstable employment. Economists, who are against concentrated power in general, find private enterprise still subject to considerable (if imperfect) competitive checks; but beyond that, it affords multiple centers of decision which—after due deduction for intercorporate relations—are genuinely independent of one another. Freedom of criticism and dissent, which economists prize above the general run of "economic values," would be subject to obvious dangers in an economy with one supreme employing authority. And the meaning of freedom of the press under such conditions would be problematical, to say the least.

This kind of consideration appears to be gaining in importance in the typical economist's appraisal of the case for private enterprise, as problems of near-monopoly and unstable employment make the customary economic arguments relatively weaker. Danger to political and personal freedoms does not prevent some economists from espousing democratic collectivism, but it probably does deter others. They may admit the reality of the danger, even while they discount dogmatic statements that freedom is one and indivisible and that political and intellectual freedoms stand or fall with business freedom and the "profit system." If pressed, a representative group might hold that the methods which a democratic and decentralized socialism could use to deal with economic problems, including unemployment, are probably sufficiently available to the mixed system we now have; and that the chance that this is true is good enough to be worth a trial. Nearly all would give the benefit of the doubt to gradual and evolutionary change, as against either abrupt and complete transformation, or a futile attempt to preserve unchanged a past in which the forces of change were an inseparable part.

Conclusion and Appraisal

The changes here summarized have transformed the American economy, and our way of thinking about it, into something which is not recognizable as the "capitalism" or "individualism" of the mid-nineteenth century. The society is taking responsibility for basic elements in the welfare of its members. This raises the problem of the effect on the individual of doing so much for him without commensurate obligations laid upon him in return. The challenges which the common man faces—not those which business faces—have been vastly lightened, at precisely the time when the society is facing the most threatening challenge of its existence. What we may fail to realize is that this challenge to a voluntaristic and self-governing society is a challenge to its members: the society will fail to meet its collective challenge if the members fail to develop the techniques and the ethics of voluntary working together. And this may impose a more exacting task on the individual than the individualistic tasks of which he has been partly freed, largely because it cannot be laid on him with the same automatic and compelling necessity. If he does his part, he does it voluntarily, as a moral act.

We can no longer rely on reaching economically correct results automatically, as an unintended by-product of what individuals do in pursuit of their private interests. We still need all we can get of such automatic adjustments; but there are growingly strategic areas in which the power of organized groups is such that, if sound terms of settlement are to be reached, people must consciously intend to reach them. This calls for some understanding of what economically correct adjustments are and a will to promote them rather than to pursue self-interest irresponsibly.[8] This element of practical ethics has become an indispensable economic "factor of production."

Disagreements are inevitable, but underlying them there must be a basic general agreement on the conditions necessary to the health of the system, and a willingness to support them and to check the pursuit of private interest short of inflicting serious damage on these basic essentials, without robbing this motive of its dynamic force. This calls for a high quality of imagination in visualizing where the danger lines come, and for loyalty to the system in the face of specific dissatisfactions. And a system of free personal competition with widely differentiated rewards is a natural breeder, not only of ambition and opportunity, but of dissatisfaction.

Adequate opportunity and a fair contest may justify unequal results in the eye of the detached observer. But not every boy can become President, and the unsuccessful individual is not a detached observer. His inferior fortune may be in some respects all the harder to bear when it is not a predetermined status, sanctioned by accepted authority, but an evidence of inferior achievement in an open contest. He may be disinclined to concede the adequacy of the opportunity or the fairness of the contest, and he can always cite imperfections. Despite these inevitable defects, the system

---

[8] This expresses the writer's personal judgment. He knows at least one able economist who would violently differ.

must somehow earn loyalty, and its constituent groups and individuals must accord it. Their loyalty must be tough-fibered enough to tolerate the amount of inequality that is an inescapable incident of a healthy economy dependent on individual incentives.

Without this tough-fibered loyalty, it will be all the more difficult to hammer out the necessary working compromise between the values of stability and the need for change. New and emergent needs must be met, without too much upsetting of the expectations on which people plan their lives. Some such disturbance is unavoidable; and a recognition of this fact is perhaps the first requirement for surmounting the resulting difficulties, some of which amount to injustice.

What remains to be seen is whether this can go on as a humanizing process rather than one of regimentation or disruption; and whether it can go far enough and fast enough to save Western society. Can we restore the saving positive value which medieval society had, by learning to act as members of one body under the strains of a dynamic, and not a static, society, maintaining the freedom and the vigor of individual incentive which are essential to progress? In short, can we do all this in ways that preserve an all-pervading basis of voluntary action, rather than replacing this with totalitarian discipline? It is a formidable assignment with destiny. Its moral requirements may well appear more exacting than those of any previous society.

CHAPTER FOUR

Forms of Economic Liberty and What Makes Them Important

Introduction

For several centuries, culminating in the nineteenth, the course of European civilization could fairly be plotted in terms of the progressive achievement of increased liberty: intellectual, social, political and economic. With the world now dominated by a life-and-death struggle between free and totalitarian systems, there is no need to remind the reader that this trend has been definitely reversed and

Adapted by permission from *Freedom: Its Meaning*, Ruth Nanda Anshen, ed. (New York: Harcourt, Brace & Company, 1940). The original essay was written at a time when mass unemployment remaining from the depression of the thirties had not yet been absorbed, as it was later under the stimulus of the rearmament drive which began in 1940. Accordingly, it was natural that the problem of unemployment dominated the discussion. In revising it for the present republication the author has eliminated statements no longer pertinent and has included brief mention of the current altered state of this problem. The discussion nevertheless continues to concentrate on unemployment to an extent that is disproportionate in terms of the conditions of 1956. For a more comprehensive view, with a distribution of emphasis more representative of the present, the reader should turn to Chapters 6–7.

that all forms of liberty are now fighting for their lives. The year 1914 stands as the most fatal landmark of this reversal.

It is true that in the economic field the growth of public controls had reversed the trend much earlier, moving toward restoring a balance between social control and private interests, which had been upset by the too-extreme *laissez faire* of the early nineteenth century. Here economic adjustment was apparently following an independent course. As a result, the essential unity of the crisis of liberty in all fields may not be self-evident. Yet I believe this essential unity to represent the important truth of the matter, wherever the issue at stake is not the balanced limitation of economic liberty, but its destruction as an effective force.

If political freedom means democracy, as may fairly be assumed, there is much reason in the proposition that it is inherently hostile to the more complete degrees of economic freedom in a developed society in which economic freedom can lead to great inequality and to insecurity for the masses; and that the two are naturally and automatically consistent only in such a simple society as is economically democratic as well as free, and in spite of being free. It has been suggested with considerable force that a political system in which power goes by sheer numbers will not naturally tolerate a free and autonomous economic system in which power is distributed according to the command of wealth. Rather, having the ultimate power, the political system will take over the economic system and remake it more nearly in its own image. If this is the natural tendency, the effect of the economic situation upon the political and intellectual system deserves more than a passing thought. In fact, it may turn out to be the vital and decisive factor in the case. We should seriously consider the possibility that, if political and intellectual freedom are used to put an end to economic freedom, they may thereby themselves commit suicide.

It should not be necessary to argue the fact that, in the

realms of action, freedom in itself implies limitations; and that not all restrictions are surrenders of the essential substance of liberty. And it should not be necessary to argue that freedom is not one thing, but many, and that some forms may need to be restricted in the interest of other forms. We have grown hardened to the opposition that has greeted every new economic restriction, on the ground that it was an interference with "personal liberty." This was, of course, both true and untrue. Business liberty is perhaps one form of personal liberty, though the modern large-scale business institutions have more the aspect of impersonal organisms. But business liberty is not, in itself, the thing which is conveyed to the mind by the general term "personal liberty." They are distinct.

Yet, while distinct, they are connected in ways which we are beginning to realize, with the help of what has been happening in the countries ruled by dictatorships and organized on a totalitarian basis. While business liberty can and must be restricted, it seems overwhelmingly probable that it cannot be wiped out, or restricted beyond its power to maintain a healthy existence, without wiping out also true personal liberty in all the more important senses. This is the most important conclusion to which the following examination of the forms of economic liberty will lead. It appears to be the paramount factor in the answer to the question, "Is economic freedom worth keeping?"

Basic Concepts

It seems hopeless to attempt to define by simple formulas the scope of economic liberty and the limits on restraints in a modern highly specialized society. The most characteristic formula of the age of individualism states that everyone is (or should be) free to use his own possessions in any way that does not interfere with the like liberty of others. But upon analysis this formula turns out to define nothing. One might be free to rob one's neighbors, the neighbors being equally free to do the same. Or all might be equally free to use a blackjack on any street corner. Of course, under these conditions no one would be free to leave his property unprotected by his private armed force and have any expectation of finding it when he returned, nor would anyone be free to walk to his place of occupation with any assurance of arriving, or returning at night. The system, which this formula was framed to fit, protects these liberties rather than those of the burglar or the wielder of the blackjack, and with good reason; but the formula does not specify them. What the formula seems to mean is that there are certain basic liberties, which the formula itself does not define, in which all alike have an interest and which are consistent with a constructive scheme of living together, in which all alike can be protected.

But these universal liberties, while basic, do not carry us far in explaining the structure of a complex industrial society. In practical terms, the liberties and restrictions of the hired worker are different from those of his employer, and necessarily so. If there is something universal underlying this differentiation—and there is—it consists of the liberty of each, if he will and can, to change his role. And in this case each acquires the liberties, and becomes subject to the restrictions, which formerly pertained to another. Any universal liberty in our system hinges on the liberty to change one's role.

Since there must be restrictions, and since their forms must change with changing conditions, there is a natural tendency to look on changes from the standpoint of the new restrictions they impose, as limitations on liberty, by which is meant limitations on its former scope. This, of course, represents a fact; but it is not the most important fact in the case. The most important fact, if we wish to know whether restrictions have gone too far, is the scope of liberty that remains. It may be, with powers and restrictions both increasing, that the sum of what we are in effect free to do is increasing also, rather than diminishing.

If we are to look at the different forms of freedom, we must ask ourselves: Freedom of whom? Freedom for what? Freedom from what? As to the first, we find that there are some liberties—like the liberty to choose what one will eat for dinner—which everyone may and should normally exercise constantly. (Actually, of course, it is in most cases the housewife who makes this choice for the family.) And there are some—like the liberty to lead a political movement or to direct a major industry—for which opportunity should be open to everyone who can qualify, so far as practicable, but for which few, in the nature of the case, can manage to qualify and which fewer still can hope to exercise effectively or successfully. It is around this latter group of liberties that some of the most crucial issues hinge today. And there is a danger, which we must avoid, of thinking that, because few exercise them at any one time, therefore they are not important in a democratic society. The conclusion is unwarranted: the reason is insufficient.

The liberties in question are those of leadership and direction; obviously of crucial importance. And while the major positions of this sort may be relatively few, nonetheless in a society with as many groups and group activities as ours, a surprisingly large number of people have the opportunity to exercise leadership in some activity or other. Under authoritarian leadership and direction, individuals may still have limited liberties within a prescribed system. But leadership and direction must be free, if the system itself is to have the quality of liberty. And if this statement sounds oracular, the remainder of this chapter will be devoted to developing its meaning. For the system itself to have the quality of freedom it is necessary, not that every individual should be a leader in every field, but that any idea or project should have free opportunity to prove its usefulness and make its way.

Freedom for what? Here we may broadly distinguish three major divisions of liberty. One may be classed as liberty to choose one's consumption goods from among those that are available (or to try to secure others which may not be available). This means not merely such things as ordering one's dinner and choosing the color and fabric of one's clothes; it means choosing one's place of residence, one's recreations and to some extent the educational environment of one's children. In a free system it includes the choosing of one's intellectual environment, at least as an adult: the pictures one looks at daily, the newspapers and books one reads, the plays one sees, the organizations one belongs to, the church one attends. And it must never be forgotten that this kind of freedom can be assured only if another kind is also assured. Someone must be free to supply what the consumer demands, or else the consumer's freedom is an illusion. And here as elsewhere the question is not whether any restrictions are imposed, but how much scope for freedom is left?

A second major division centers on the choice of an occupation. This commonly means choosing from among the occupations which the existing system holds open. But full liberty includes the liberty of the rare individual to blaze a new trail and to do something that has not been done before. And the importance of this form of liberty is out of all proportion to the number of those who have the genius to take advantage of it. Many, of course, are cranks. But the world could not afford to do without the group which has included Johnny Appleseed, Luther Burbank, and Frederick Winslow Taylor.

Full liberty calls for something more. One may be free

to choose whether to be an electrician or a garmentmaker, without having any part in the decision whether electricians shall produce radios or something else, or what kind of garments shall be made and how many, or under what kind of shop conditions. Beyond the choice of an occupation there lies the choice of what the array of occupations in the system shall be, and what shall be produced by them. We may have freedom for one kind of choice, but not the other. In fact, socialistic systems are likely to afford a good deal of liberty of the first sort, but little or none of the second.

Under a system built on exchange, liberty includes liberty to alienate things, and partially to alienate one's liberty for the future, by binding oneself to contracts or by accepting the discipline that goes with industrial employment. But some minimum of liberty must remain inalienable, and the liberty to alienate must be correspondingly restricted. The contract of employment must not be allowed to create irrevocable servitude. This inalienable minimum is gradually being extended and includes education, some rights to health and, in effect, a minimum of material goods and services. Traditional individualism, and the legal system that went with it, overstressed the liberty to alienate at the expense of the need that the essential conditions of liberty be inalienable. But this represented merely one concept of liberty, and is not the one now prevailing.

Freedom from what? Certainly not from all outside forces conditioning one's actions: that is unthinkable. Primarily, we mean freedom from coercive authority wielding irresistible power and prescribing positively what the individual shall do. The liberal theory is that government tells people what they must not do, and leaves them free within the limits thus drawn. Naturally, the area of the *verboten* must not grow until it leaves insufficient range of choice open. Also, some positive requirements are necessary. Even an individualistic state properly requires parents to care for their children and send them to school, while anyone who chooses to operate a factory must meet the requirements of the safety-appliance laws.

There must also be freedom from undue and organized private persecution, and to this end the state must set some limit on the liberty to persecute. Not that anyone ever is, or should be, free from the pressure of the opinion of his fellows. Such pressures are omnipresent, whether in Tennessee or Greenwich Village, making for conformity of some sort. And if an individual does not care enough for an independent course of action to withstand these pressures in their more ordinary forms, he has simply not earned his liberty. When someone does withstand or disregard them, they have a surprising way of vanishing. If someone argues with you that because of these pressures all freedom is an illusion, he is probably either speaking the language of metaphysics or trying to persuade you to surrender what liberty you have to some form of authoritarian control.

Our present economic system is geared to favor innovation of certain sorts, largely as to technical methods of production and the introduction of new products. Innovation as to industrial relations is perhaps less easy, but by no means impossible. Liberty as to styles of living in general seems to be greater than it was. It is chiefly radical proposals as to the social system itself that have to meet the stronger pressures toward conformity. But on the whole we have established a popular attitude that is sufficiently tolerant of nonconformity to permit it to exist, and even to flourish; and that appears to be the main thing. This state of things could easily be overthrown. The preservation of it requires the proverbial "eternal vigilance." [1] We may not be too well satisfied with what we have in this respect, but it is a pre-

---

[1] This passage stands as it was originally written, a decade before the beginning of the excesses called "McCarthyism." (Footnote written in 1956.)

cious achievement, imperfect as it may be, and one not lightly to be abandoned.

There is also freedom from the limitations imposed by poverty, disease, ignorance, weakness, and lack of opportunity. Full protection is impossible, mankind being what it is. And such protection as is possible of these forms of liberty requires some restrictions on some at least of the other forms of liberty. Protection of freedom from disease requires a public health service with powers of quarantine and various compulsory preventive measures. Disease carriers should not be free to be handlers of food. Rigorous application of the principle of individualistic liberty would sacrifice many of these other forms of freedom. And those who reach a socialistic position via humanitarian and democratic ideals do so because they believe that our traditional forms of economic liberty are at war with these other forms, and that the other forms are the more important. This is a serious issue, and not to be dismissed lightly.

Such persons are likely to hold that the traditional individualistic liberties are formal merely; and that the substance of liberty as distinct from the form depends on what one can do (with the help of one's formal liberties) to promote and protect one's substantive interests. Where so many of us are able to do so little, there is much reason in the claim that persons so limited possess the form of liberty without the substance. Any real answer to our present problems should face this issue squarely. It seems clearly impossible for everyone to possess both complete formal liberty and complete protection against disease, poverty, ignorance, and folly. The real issue is whether a sane balance can be struck between formal liberty and protection of its "material content," or whether we must go to one extreme or the other.

To what extent, if at all, does real liberty to do something require that one should also have the ability and the means to do it? We are not here concerned with attempting to solve metaphysical problems, but rather with giving such clarity as may be given to the ideas prevalent among common men: the ideas they work by. And on this basis it seems clear that real liberty implies opportunity and ability to do something meaningful directed toward a given end; but that in the nature of the case, it does not carry a guarantee of success. In this sense liberty and ability are not synonymous. The content of liberty can be enriched by increased opportunity and ability to command the material means of success, and it can be impoverished by the opposite; but the fact that there are severe limitations on opportunity and ability does not mean that liberty does not exist.

My liberty to buy the United States Steel Corporation may mean nothing; but it is part of my liberty to acquire a business enterprise or an interest in one. This may mean more, though perhaps not enough to make very much impression on a large-scale economic system. It is in turn part of the general liberty of any who will and can, to acquire and direct business enterprises, large or small. And this means a great deal, whether or not we are wholly satisfied with the results. It affects the character of the United States Steel Corporation, whether or not I personally play any part in this. It affects me if I buy a loaf of bread baked in an oven made of steel produced by the Corporation. From the standpoint of liberty, my inability to buy the Corporation is a serious matter only if liberty to do this is one of those liberties which do not have their proper effect unless everyone actually exercises them. Apparently it does not belong in that class.

A more serious matter is what happens to the liberty to choose an occupation, when the system is unable to afford jobs to some millions of the population who need them. This is one of the liberties which the system requires most of us to exercise; and such widespread inability as existed during the crisis of the 1930's was a grave impairment of the substance of this liberty. A system of full-scale collectivism could, if it would, increase tremendously the effective content of this particular liberty. And it is this one fact, more than any other, that gives ground for the contention that there would be more real personal liberty under full collectivism than under the system of private enterprise. There would, of course, be a price to pay. In the first place, the assortment of occupations itself would be prescribed, not freely worked out (at least not under collectivism of the centrally administered type). And in the second place, the selection of candidates for jobs and for advancement would be made by a different kind of agency, under different motives and pressures. How important this would be, we will inquire into later.

Liberty is always a matter of choice between available alternatives; and the available alternatives represent the range of opportunity. The requirements here are that the range of alternatives shall be as rich as possible, as responsive as possible to the preferences of the people, and as accessible and well-known as possible. This requires the equivalent of a well-organized market, under any economic system, collectivist or individualistic. The collectivist market might be better organized than the individualistic, though also probably less rich and less responsive. And the individualistic market is capable of being much better organized than it is, without ceasing to be individualistic. The range of market opportunity can be much improved.

One pair of concepts, the relationships of which are perhaps most difficult to trace, is liberty and security. Liberty implies some insecurity, because at bottom it implies that people are testing their capacity to make effective use of available powers and resources, with no absolute guarantee of a successful outcome. They may succeed or they may fail, and this uncertainty spells some degree of insecurity. It also implies, in an interdependent society, that the experiments which some of us try may have unexpected effects on the rest of us, and they may make the rest of us to that extent insecure. Yet liberty also requires some degree of underlying security if it is to have much effective meaning and content. We must be able to count on something, or our experiments can end only in disaster.

This issue is harder to formulate in a satisfactory universal generalization than to settle in particular cases. We can afford purchasers security against physically harmful foods, and let them govern their own diet within the very wide range of choice that would be left; while the range of liberty that would be left to the food-producing industries would not be limited in such a way as to cripple any of their defensible activities. On much the same terms we can control individual behavior sufficiently to afford a degree of security against epidemic diseases which would come much closer to the standard which our medical knowledge permits, though this would require much more restriction of personal liberty; and a perfect result (within the limits of existing medical knowledge) might not be humanly possible. We can guarantee everyone security against absolute economic disaster and still leave individuals free to achieve what status they can, above the assured minimum; but there can be no general guarantee against failure to achieve the sort of economic position people choose to strive for, or the sort they set as a satisfactory standard.

The security to which people generally feel they have a just claim is the opportunity to do some work of a worthwhile character and to receive a reward bearing a proper relation to the worth of what they do. Recognizing the difficulty of defining worth, it seems clear that this claim is not easy to satisfy, consistently with leaving private enterprise a fair opportunity to reabsorb the unemployed. It may be able to offer only jobs calling for a change of industry, or of skills to a lower-paid job, or of residence; and all these changes may mean a sacrifice, measured by one's previous status. Security cannot properly mean protection against all such sacrifices, but how high can its standard be set? One theoretical answer might be the assurance of such a level of income that the worker would feel that in accepting any offer that might be made by private enterprise, he was not being coerced by the force of hard necessity, but was free. In practice this standard would be hopelessly indefinite; and any attempt to construe it by political processes is likely to set it too high for private industry to outbid successfully, with some of the job opportunities it is actually able to offer, in the readjustment from a depression. All these problems are bound up in the requirement that an applicant for un-employment compensation must stand ready to accept a "reasonable" job offer.

It appears that we are not in a position to guarantee universal security, if this is defined as freedom from the fear of losing one's job, and of being forced to accept something poorer, or even of enduring some real hardship and privation, if one does not meet fair standards of performance. Even a collectivist society would have unequally attractive jobs. Some might be of a disciplinary sort, involving hardship; and many others would be of a distinctly unsatisfactory sort, for those who do not succeed in qualifying for the better positions. There would be the likelihood, too, that the assignment of these jobs would be governed to a large extent by considerations other than industrial capacity and performance—in short, by political considerations. And this would introduce another kind of insecurity, some aspects of which might be even more serious.

Liberty is a burden as well as a privilege; and the actual exercise of undictated and unguided free choice in every act of life would overburden all of us. Therefore the most basic form of liberty is the liberty to choose how much liberty one will exercise and what guidance one will accept. The really unfree system is not the system without guidance and direction, but the system which deprives the individual of this basic liberty of choice.

Such a system, imposed on a population in which the urge to decide things for themselves is not too deeply ingrained, and managed with the greatest skill, might produce the illusion of liberty, in the sense of action in accordance with one's nature, not by leaving action free but by regimenting human nature to conformity, from childhood up. Where the leaders of such a system would ultimately come from, remains a problem; unless all real leadership were relegated to an infallible tradition or "ideology," set up by the original founder or founders. And how long this could endure is another problem—the answer to which, let us hope, this country never has occasion to discover for itself.[2]

To escape this suicide of liberty requires a people with a sane balance in their natures. They must have enough of the urge to independent decision to reject complete regimentation. But they must have enough underlying like-mindedness to make most of them accept, without formal coercion, fundamental ideas and moral codes calling for action in harmony with the interests of the community. This is the indispensable moral basis of liberty, no less in the economic than in other realms.

A recalcitrant minority will always have to be coerced; and the majority will necessarily be subject to direction in many things which require more definite conformity than mere moral codes will bring about, and in which they will accept direction, not because they would voluntarily choose to act in the particular way the authorities decide on, but because they are intelligently law-abiding and recognize the

[2] The present "new look" in post-Stalinist Russia—as of 1956—appears to involve some slight relaxations of the Stalinist degree of regimentation. These will be watched with great, but cautious, interest.

need for this kind of conformity. If the controls go beyond what this law-abiding spirit will voluntarily support, then there is trouble ahead. To repeat, the question is not whether there is specific direction, but whether the sphere of liberty that remains is adequate.

Wartime and Peacetime Economies

Normally, a fairly sharp distinction can be drawn between the peacetime economy and the wartime economy, the latter being, in democratic countries, ordinarily a temporary interlude. In wartime the advantages of the free economy are to a large extent in abeyance, for several reasons. In the first place, in wartime the dominant purpose of the economy is no longer to give individuals as much as possible of the means to liberal individual living, but to concentrate as much as possible of the country's resources on a single national end: the winning of the war. Any unnecessary surplus for individual citizens becomes, temporarily, an undesirable thing. In the second place, the wastes and fumblings of the market's trial-and-error methods become inappropriate as compared with the method of centralized statistical canvassing of resources and needs. And in the third place, the shortages of essential materials and of labor and resources for essential purposes are such that the unchecked forces of supply and demand would raise prices and rewards far beyond the level that is necessary for the most effective stimulus to the needed mobilizations. If increases in prices are limited short of the level that would equate supply and demand, rationing of the more essential scarce supplies and resources becomes necessary and is tolerated as a temporary emergency measure.

The peacetime "war against depression" is sometimes spoken of as if the same general kinds of measures would be appropriate to it. But it seems on the whole more nearly true that the essential conditions are here reversed. In wartime the effective demand for goods and services is excessive; in depressions it is deficient. In wartime, more-than-adequate purchasing power is forthcoming via deficit-financing and credit expansion, with no serious effects on business confidence. In depressions the reverse is the case; business confidence is weakened to start with, and deficit-financing beyond a moderate limit serves to make the weakness worse. In wartime the economic energizing forces are superabundant, and it is a question of directing them into the most essential channels and restricting their action in other directions. In depressions the basic problem is a partial paralysis of the energizing forces. For all these reasons (which could be much elaborated) it appears that the same measures will not work in the same way in the two situations. The peacetime economy requires a fuller measure of liberty, unless the whole system is to be revolutionized.

Liberty in the Individualistic Scheme

It is perhaps not necessary to sum up systematically the place and forms of liberty in the individualistic scheme of theory and practice. Among economists, at least, the emphasis shifted early in the nineteenth century from liberty as an inherent "natural right" to liberty as an instrument of economic plenty. There is much to be said for the contention that liberty of some sort *is* a natural right in the sense that it is such a vital need of humanity that it cannot be denied without serious or even disastrous social consequences. But while this means that everyone should have liberty of some sort, it does not necessarily mean that everyone must have economic liberty (though it creates a strong presumption, the economic realm being so important). And it certainly does not in itself mean that there should be the precise variety of economic liberties that has constituted the historic system of individualism.

The individualistic system was based on freedom of consumers to choose among products and among competing producers of any one product. Everyone was free to attempt what only a limited number could succeed in: namely, the working-out of improved methods of producing goods, or the development of new products; and he was free to imitate the pioneers and compete with them (except as limited by patent rights). And all were free to secure the co-operation of labor and capital by individual bargaining in a free market, whereby each would get as much as the market could afford. Access to all occupations was to be similarly free. Parties were bound by contracts they had made, but the contracts were free, and contracts unduly limiting liberty for the future were not enforced.

In this system freedom was an instrument for the production of plenty, and the plenty was to be distributed on the basis of freedom for each to get as much as his services, or those of his property, were worth in the market in some economic employment. A wide distribution of the plenty was desired, but economists were not always too hopeful as to the possibility, under either individualistic or socialistic systems, of freeing the undistinguished masses of humanity from the burden of poverty.

The system was one of voluntary co-operation, which the co-operators were free to withhold at any time (except for the performance of existing contracts). This freedom to withhold was the basis of their power to bargain for the price of their co-operation. The fact that if they held their resources idle they lost all income from them was the only compulsion laid upon them to co-operate with someone or other and not to let their resources lie idle. Aside from this compulsion, they were free to produce what they chose, or not to produce: to work for whom they chose or not to work; to buy from whom they chose or not to buy, at a particular time or ever.[3]

This freedom not to co-operate seems to be an inseparable part of the freedom to choose with whom one will co-operate, and the manner of one's co-operation, and to bargain for remuneration. The state can hardly order people to co-operate without assuming considerable responsibility for the manner and matter of the co-operation, and thus, in effect, introducing the essentials of a collectivist system. Yet this freedom is clearly dangerous; and any widespread failure to co-operate, or the withholding of co-operation, can produce serious industrial paralysis. Therefore this form of freedom is no longer a purely private affair, but has become a matter of vital and recognized public interest.

Employers can be trusted not to suspend operations as soon as profits become unsatisfactory; they are under economic pressure to continue operating so long as they can cover actual current operating expenses. The more stably established among them are under pressure to go further and to operate at a loss, so long as financially practicable and so long as recovery is in prospect, rather than disband their working organizations. These pressures are strengthened by a growing sense of public obligation to maintain employment. But the employers are also under pressure to avoid bankruptcy or unduly heavy losses. And as the price system operates, a moderate decline in demand often takes effect more largely in a decline of output than in a radical reduction of prices such as might result from a resolute attempt to maintain full production and employment at all costs. Thus, despite strong pressures to maintain operation, the liberty not to co-operate remains an important factor.

Central features in this problem are the timing of pur-

---

[3] This is, of course, qualified in the case of public service industries by a positive obligation to render service.

chases of durable consumers' goods, such as houses and automobiles, and of the installation of durable productive equipment. We have learned the explosive possibilities of irregular timing in these matters; yet the state can hardly step in and prescribe regular timing by public fiat without destroying the basis of the voluntary economic system. If it is to work toward this end, it must do so by indirection, acting on the causes of the irregular timing; and the manner of doing this represents no easy problem, especially as the economists have not yet reached certainty as to some of the fundamental causes at work.

Yet the cumulative result of this freedom to withhold economic co-operation has at times been to deprive millions of the opportunity, and in effect of the liberty, to earn a living, reducing them to dependence—which also undermines the basis of the free economic system. This constituted the central dilemma of economic liberty during the decade of the thirties. Since then we have passed through World War II and the Korean War, and entered the period of armed "cold war," with this country acting as the principal "arsenal of democracy," military and economic. Under the resulting stimulus, our national product has increased hugely, and we have had high-level employment, with only moderate fluctuations.

Furthermore, our economy has gained certain protective features, permitting us to hope that it has become inherently less susceptible to fluctuation and depression. These protections include "built-in" fiscal stabilizers, a notably broadened distribution of incomes, and the public implementation of stabilization policy, established by the Act of 1946 and centering in the President's Council of Economic Advisers. This is backed by a new understanding and acceptance of fiscal policy as a means of stabilizing total demand, while leaving its allocation to the forces of private interest. On the side of private industry, long-run programs of capital outlays seem to offer interesting possibilities of stabilizing effects. All in all, our prospects for stabilization appear distinctly improved.

But these improved protections remain to be tested. For example, a substantial reduction of public outlays for defense and overseas aid might put a greater strain on them than they have hitherto experienced. It is still pertinent to ask what might happen if we were to encounter a real depression, even one considerably less severe than that of the thirties.

If this should occur, it would not be appropriate to lay all the blame on the principle of individualism. One answer to this is like the proverbial answer to the claim that Christianity has failed—namely, that it has not been tried. The individualistic principle has not been consistently followed. The aggravation of our troubles is at least in some considerable part due to just the sort of restrictions on free competition, and obstacles to free movement, against which Adam Smith directed his heaviest artillery. This includes not only barriers to free international intercourse, but a host of internal restrictions on free competitive bargaining. Trade unions set a standard wage and maintain it, even though industry may not be willing or able to employ all their members at that wage level. Industrial producers do something similar with prices. Both are, quite understandably, protecting themselves against what could otherwise degenerate into competition of a ruthless and cutthroat sort.

Among economists it has come to be generally regarded as more than doubtful whether, for example, an indiscriminate slash in wages would be a useful measure of recovery in any and all situations of depression, in a country as largely self-contained as our own. The problem is not as simple as that. For wages constitute not only a major part of the cost of producing goods, but also a major part of the purchasing power on which the demand for goods depends.

Hence the effect of an indiscriminate reduction in wages and prices might largely cancel out. Particular adjustments may still be needed; but we are leaning toward the view that general reductions are of relatively little use as recovery measures in industries and trades that serve consumers directly. And in those that serve producers, such measures may be fully effective only in connection with other measures of a more positive sort. In any case, we shall probably have to shape our future course on the assumption that any future recessions will not be met by ruthlessly competitive slashing of wages and prices. Instead they may be so successfully pegged as to create an opposite danger: that of creeping inflation, with wages and prices rising in good times and resisting decline in recessions.

Under such conditions, what can we hope to do, within the framework of the free economic system? We can hope to manage a social security program in such a way that it will not only help the victims of depression with a maximum of preservation of self-respect and a minimum of "pauperization " and demoralization, but will also have some stabilizing effect via the steadying of the flow of purchasing power. For further stabilization, we can attempt to fill the gaps in private spending for consumption and investment by public deficit-spending or to stabilize private spending power by adjustments of taxation. Such policies can have some effect in mitigating industrial fluctuations of moderate extent and duration, if well planned and timed, and placed on a basis which does not create distrust and fear of endlessly accumulating public deficits. But a prolonged depression would probably exceed the limits of usefulness of this policy. It is a more than doubtful reliance for combating a state of chronic partial stagnation.

For the longer future, we can hope for improvement in the partial stabilization of investment spending, possibly fortified by voluntary mutual arrangements between different industrial groups, which have a common interest in this matter. This last is probably a matter for decades of education, experimentation, and difficult adjustment, and at best it can hardly be hoped that it will achieve perfect success. In short, under the free system we may hope to mitigate the severity of economic stagnations, especially if we can establish a sound basis for international peace, and to cushion their incidence on the chief victims, but hardly to cure them completely. Ultimately, a liberal cannot help believing that the organized common sense of humanity and man's common interest in uninterrupted production will succeed in reducing the evil of depressions to proportions that will not be seriously harmful. But some burden of this sort appears to be a part of the price we pay for the system of economic freedom.

If this burden once more becomes substantial, many will ask seriously whether it is worth the price; and some will presumably decide that it is not. Then we might be seriously confronted with a choice between private enterprise and collectivism, not on the Soviet model but of a democratic sort. In terms of freedom, what would such a choice involve?

Economic Freedom Under Collectivism

A collectivist system might develop less productive power than the individualistic system, but it would be likely to utilize far more completely such productive power as it did develop, and to afford practically complete opportunity for everyone to get a job. On this basis alone many would rate it above the individualistic system on a scale of human liberty—always assuming that it need not follow the Russian model, but may be democratic, and as hospitable to personal freedom as its essential nature permits. This raises the question what effects on freedom are bound up with the essential nature of economic collectivism. In such a matter we can, of course, deal only with probabilities, not certainties.

As already remarked, under collectivism consumers would presumably continue to exercise free choice among products offered for sale, though within narrower limits as to amounts and assortments of goods available and presumably as to the time of delivery, especially in the case of durable goods. And workers would presumably have considerable freedom of selection among occupations, within a range somewhat more limited and standardized than at present. The question of what goods should be produced would be affected by the consumers' choices as expressed in the market, but with a difference, since the determination of what wants should or should not be satisfied would in the last analysis rest with a governing bureaucracy, modified by whatever democratic machinery might be set up for determining general policies. It is here that the great difference would lie—always provided the state did not prescribe the personal, cultural, and intellectual activities of the people as the Russian state does at present. Into the probabilities bearing on this question we will inquire in a moment. The chief liberty that is sure to be given up is what we know as business liberty; and the question is whether this particular form of liberty is important enough to be kept, at the price we have to pay for it.

The Choice: How Important Is Business Liberty?

Considering how heavy this price can become, it is not too easy for an impartial observer, accustomed to the principle that the welfare of the greatest number weighs most heavily in the social scales, to justify a decision to keep the continuity of development, building on the core of the existing system and working for betterment within these limitations. Many persons are actuated to such a decision for a variety of reasons that will not stand the test of critical scrutiny.

One such reason is the fact that many persons who are now prosperous and able to live lives of much freedom and generous proportions would be less prosperous and more limited under a collectivist system. If the price to be paid includes the economic displacement of some millions of unemployed, this reason would appear to rest on a warped scale of values. If it is to be defended, it must be not on the ground of the enjoyments or welfare of the fortunate groups taken by themselves, but on the ground that it is indispensable to society that there should be as many as possible who are able to live really generous lives and be free to cultivate the accompanying interests and capacities.

This contains a large measure of truth, even where there is not enough to give everyone this privilege, and even if many of those who enjoy it put their advantages to futile or unworthy uses. The same liberty which these individuals misuse leads the best among them to make imaginative and invaluable contributions to society, of a sort that no bureaucracy would accomplish. Society needs such contributions. On the other hand, while it is not safe to take for granted that the creative leaders of a collectivist system would be penuriously paid, they would not be in a position, out of their private funds, to endow expensive enterprises of social pioneering. This last is a really important matter from the standpoint of free social experimentation. But on the whole, while the argument has important force, it does not seem sufficient: this reason for retaining business liberty is not as bad as many radicals think, but it is not good enough.

Another argument is that one of the primary objectives of collectivism, namely, the abolition of class inequalities, would turn out to be an illusion; and that the result would simply be to set up new class divisions, with a fresh starting point and an altered basis of selection. To speak in unduly simple terms, a bureaucracy would replace a "plutocracy." One might grant this point fully, and still hold that the most decisive element in the case for collectivism is not affected. This argument also hardly seems good enough.

Another argument is that the selection of industrial leaders and directors would be on a basis that would afford a less rigorous test of efficiency in doing the job, and especially a less rigorous weeding-out of the less obvious grades of inefficiency, which could not be proved by bureaucratic records of performance. The force of this argument is necessarily conjectural. The existing system is far from perfect on the score of efficiency. Tendencies to nepotism and bureaucracy exist. But they are under a pretty severe check: more so than bureaucratic tendencies in government. With the Russian example before us, we may admit that a collectivist dictatorship *can* be ruthlessly efficient, though the element of ruthlessness may itself involve a very considerable sacrifice of the possibility of the higher and more creative forms of efficiency. But there seems no point in discussing such a system in a study of which the main concern is liberty. And democratic collectivism would presumably involve a considerable sacrifice of efficiency: possibly more than would be involved in periodic moderate depressions. This argument has force; nevertheless it does not seem to prove its case quite beyond question.

More serious, perhaps, than a loss of efficiency in the current work of production, is the cumulative effect over generations of a slowing-down of the rate of technical progress; and this also might be expected under a system of democratic collectivism. Yet it is not likely that progress would stop; and there is much evidence that our present speed of technical advance is greater than we can assimilate with complete success, in terms of its social impact. On these grounds alone we might be better off if the rate slowed down somewhat. But this is a luxury we cannot at present afford. With the free and communistic worlds immersed in a contest of economic productivity, a deliberate slackening of the rate of technical progress is unthinkable for either side. If business liberty can contribute to technical progress, we need all the contributions it can make.

What would be the effect of a collectivist system on those forms of freedom which are properly designated as "personal liberty?" Is there any reason why personal liberty, as distinct from business liberty, should not be as unrestricted under socialism as under the present system, or more so? I believe that there is; and the reason centers upon the coercive potentialities of a central administrative authority that has ultimate power over the livelihood of every citizen. This is a power of whose full impact we in this country have no direct knowledge, though we have recently had some hints, and elsewhere people have learned its full meaning by experience.

Advocates of the looser federative forms of socialism might deny the necessity for such a central authority; but without it there is no clear way of settling the terms of interchange between the industrial units that would be set up. Each can hardly be sovereign; there must be an ultimate sovereign power over them. This power must be predominantly of an administrative character; and the policy-forming decisions that might be made by a democratic (or nominally democratic) legislative authority would, even more than in our present system, have to be applied to such complicated situations that continuous and detailed democratic scrutiny would be even more impossible than with us. These policies would be extremely dependent on the administrative organization for their concrete interpretation and embodiment in action. And the administrative organization would include—how much? In a real sense it would have no limit, short of every citizen. What would be the tendencies of an organization with such possibilities of power?

The probability is that the system would start with a requirement of universal espousal of some officially formulated "ideology"—perhaps the Gospel according to Karl Marx, as expounded and interpreted by an infallible priesthood. But for the sake of argument, let us pass this by. Aside from this, what would be the natural tendencies of such an organization? A naturally defensible principle would be to permit criticism of the performance of the administration in the carrying out of the fundamental purposes of the system, but to suppress attacks on these fundamental purposes. If a more liberal principle were formally adopted, one can hardly imagine it being carried into effect by an administration of the character this one would necessarily have. But who is to decide where criticism of performance ends and attacks on fundamental principles begin? The real power would rest with the administration itself.

Some offenses and penalties might be in the hands of a judiciary, and the judiciary might be theoretically independent, though it is hard to see how this independence could be a working reality under such a system. But the administration would not be dependent on judicial penalties. It has the most irresistibly powerful system of rewards and penalties in its hands already in its power over occupational opportunity. If American political administrations held such power, how long would it be before an administration came into office which could not resist the temptation to exercise it and to construe faithfulness to the administration as an indispensable test of fitness to hold the positions it had in its gift? (Note that under full-scale collectivism this means all the real jobs in the country.) And after that happened, how long would it be before the formal guarantees of liberty ceased to be of any effect?

A radical nonconformist often has difficulty under our

present system in keeping his job or in getting another of similar quality; and this is a serious matter.[4] How much more serious would it be if there were, in the last analysis, only one employer? The sad imperfections of personal liberty as we have it are often used as arguments by radicals. Yet they seem to be the poorest of reasons for adopting a system under which such avenues of escape as now exist would be cut off and such liberty as we now have, extinguished. "Disciplinary jobs" have already been mentioned, but the term conveys no faint impression of what such discipline could amount to. It has the power to rob martyrdom of its dignity and to reduce it to bald sordidness and the breaking-down of personality itself.

In short, it seems that the existence of genuinely independent employers, with some one of whom the nonconformist can find employment, is not merely a matter of business liberty, but is one of the indispensable safeguards of true personal liberty. And this may be the one most decisive reason for refusing to make the irrevocable shift to full collectivism, despite the admitted and ominous defects of the system we have.

Conclusion

One word in closing, by way of safeguard against a possible misapprehension. This argument should not be taken as a brief for "preserving the existing system." That is a straw man. Existing systems are not preserved unchanged, no matter what we decide about them. They change of them-

---

[4] The above was originally written long before pressure was put on an increasing range of occupations to exclude anyone suspected—rightly or wrongly—of being a "security risk." The use of derogatory information from secret and unchecked sources has added to the sinister features of this situation. It would appear, as of 1956, that the worst excesses are over.

selves, if they are not altered by outside forces; and our present system is not exempt from this law. No single form of existing business liberty is sacred. But this argument is a brief for continuing to struggle onward with a system embodying the principle of liberty, economic as well as personal, in spite of the difficulties. This does not offer a quick cure of basic evils. It offers rather a prospect of generations of effort, with patience, persistence, and tolerance, to strike a sane balance between liberty and control, and to reduce our worst evils to tolerable proportions by a process of adjustment, using voluntary means to the utmost of their capacity, the whole being subject to free discussion, not directed by arbitrary fiat and suppression of dissent.

It is conceivable that at some point in such a process we might achieve enough co-ordination to reduce unemployment to minor proportions and to maintain stability in other respects without making everyone an employee of the state. At that point it would make little difference whether we called the system "socialistic" or not. "Socialism" of such a sort, reached by such a process, could still leave room for true personal liberty: it could still be democratic. But this can only be attained by a process that does not go too fast for business to adjust itself without catastrophic breakdown or violent revolution. If such a process is to continue, we must avoid committing ourselves to the experiment that would mean the end of free experimentation.

CHAPTER FIVE

Economic Welfare in a Free Society: I, Basic Conceptions

Summary Statement

Fourscore and eleven years ago Abraham Lincoln de-
livered a notably brief address, which he modestly, but mis-
takenly, predicted that the world would little note nor long
remember. This address signalized the internal struggle of a
nation that could not endure permanently half slave and half
free. Now, when our national experiment in self-government
has attained exactly twice the age it had when it won the war
over slavery, this strangely shrunken world is locked in a
wider and deadlier struggle against a more inclusive form
of servitude: a struggle testing whether the world itself can
endure half free and half implacably-aggressive totalitarian.
In this chapter we are dealing with some of the economic

Chapters 5, 6, 7, and the Epilogue with which this volume closes,
are adapted by permission of the Trustees of Columbia University in the
City of New York from "Economic Welfare in a Free Society," appear-
ing in *National Policy for Economic Welfare at Home and Abroad*,
Robert Lekachman, ed. (New York: Doubleday & Company, 1955)—
the proceedings of Columbia University Bicentennial Conference No. III,
held in May, 1954.

problems involved in the survival of the free sector of the world; and we are asking whether a free economy, evolved out of nineteenth-century private enterprise, can be adapted to meet twentieth-century standards of welfare. If not, the next step is presumably a collectivist transformation, with unforeseeable consequences for freedoms outside the economic realm: freedoms of mind and spirit, of personal attitude and political action.

If it is true that a theory can be overcome only by another theory, then our great need is to formulate, in its simplest and most basic terms, the theory that unites welfare and freedom. Doctrinaire totalitarianism cannot be overcome by an equally doctrinaire individualism; the time for that is past. To use Hegelian terms, that was the thesis to which modern totalitarianism is the antithesis. And what the West is building has the chance, at its best, to become a successful synthesis—if it can sound the keynote that can organically unite the valid elements of the opposing doctrines, and not merely try unconvincingly to hyphenate them.[1]

That unifying keynote is man, as we are learning to know him in the twentieth century; and a concept of welfare which affords balanced expression to the different sides of his nature. For he is not the kind of being that underlies either of the extreme and one-sided doctrines—not exclusively a collectivist animal or a political animal, nor exclusively an individualist animal or a bargaining animal. He is both an individual, solving problems, making decisions, meeting personal challenges, and he is, or needs to be, an actively participating member of a group that cares what happens to him and shows it in practical ways.

A system that is to give expression to his nature must

[1] It should be obvious that Communists would violently reject the version of the "Hegelian dialectic" here presented, which is poles removed from their own inversion of Hegel's principle.

somehow include both sides without crippling either. Though I have tried to define the concept in Western terms, it has room in it for diversities of emphasis in different cultures; and for a wide variety of agencies—business, political, civic, and professional—which may be found appropriate to different purposes. Propaganda-wise, this synthesis lacks the force of dogmatic certainty and logical single-mindedness which the most one-sided doctrines possess. Against this it pits the force of realism and adaptability.

If men must undertake the dangerous business of guiding their collective destinies, with all the unexpected consequences that are bound to accompany social experimentation, they are safest on a basis that leads them to respect one another's values, and to try to understand them. The experiment has so far meant both increased activity of government and increased demands on our ethical standards. And we do well to be watchful lest the combination of mass industry and the "welfare state" erode some of the independent qualities that citizens need if they are to maintain as a going concern a society that is both free and interdependent.

Soviet propaganda can be trusted to do its formidable best to persuade that part of the world which the Soviets have not yet absorbed that the union of freedom and welfare is impossible: that the only alternative to their form of slavery is private exploitation, by feudal powers in the underdeveloped countries or by plutocrats in the industrially developed countries, in either case building the prosperity of the few on the poverty and neglect of the many. For the underdeveloped countries, this challenge may be peculiarly difficult to meet. It is the industrially developed countries that have the chance to prove, to themselves and to the rest of the free world, that a free economy can not only produce wealth but diffuse it more widely than other great societies have ever done. The resulting mass demand has reinforced the economies of mass production in a cumulative spiral,

while the lack of it can be a stubborn obstacle to low manufacturing costs: in fact, a vicious circle. Finally, these favored countries have the chance to prove that they can in-
corporate safeguards for the means of welfare for the many,
while preserving the essentials of their free character.

This question is the main theme of this discussion. In
pursuit of it I have briefly examined a number of problem
areas, asking in each case whether reasonable policies of the
general sorts actually followed are consistent with the essentials of a healthy private economy. The general conclusion
reached is that there are, in any of the areas which have been
successively examined, plenty of difficult problems, and
some dangers, but no irreconcilable conflict between the requirements of welfare and those of a healthy private economy.

Perhaps the chief omission in this treatment is an attempt to appraise the simultaneous and cumulative impact
of all these policies taken together. And for such an appraisal, criteria are even more difficult to set up. It appears
that the price of freedom is not only the proverbial eternal
vigilance as to important evils, but a sense of proportion as
to what evils are most important, a renouncing of precision-
ism and perfectionism, and acceptance of the idea that freedom is worth some imperfections. These will always leave us
problems to work on. The limits of what we can safely attempt may be pushed back, but only if we succeed in growing as our problems grow.

The Central Theme of the Present Study

Is man's ambition to mold his destiny through his own
intelligence dangerously presumptuous? Freedom includes
freedom to go wrong, and the consequences could be as
shattering in the human and social spheres as those of the

atom bomb in the material realm. It is a commonplace that the growth of man's applied power seems to have outstripped his wisdom in the use of it. To many, he seems today less like the master of his fate than like the Sorcerer's Apprentice, who has loosed forces he cannot guide.

Any society today must be, at least ostensibly, dedicated to the welfare of its members. A free society proceeds on the faith that this dedication is least exposed to perversion if the members have plenty to say about it. The members act voluntarily and privately to multiply economic products—that is part of our idea of the means to welfare. But the method—mass production—generates concentrated power and a kind of private regimentation, as well as numerous other abuses. And men are also free to use means that are public, political, and compulsory; to control this private power—if they can—to protect individuals from the results of their mistakes, and generally to pursue whatever ideas of interest and welfare their political organs are adapted to express and promote. And the question is raised whether this combination of private and public power may end by doing so much controlling as to impair or destroy the free character of the society. Is this the destiny of the "welfare state"? If the process gains the reinforcement of a full-blown "science of man," will this be a liberating force or will it be perverted into an instrument of Orwellian regimentation? [2] Are we witnessing the suicide of the liberalism that was born of the eighteenth-century Enlightenment, under the impact of its own mechanistic creations? Or can such a fate be avoided?

Let us try to reduce part of this unanswerable question

[2] After writing the foregoing, I find Dr. Robert Oppenheimer quoted in *The New York Times*, May 23, 1956, as saying: "Science leads to powers whose exercise spells disaster and nuclear weapons are not the deepest of these. In the great strides in the biological sciences, and far more still in the early beginnings of an understanding of man's psyche, of his beliefs, his learning, his memory and his probable action, one can see the origin of still graver problems of good and evil."

to more specific terms. Given the standards of welfare current in the free societies, can these standards be maintained by a combination of public policies and voluntary private action which will not undermine these societies' essential freedoms?

First, will such policies act directly to wear down the incentives of individual persons for assuming the burdens of responsible decision, and limit its scope in a way that may undermine their capacity for exercising the personal, intellectual, and political freedoms essential to democracy? Second, will such welfare policies be incompatible, in the long run, with preserving a healthy sphere of private economic enterprise? It is worth noting that free societies, even those characterized as socialistic in tone, typically continue to place heavy reliance on private enterprise. Third, is a healthy sphere of private enterprise necessary to the personal, intellectual, and political freedoms, to which we have given first priority?

The second and third questions are interdependent. If the answer to the third is "yes," then the second must be answered by harmonizing our welfare standards with a healthy sphere of private enterprise, if a free society is to continue. Even if the answer to the third question is merely "we do not know" (as I suspect is the case), still the *assured* continuance of a free society depends on avoiding policies which, in the name of economic welfare, would wreck the free sector of the economy. But if adequate welfare policies would not wreck it, or need not wreck it, they may be followed without too great fear for our essential freedoms on this score, even if we lack a sure answer to the question whether private business enterprise is necessary to human and social freedom.[3]

For these reasons, I shall focus mainly on the first two questions, and especially on the second, which is both more

---

[3] This question will be encountered later: see pp. 125–6 below.

immediate and more appropriate for an economist, and has been forcefully raised, in various ways, by Henry Simons, Hayek, Mises, Roepke, and others. But one must note that it presents a two-sided problem of mutual adaptation. Can public welfare policies adapt themselves to the requirements of the health of the private economy? And can the private economy adapt itself to the goals of welfare?

Our approach will be to examine, briefly and in general terms, certain key areas of economic problems and policies, in the light of the two-sided question just indicated. As to welfare, I shall try to avoid theoretical controversy by confining the discussion to aspects that I hope will command general agreement. The areas of policy discussed will include the protection of welfare in connection with consumers' free choice, workers' freedoms including free choice of occupation, the human conditions of work itself, diffused gains and costs and the limitation of parasitism, conservation of exhaustible resources, ample and stable employment opportunity, prevention of inflation, and the scope and maintenance of competition.

The Setting of the Problem

The free Western world, after an early overdose of economic *laissez faire,* which may have been inseparable from the introduction of the Industrial Revolution, has for the past eighty years or more been groping toward an altered balance between private enterprise and community protection of human and social values. Complete *laissez faire* has never existed, but we came close enough to it in the early and middle nineteenth century to incur outrages on human welfare and dignity which no humane and enlightened society could long tolerate. Our groping started with piecemeal remedies for particular abuses which, from the standpoint of the basic market mechanism, were of a "fringe" character, not threatening the essential functioning of the market. From these we have moved on to policies affecting the heart of the market mechanism—to the minimum wage, farm price supports, various policies having broad effects on the distribution of incomes—and ultimately to trying to influence or control the general level of prices and the total rate of production and employment.

This has been accompanied by vaguely disturbing talk about "economic planning," which was suspect, with only partial justification, as being a semantic disguise for socialism. It is no wonder that some able economists call for a halt. But it is also no wonder, in the light of the defects of unrestricted *laissez faire* and the inevitability of large departures from it, that no one has successfully specified just where to stop, or how far to turn back the clock of history.[4] I shall attack this baffling problem, not expecting to solve it, but trying to make some contribution toward at least formulating it in reasonably concrete and realistic terms.

There appear to be a few propositions with which one may start.

1. Complete freedom is an anarchist's myth.

2. The less-complete freedom called *laissez faire,* in its full sense, is at present largely a myth of the ultraconservative wing of business men, with much-qualified support from some forms of economic theory.

3. The idea that a fully collectivist state, by centering

[4] The "Liberal Manifesto" (International Liberal Conference, Oxford, 1947) seems clearly to sanction social security, indicates that something should be done about housing but not by state ownership, and indicates that both private monopolies and public controls must stop short of "suppression of economic freedom," specifying "freedom to associate or not to associate," but not otherwise defining where the critical deadline comes. It is deliberately drawn in general terms which might cover a variety of policies.

on the administration of things, avoids the coercion of people, is a Communist myth that must be wearing somewhat thin, even in Communist circles.

4. If the economic system is to justify itself well enough to survive, it must serve the dominant concepts of welfare better, and more consciously, than old-fashioned "individualism" did. Otherwise it will be changed.

5. Some observers appear to hold, or at least imply, that once the change from individualism starts, it can find no logical point of rest short of complete collectivism. As against this, I shall regard it as more probable (though naturally unprovable) that a society of Western type, which has once thoroughly tasted the spirit that combines democracy with economic freedom, and has gained prosperity under it, would check any trend toward collectivism without reaching a "point of no return." This would mean that its natural state is one of uneasy balance between private and community action. Complete collectivism could be imposed by alien conquest or dictatorial *coup d'état,* backed by the full Soviet basis of force, terror, and coerced acceptance of the "big lie." But I have faith that this system of totalitarian coercion contains inherent weaknesses that are ultimately bound to bring it to an end, even in Russia. This could most safely happen through a gradual humanizing and liberalizing transformation. In such a transformation rests the chief hope of avoiding another, and fatal, World War. Or collectivism could come through a breakdown of the free economy; but I hold to the probability that, in a Western free society, even if something close to a breakdown should occur, it would be temporary.

6. Last, and most directly pertinent, for the next few decades the symptoms of a possible "creeping socialism" will not be chiefly found in an actual increase of literal collective action. We are not likely, within this period, to get more of this than private enterprise can make terms with.

The more significant danger signals, for which we need to be on our guard, will, I suspect, be any signs of a weakening of private action for the performance of its essential functions. This includes action by persons and by business, and it leads naturally to the question of what these essential functions are, as distinct from the nonessential features which welfare policies can safely modify, as they are bound to do.

One ultraconservative type of answer condemns any reduction in the customary scope of free choice (but may accept the reduction after it has in turn become customary). This attitude is exemplified in the early objections to social security—which some of us may vaguely remember. Initial reactions to fresh extensions of welfare policy are likely to be of this sort. The real question is not whether customary definitions of freedom have been altered, but whether a healthy scope and conditions for free action remain. Under social security the individual still has his spending to manage, and so far he has plenty of decisions left to make, while the conditions for making them are improved. Effective free choice is not impaired by lightening a burden which too few could handle successfully.[5] And so far business has been able to assimilate its share of the burden. Remaining questions are those of method and extent. Conceivably, social security, like any welfare policy, could be carried too far.

This brings us back to the question of what the essential business functions are, which mistaken welfare policies might weaken. They seem to include opportunity and incentive to produce, to produce the things people are most ready to pay for, to produce efficiently, to pioneer improvements and new products, to employ labor and capital and to move them where they can be most productive by market standards. As to furnishing employment, the business record is

[5] This view is corroborated by the findings of the American Assembly, conference on Social Security, 1953. See *Economic Security for Americans*, 1954, especially p. 9.

obviously vulnerable; the present point is that public welfare policies—even employment policies—cannot afford to disregard their effect on the employment that business already furnishes. As for incentives for the workers, they must include differentials, and these are compatible with an underlying social dividend not based on personal performance. However, if the social dividend gets large, the added personal incentives may lose a good deal of their force.

It is also desirable, and may be essential, that private gains, including the differentials, be reasonably related to contributions to the national aggregate product. This function the market performs crudely, with many imperfections, but maintaining a fair degree of mobility and of effective competition. It furnishes incentives under which the powers of applied science have been unleashed in production, affording spectacular increases. The unlimited competition we call "war" has been both an interference and a stimulus. It can claim credit for numerous useful achievements, and it is clearly chargeable with the most ghastly menace that now hangs over humanity: the menace of the atom bomb.

In this process of technical and economic advance the economy of the United States has, as a result of a number of historical circumstances, afforded an uncomfortably unique exhibit. It has felt the stimulative effect of two world wars, while being spared their most destructive impact. A large market and mass production have reinforced one another, culminating in a spectacular "economy of high wages." Preeminent gains in per capita real income have been matched by almost equally notable reduction of inequality in distribution. There is ground for the view that the real reduction in inequality is greater than the statistics show, though this is not proved.[6] This record challenges comparison with that of

[6] This rests on the view that, by and large, the economies of mass production apply more to goods consumed by persons of moderate incomes than to the quality products, and especially the personal services, consumed by the wealthy. Producers of these goods and services are paid

democratic collectivism. The qualities of the market system that are responsible for these positive achievements are the qualities we should like to preserve as "essential," while endeavoring to remedy its well-known and well-advertised defects.

Welfare Through Economic Spectacles

The phrase "economic welfare" links the concepts of welfare and economics: a linkage about which current thinking among economists is in a notoriously unsettled state. The phrase is troublesome, chiefly because it suggests a special kind or measure of welfare different from the kind envisaged by those who look at welfare directly, without first putting on the particular economic brand of spectacles, with their special polarizing quality. This implication seems unfortunate, and I shall assume that the wording of the title does not intend it. Thus I shall avoid discussion of current forms of theoretical "welfare economics"; largely because I am too profoundly concerned with welfare to be willing to accept the restrictions—or the polarized spectacles—which this variety of "welfare economics" imposes on its treatment.

These seem to point, in effect if not in conscious intent, to limiting one's study to exchangeable goods, as measured in markets. And *this is not welfare,* but one class of means, which may be used for welfare or the opposite, according to the users' wisdom and circumstances, conditioned as these are by their whole culture, of which their economic system is

more but their physical productivity has not risen proportionately. Therefore their products have become more expensive, and this does not show in the price indexes, which are not designed to represent the costs of these levels of consumption. Therefore the real buying power of the upper incomes is less than is shown by statistics of disposable money incomes, deflated by existing price indexes. This view is, however, questioned by R. J. Lampman, "Recent Changes in Income Inequality," *American Economic Review,* June, 1954, pp. 251, 264.

a formative part. As indicated elsewhere, I shall not equate "welfare" itself—which is an end—with the means for its attainment as dealt in and valued in markets. "Economic" will point not to exchangeable goods but to elements of welfare that are definitely conditioned by them, or by economic processes (for example, methods of production as directly affecting human life).

In considering the nonmarket factors affecting welfare, including the quality of human relations and conditions on the job, one notable feature is that they affect welfare directly, for better or worse. Once an economist considers these matters, there is no intermediate, measurable economic quantity, like the national dividend of marketable goods, with which he can terminate his inquiry, if he wishes to remain purely an economist in a conventional sense. There is no conveniently logical stopping place short of asking the searching question, "How do these things affect welfare?" Even if one tries to limit the inquiry, and preserve the economist's traditional *wertfrei* attitude, by accepting people's existing ideas of what they want, there remain questions of balancing values and costs which cannot be resolved by appeal to valuations established in markets. Wants which cannot be expressed through markets are just as real as those that can be so expressed.

One must look outside of markets to complete one's picture of the evidence of people's actual valuations; and part of the evidence will be found in dissatisfactions expressed through political channels. So one may find one's self comparing the imperfections—the strong and weak points—of markets and of politics, and using the strong points of each to redress the weaknesses and biases of the other. To deal with that peculiar economic-political hybrid—collective bargaining—will require both kinds of understanding. In short, this inquiry, even if—or especially if—it aims to be *wertfrei* in spirit, leads inexorably outside the conventional area of

"pure" economics, and forces one to recognize the interpenetration of the two kinds of forces and values. These are
difficulties, but they seem inescapable in the attempt to deal
with welfare in a way that is meaningful.

Once one goes this far there is a temptation to go further, looking behind the standard of a large, widely diffused
and progressively increasing national dividend of marketable goods and asking whether this increase in wealth leads
to welfare. Does it lead to higher activities and a better life,
or to activities that are of pettier significance, because what
is at stake at the "margin" is no longer the necessities of life,
but the superfluities? The answer, of course, hinges on the
quality of the people themselves, and it involves an ethical
judgment on the indefinite and conflicting scales of values
which they embody in their aggregate behavior. But these
scales of values are themselves influenced, for better or
worse, by the discipline of their economic processes and
mechanisms. So, if we are to appraise an economic system
in terms of welfare, we need to ask not only how much of
gratification it furnishes, but whether it improves or deteriorates our systems of wants.[7]

This effect on the quality of people's values is so important that it constitutes one major reason why so many intellectuals are moved by powerful revulsion against the business system and doubt whether a very high national income,
secured by such a system, makes for a good life. Whatever
the answer, in a war-threatened world we need all the productive power which mass production can give us; and I
shall not question this need. But an economist does well to
remind himself that the effect on personal welfare is not self-
evident.

[7] Cf. Paul Streeten, "La Théorie Moderne de l'Économie de Bien-
Être," *Économie Appliquée*, 1953, pp. 429, 450. Cf. also David M. Potter, "Advertising: the Institution of Abundance," *Yale Review*, Autumn,
1953, pp. 49, 59–60, 65–70.

Welfare as This Study Conceives It [8]

While the proposed method of analysis attempts to confine itself to policies for the protection of values that are generally accepted as *elements* of welfare, this does not settle the question of their relative importance and place in a concept of welfare as an organic whole. Therefore it still appears pertinent for the writer to make declaration of the general conception of welfare that underlies his discussion. Welfare is here conceived in terms of needs, rather than of an undiscriminating list of desires. It calls for healthy and responsible individuals, organized in a healthy society which in turn is responsible to and for its members. To inquire into needs, as distinct from desires, implies that somebody can distinguish between them; that is, that society can command specialized knowledge or wisdom, or both, which has a validity superior to the uninstructed choices of all or most of its unspecialized members. Such knowledge is available, for a growing number of purposes. Even the best of us can benefit by the advice of specialists—though we do not always act in accord even with our own maturer judgment of our own welfare or of that of society.

DEVELOPMENT OF CAPACITIES

I shall assume that, for welfare, development of capacities and their well-balanced exercise are more important than passive receipt of gratifications—or perhaps one should say that this is the way to the most solid and secure gratifications. And for such development most of us, at least at times, benefit by challenges requiring us to do things we would not otherwise choose to do. Needless to say, welfare calls for a

[8] Cf. J. S. Davis, "Economic Potentials of the United States," in *National Policy for Economic Welfare at Home and Abroad*, R. Lekachman, ed., pp. 128 ff. Dr. Davis's treatment is notable for including qualitative aspects and nonmarket values.

rounded development of the different sides of man's nature. If there are capacities that are inherently antisocial—a debatable point—welfare, of course, does not include their development. Impulses to power, conflict, and invidious prestige are obvious examples; but these capacities are probably better interpreted as impulses that can take forms that have their uses if properly channeled and attached to serviceable objects. For this, the psychology of sublimation is pertinent.

The brand of welfare here described is one typical of modern Western civilization. It is not synonymous with contentment, which is probably best secured by reducing one's wants to the scale of one's means and accepting the limitations of one's status and opportunities. It implies rather the kind of discontent that finds outlet in constructive activities that are rewarding in themselves and that lead to a sense of achievement. But this is easier said than done, and Americans would do well to recognize that social experiments with the economy of unlimited material aspiration carry serious dangers. They may generate an aggregate of ambitions too far in excess of what the system can gratify. (One tangible aspect of this will appear in later discussion of the problems of inflation, but the most explosive case is presumably the "awakening" in the underdeveloped countries of discontent with their low level of living, in the light of the far higher levels prevailing in Western industrialized countries.) Or the activities that increase production may not all be rewarding in themselves—to put it mildly. Both these conditions can lead to destructive frustrations.

The challenges must be difficult, but not so difficult as to destroy all hope that they can be adequately met. If they are severe enough, there will be a percentage of individual failures. And one of the challenges a free society has to meet is that of dealing with these failures in ways that will not be destructive either to the balance of their own personalities or to their loyalty to the society. Those who fail in one role should find another without undue discredit. The extent to which they are thrown on their own resources must not be such as to deprive them of the sense of support that comes from "belonging" to the social group—as theoretical "individualism" in its most extreme form would be likely to deprive them.

Man has a dual nature, individual and social; and however much individuals may differ in their relative emphasis on these two sides, none is a whole man in whom either side is completely repressed. And since individuals differ in their capacity for independent decision and in their competitive disposition, the assortment of challenges presented by the various roles in a differentiated society needs to be correspondingly differentiated. Many are probably adapted to a considerable amount of routine in economic matters, though not as much as this type would be likely to prefer. People do not like as severe challenges as are good for them, witness their tendency to seek shelters from the rigors of competition, if given the chance. And some kinds and degrees of shelters are warranted.

ROLE OF DEMOCRATIC ACTION

Furthermore, our ideals include the conception that people should feel that they have something to say, collectively, as to the kinds of challenges the system requires them to meet. Will they then provide too much shelter, and of the wrong sorts, reducing incentives and replacing dynamic progress with stereotyped stagnation? This question expresses what may be one of the basic difficulties in combining welfare with collective freedom. To find the right answer implies leadership which recognizes the need for challenges, plus a willingness of the people in general to follow such leadership.

NEED FOR INEQUALITY

This conception of welfare calls for some inequality rather than complete equality, and only partly for reasons of incentives. Inequality—of some sort—need not be merely an evil tolerated because it stimulates people to develop their capacities. It is, or can be, an element of welfare in itself, because human nature includes an impulse to attainment which is inevitably unequal and involves comparisons. Everyone aspires to attainment that will be superior to that of *some* others, in *some* kind of activity, and will secure recognition as such.[9] We also have an impulse to recognize the superiority of *some* others, from whom we accept leadership. An absolutely flat plain, and a sharp peak higher than everything else in sight, are both, for the majority of people, uncomfortable places on which to stand.

If complete equalitarianism is abandoned, there remains the agnosticism embodied in the prevalent economic idea that there is no scientific way to compare the subjective gratifications of different people, hence no possible judgment for or against equality. This appears not so much incorrect as a mistaken way of approaching the problem of inequality. I suggest that the key to a rational answer is not subjective gratifications (especially if limited to consumption) but the functions people fulfill.[10] From this standpoint there are physical needs, not strictly equal but related to physique, climate, and type of work, about which scientific

[9] In view of the many degrees and areas of attainment, universal gratification of this impulse is not so nearly impossible as might superficially appear. Most people can find something at which they will be better than the poorest, and those who are poorer at this may be better at something else. Some absolute and noninvidious sense of achievement ought to be accessible to everyone.

[10] If challenged, I would defend the concept of "productive consumption" as having been wrongly discredited by a too-rationalistic theory on the mistaken ground that if something is an end (as consumption is) it cannot also be a means (as consumption surely is also).

knowledge is available. In an advanced society these needs can be met by a minimum standard of living, leaving room for performance differentials. There are further needs, beyond the strictly physical, for the means and capacity to perform various functions in a differentiated society. Posts of leadership call for a more liberal standard of living than the minimum needed for routine labor. This is in addition to the nonequalitarian impulses just mentioned.

NEED FOR EQUALITY

Gratification of these needs, which vary widely from one person to another, must be combined in some fashion with an underlying equality in some rights and dignities. As to how much inequality this calls for, and how the underlying equalities shall be defined, this can vary largely with the traditions of the society, its degree of wealth and of specialized organization, and other factors. One method of analysis, worth considering because different from that usual among economists, might begin with the functional requirements of the classes holding leadership. By this standard the great fortunes of America's gilded nineties were excessive, and so are those of the ruling classes of the underdeveloped countries, where inequality is typically greater than in the United States. From this starting point a rich society can afford more leveling than a poor one and still give its leaders an adequately generous existence.

Problems of equality lead naturally to the question of economic security. This is handled informally in very simple societies, but in more developed ones it calls for formal arrangements. It may be broadly divided into two categories, with some vagueness and overlapping of boundaries. One consists of assuring that goods and services or funds are available to meet certain needs and contingencies, without directly altering the basic terms on which the individual secures the income he derives from economic functions. Examples would be compulsory insurance and direct relief or aid. The other category consists of shelters from the full rigors of competition, or from unmitigated exposure to loss of status and livelihood, within the individual's economic activities. Simple examples would be farm price supports and the protection of workers against arbitrary discharge. This second kind of security obviously interferes, more than does the first, with the "free market" system of incentives and of direction and allocation of economic resources and efforts.

NEED FOR ADVENTURE

Over against the need for some sort of underlying security, and needing to be harmonized with it, is the craving for some experience of adventure in one's life. Complete denial of either of these can lead to unstable states of personality. Old-fashioned personal business enterprise undoubtedly afforded one form of gratification of the adventure-craving in certain types of persons. Modern large-scale enterprise may contain the same element but in different form and degree, with the factor of personal independence much reduced. Some persons find this kind of outlet in gambling, or crime, or politics; a few risk their lives on dangerous mountains or cross the ocean in small boats; more find it in hunting or fishing, in institutionalized sports or in "escape literature" or movies of adventure. The entertainment industries stand ready to furnish the thrills vicariously, without personal activity or personal risk—for whatever this sort of *ersatz* may be worth psychologically. There should be more emphasis on the actively participating ways of gratifying this impulse without risking the substance of personal or economic safety.

ACCEPTANCE OF SOCIAL STANDARDS

For the society, welfare requires loyalty to it on the part of the members, and the system must be such as to command loyalty. While it seems probable that no system, as such, can guarantee this, the most necessary condition appears to be that the individuals have a lively sense of making a distinguishable contribution to a joint enterprise with a worthy common purpose. This implies that the individuals' (unequal) rewards be not wholly unrelated to a common end. Negatively, it requires that parasitic and predatory activities be circumscribed sufficiently for this purpose, without reducing private discretion to zero; but this negative requirement is not sufficient—something more positive is called for. Finally, the changes involved in progress must not be so rapid and complete as to shatter the inherited framework of social standards. Rapid and revolutionary reconstruction of such standards appears to be too severe a challenge to be met without disastrous social costs. The kind of welfare here envisaged calls for evolutionary, rather than revolutionary, change. This applies with peculiar force to attempts at aiding underdeveloped countries to modernize their economies. It may not be easy to avoid destructive cultural impacts.

A "Free Society"

Finally, what is the meaning of a "free society"? This carries a double implication: freedom for the society itself and freedom for its members. The most difficult dilemmas in the attempt to combine these requirements apply to some of the underdeveloped countries, where freedom of the society from external domination may leave it in the control of an internal autocracy. Such countries face multiple alternatives, all dangerous. The urge to nationalism is genuine and spontaneous—also it is incessantly and effectively played on by those whose sole purpose is to split the country off from all allies and leave it a helpless prey, to be picked off and added to the growing Soviet Empire when the opportune moment arises. This opportune moment may be hastened by internal chaos if the indigenous autocracy is either too stubbornly exploitive, or merely too inept, to carry out effective reforms. The Western aspirations to aid these countries to maintain their independence must either make the best of supporting the indigenous autocracy or run all the risks of tampering with another country's social system. In such cases the most stubborn obstacle to economic improvement may be the pressure of unchecked population, and this may have religious involvements. The risks of social tampering are, of course, compounded with the risks of rousing nationalist hostility and so playing into the hands of the waiting Soviets.

For purposes of this discussion, we may be content to recognize these problems without attempting to resolve them, confining our present attention to more developed societies in which the basic conditions of internal freedom exist and merely need to be defended against the threat of internal decay or external domination stemming from Moscow. This latter threat, of course, severely limits the freedom of both opposing groups of countries by requiring them to devote resources to armament that might otherwise be used to raise standards of living. Also, as already noted, it makes the efficiency of mass production imperative, whether we like mass production or not. This limitation the free world must accept as the price of continued freedom.

KINDS OF FREEDOM

Freedoms may be, very imperfectly, classified into economic and noneconomic, recognizing clearly that there is much interpenetration between these groups. Another basis of classification, equally imperfect, would be between personal and business freedoms, the personal freedoms including the "noneconomic" ones, plus a number of the economic.

The noneconomic freedoms include freedom of religion, thought and its expression, and political action.[11] The personal sector of economic freedoms includes mainly freedom of consumers' choice among economic goods and of choice of occupation, plus freedom of the individual from arbitrary domination within the occupation chosen. I shall assume that these personal freedoms are the most vital ones; and that business freedoms, especially those involving large-scale business organizations, stand on a different basis, being mainly means, to be judged by their effects on the welfare of actual individuals. In the spirit of the English classical economists, we should avoid the pseudo-individualism which transfers the principles of individualism directly to large-scale organizations, corporate or other. Economics is just beginning to replace this pseudo-individualism with a more realistic attitude toward organizations.

LIMITS OF FREEDOM

The essence and scope of freedom (always limited) may be defined as a range of alternatives open to the individual, his choice being determined by forces acting through his own personality rather than by external compulsion exercised by other persons or agencies, including government. Compulsion needs to be distinguished from mere social pressures, which can be resisted if one has the fortitude and which are resisted by those independent spirits on whom a free society depends for breaking new paths. The spirit of the society needs to be one in which these social pressures are leniently exercised. Tolerance of diversity, and within wide limits tolerance of honest heresy, must be established

[11] Obviously, organized exercise of these freedoms requires economic means, but this economic relationship appears less integral to their character than is true of the personal sector of economic freedoms. The essential thing is that the distinction between these kinds of freedom appears meaningful, aside from the terms used to label it.

institutions, woven into the texture of people's attitudes and lives.[12]

Freedom itself—the range of things one *may* do—needs to be distinguished also from the effective capacity to use it —the range of things one *can* do, having the enabling means and ability. Means and ability determine the effectiveness of freedom; but to identify them with freedom itself—as is sometimes done—could lead to the conclusion that the only free system is one in which all resources are socially distributed, so that no one's freedom is defeated by (avoidable) lack of means. Thus a free system would be identified with a paternalistic one. And, after all, the two are not the same!

Freedom operates within a framework of compulsion and informal pressures. A "free system" is one in which many of these, at least, take the form of telling the individual what he may not do, leaving a range within which he may choose what he will do. Such prohibitions can bar the more obviously harmful acts, but not all undesirable ones; hence co-operation in such a system cannot safely be left to irresponsible personal self-interest, even with formal controls, but requires also a moral basis. And with group organization in the society the scope of this necessary moral basis is enormously extended. The maintenance of freedom depends upon it, and this is perhaps the most crucial internal problem of a free society today.

It is interesting to speculate whether personal and political freedom could be maintained in a system of complete economic collectivism, if operated by a democratically minded people. Such speculation may, however, be academic, as the problems appear unlikely to be encountered in such an absolute form. It seems conceivable, though debatable, that the most securely democratic of the Western coun-

---

[12] The obvious limit comes when heresy embraces conspiracy to abolish freedom and ceases to be honest.

tries might possess the necessary qualities for such an achievement, but the achievement would be difficult and exacting at best. As for the United States, its experience with "McCarthyism" seems to bear witness that the necessary and fundamental qualities for maintaining freedom and democracy under unusual stresses are not firmly enough entrenched to promise success in the face of the powers of abuse which economic collectivism would carry with it. Without this basis formal constitutional safeguards would be insufficient.

There would be need for requirements that opinion should not be a condition of employment, and these would be all the harder to maintain because it would be necessary to make exceptions for high policy-making positions. There would also be need for decentralization of employing authorities. All this for the basic reason that economic coercion, via power over the victim's job, is too obviously easy and tempting. And a free press, operated by the government in power, is almost a contradiction in terms. In any case the means of preserving personal freedoms in such a system are political and social, rather than economic, to an extent that may place them outside our immediate agenda. Thus the present discussion will construe a "free society" as one involving at least a large measure of freedom of the business type, with its characteristic economic problems.

CHAPTER SIX

Economic Welfare in a Free Society: II, The Roles of Consumers and Workers

Welfare and Consumers' Choice

Short of the most all-out kind of war, any conceivable economic system is bound to place major reliance on letting consumers have purchasing power and choose what they will buy with it. Even the Soviet system does this. And any conceivable modern system is bound to set some limitations on consumers' freedom to choose what they will, and will refuse to let health, private and public safety, and morals depend solely on the maxim of *caveat emptor*. For both these opposite policies there are reasons that are completely conclusive. The options of policy that are open concern where the line between freedom and control shall be drawn, what methods shall be used, and what standards or authorities shall be relied on, other than the consumers' own choice. This last is highly important because public policies in this area are notably exposed to being weakened by the pressure of business interests with which they interfere or perverted into instruments for restricting legitimate competition. Building codes and milk-inspection areas may serve as examples.

STANDARDS OF CHOICE

Proper standards are a compound of socially accepted values and scientific, or at least professionally competent, judgments of fact as to what free consumer-choice does to these values. It is not a matter of broad generic values alone; the judgment does not, for example, take the form, "health is more important than freedom"; but rather, for example, "the protection to health afforded by preventing the sale of milk from tuberculous cows outweighs the interest of the owner of the cows and gives effect to what the consumer would want if he knew the facts, he being in no position by himself to give effect to his desire for healthy milk." The alternative view would be, "the producer has a right to sell his milk if he can find consumers who know no better than to drink it"; and this would be a *reductio ad absurdum* of the dogma that the consumer is the final judge of values.

To the extent that economics adopts this dogma, it disqualifies itself for saying anything meaningful about the real problems of consumers' free choice. The reasons for this dogma are understandable in terms of the specialization of academic disciplines and the desire to make economics objective and "scientific." But from the standpoint of the purpose of this discussion, it represents an unfortunate limitation on the contribution economics can make to the pursuit of human welfare.

It may appear paradoxical that things seriously affecting health are too important to be left at the mercy of consumers' free choice, while food for the mind is regarded as too important *not* to be thus left free, under the principle of freedom of speech and press. The paradox can be resolved by noting that in the one case the end value—health—is something we may safely assume that all sane persons want; while the dangers are often invisible, and it takes trained specialists—who are available—to diagnose threats and safeguard against them, thus giving better effect to the consumer's wishes than he could do for himself unaided. In the other case it is precisely the end value that is in question—do we prefer Theodore Dreiser or P. G. Wodehouse—and scientific standards cannot tell me what I want; this defines the area of personal free choice, alike for trifles and for matters of the profoundest social import.[1]

CHOICE IN RUSSIA

In the Soviet type of system the handling of the question of what kinds and amounts of goods the consumer shall and shall not be allowed to buy is, in principle, quite simple. The planning authority decides it. What remains is the—very sizeable—administrative problem of giving effect to the decisions made. If, among the goods made available, the consumers prefer some to others, there may be a shortage of the preferred goods and possibly a temporarily unsold surplus of the others; and this may lead to an alteration in the proportions produced. To this rather doubtful extent, demand may influence supply. But the Soviets appear to minimize this by tending to keep the aggregate volume of buying power in excess of the total supply of goods at the prices set, thus reducing the likelihood that the less-preferred goods will remain on the shelves.

[1] There is significance in the current use by some theorists of the word "taste" in ways that imply that all consumer choices are matters of taste, about which there can be no meaningful argument. If the above analysis is correct, the word "taste" applies to a large part, but only part, of the values in which consumer judgments are final, and these in turn are only part of the whole field of consumer choice.

THE PLACE OF PRODUCERS' FREEDOM

More important, any purely potential demand, for goods not offered, has no way of expressing itself. Individual would-be producers do not have the chance to explore such potentialities and satisfy them. This brings out the crucial fact that consumers' freedom requires producers' freedom as a complement, including free and competitive innovation, if it is to have full effect. Then any known article, for which someone will pay, can get produced, anything many will pay for can get produced on a large scale and hence cheaply, and things the buyer does not know about will be brought to his attention. All these points are especially pertinent to that most basic of freedoms, freedom of speech and press. And it is an illuminating way to approach the general problem, because it starts from the consumer's freedom to receive—defined in terms of adequate alternatives—and proceeds from that to the producer's freedom to produce—in this case, to utter or publish.

Producers' freedom is especially important in an economy with a large and growing per capita income, in which science is providing—and must provide—constantly new goods in which the growing income may be embodied. And this leads to another factor, namely, advertising. In some form or other this is necessary as a means of bringing new, improved or altered goods to the attention of consumers and enabling them to know at least something about the available assortment within which they may exercise choice. Where the new goods are privately produced, there is powerful logic in letting the producers devise their own means of appeal. This in turn affects the nature of the known alternatives which determine the content of the consumers' freedom.

Some would say it circumscribes this freedom by making the consumer the plaything of the arts of interested advertising propaganda. Certainly it is a powerful and not-too-responsible force affecting the quality of our values.[2] It involves much that is wasteful, misleading, and banal; much bad taste and vulgarity. But these appear to be the natural accompaniments of a free and democratic system, in both the political and economic realms. We pay this price for fluidity and progress, and for our own ultimate right to make our individual choices, as best we can, from among appeals which, while they may influence us, stop short of final power to coerce us. The price grows large in a system that is rich enough to afford it, at least in quantitative terms. Qualitatively, some at least of its abuses are susceptible of control, as the Federal Trade Commission controls false statements in advertising, or as the Bureau of Standards has on occasion exposed false claims, or as Consumers' Union offers services of testing on a private basis. And in a society in which citizens have to vote and in which there are no very effective rules for honest labeling of political proprietary remedies, the citizen needs some practice in scrutinizing and exposing false claims by his own shrewdness. This faculty —which under the Soviet system must be exercised in secret if at all—is one of the earmarks of a free and democratic society.

Finally, there is the consumer's freedom to spend or not to spend, which has a crucial effect on total economic activity through determining whether a highly productive economy will spend all its income, for consumption plus investment, and thus maintain its rate of production without erring on either side and incurring either unemployment or inflation. Welfare-oriented policies affect this factor chiefly indirectly, through taxation and other measures affecting the distribution of disposable income. These affect both sides of the balance between saving and investment; and it seems

[2] Cf. David M. Potter, "Advertising: the Institution of Abundance," *Yale Review*, Autumn, 1953.

likely that their most important effects are on the side of investment. These matters will be dealt with in connection with policies for maintaining employment.

Welfare and Choice of Occupation

Workers' free choice of occupation is an element of welfare in its own right and is basic to a free economic system. It is peculiarly strategic for the individual, and contains a considerable element of irrevocability, which makes wise guidance especially important. Much is already done in this direction, in connection with educational institutions and otherwise, and there is much room for extension and improvement. Such guidance of voluntary choices improves the free market system, rather than threatening it. Even in wartime the free economies have done very little that could be classed as compulsory allocation of labor. The possible impact of total atomic warfare on this practice is something we must hope never to have to learn of by experience.

Choice of occupation, like consumers' choice, involves not only choice between existing occupations, but also the opportunity to create new ones. This last, like all creative leadership, is important out of all proportion to the small number who can hope to do it successfully. But in our kind of society it carries complications, largely because it is generally the employer who makes the innovations, and these involve changes in the occupations of the employees. These changes may raise qualitative questions which will be discussed in the following section. Or an existing occupation may be threatened with displacement, in which case the workers have claim to equitable consideration, including preferential rights to qualify for new jobs. New forms of production, providing new occupations, generally start as small enterprises; and it is important that they have a chance to grow.

A broader problem can arise from the general raising of the level of education, coupled with a failure of the number of "higher" occupational openings to correspond with the numbers who seek them and who feel themselves qualified for them. This is combined with the effect of labor organization in raising the rewards for manual work, while numerous "white-collar" and intellectual occupations have not kept pace. Frustrations can result, including those of the "intellectual" who does not attain the status he feels he has a right to expect. The ultimate answer should include the raising of the cultural level of life for those in all occupations, so that an "intellectual" need not feel out of place in occupations in which his grandfather would have felt unclassed. We are groping in this direction, though without conspicuous success so far. The process will not be quick or easy.

A further question is that of setting proper standards of competence for professional and other responsible occupations. Here the general welfare obviously calls for adequate standards, set by qualified bodies, animated by a sense of public responsibility for both the number and quality of those admitted. There are plenty of problems here, but they do not call in question the principle of setting standards of competence. Full opportunity to qualify, including scholarship aid in appropriate cases, is presupposed. The problem is one of safeguarding quality of service without setting up monopolistic restrictions which unduly limit supply in the interest of the members of the trade or profession and in opposition to those of the consuming public. And for this delicate balance of values no simple formula is easily apparent. In our present system dependence must rest heavily on the conscience of the quasi-private examiners and on an informed and intelligent public opinion. If these safeguards fail, resort to public controls may prove inevitable in the interest of greater freedom, but involving a fresh assortment of problems and difficulties. Similar principles apply, in varied forms, to union practices that set limits on access to trades.

Welfare of the Worker on the Job [3]

The effect of the job itself on the worker's welfare falls within what is probably the largest blind spot of traditional theory because, though it is a product of industry of co-ordinate importance with the goods turned out and sold, it is not a marketable product.[4] It has suffered neglect in practice, partly for this reason and partly for lack of understanding of what the effect was, under modern industrialism. Progress is being made toward remedying this neglect, but more is needed, grounded in better understanding. This problem may well prove to be the most important area of exploratory welfare thinking and experimentation on the agenda of the present generation.

Starting with the most tangible matters, there are controls requiring safe and healthful working places and conditions and limiting hours of work. For more intangible

[3] Cf. J. S. Davis, "Standards and Content of Living," *American Economic Review*, March, 1945, pp. 1–15, especially 7–8.

[4] Though careful analysis would require some qualification of this statement, it appears essentially warranted. The key to the myopia of formal theory lies in its concentration on the marginal hour's work and the balancing of its disutility against the utility of added product—or of the workers' share of it. For a germinal formulation, recognizing that work may have positive value but diverting attention from this to the marginal equilibrium, cf. W. S. Jevons, *Theory of Political Economy*, 2nd ed., p. 187. Further questions may be raised as to the pertinence and realism of Jevons's treatment of the marginal hour but these are not essential for our present purpose. "The State in Relation to Labour," by the same author, but not written as a work of theory, has the appearance of coming out of a separate compartment of the author's mind.

conditions, such as freedom from the kind of arbitrary discharge to which workers were exposed in the days of too-extreme individualism, reliance is twofold, on collective bargaining and on an altered attitude in management. I venture the estimate—which may be mistaken—that collective bargaining has accomplished more in this area of the workers' human rights on the job than it has in raising real wages faster than they would have risen without it. And union pressure has presumably been one of a complex of factors leading to a growing realization on the part of employers that the safeguarding of such rights of the workers is an essential part of their function.

Each employer holds a kind of trusteeship for a sector of the nation's assets of labor; and it is to his long-run interest, as well as his responsibility, to conserve it. This means doing his utmost to find a place for the ill-adjusted worker, resolving his maladjustments and using discharge as a last resort. Unions, in exercising the powers that they have gained in this area, have an obvious responsibility to support the necessary and proper disciplinary powers of the employer. The best unions appear to meet this responsibility, though there is clearly much room for abuse of power on both sides. On the whole, existing methods appear to afford a salutary, though imperfect, scheme of "checks and balances," without seriously interfering with the essentials of a free economy, though they carry a centralization of power that needs to be closely watched.

QUALITY OF WORK AS AN ELEMENT IN WELFARE

There remains a problem that may be more stubborn: "Do the processes of work itself make for the workers' welfare or the opposite? Do methods designed for mechanical efficiency do violence to the workers' essential needs, sacrificing quality of life to quantity of product?" Since Adam Smith's famous passage on the subject and Ruskin's "There is no wealth but life," this has been recognized as a danger, without an "obvious and simple" antidote, of assured adequacy, inherent in the system.[5] A list of typical complaints includes monotony, lack of rounded exercise of capacities, replacement of balanced skills by specialized dexterities, isolation from personal contacts during work hours, "being a mere cog" in a vastly impersonal organization, ignorance of the product or the purpose served by one's work, lack of chance to develop or advance, or to put one's personal stamp on one's work, and fear of working one's self out of a job or into a cut in piece rates. The conditions complained of are far from universal—it has long been noted that as monotonous jobs invite mechanization, the "trouble shooter" who replaces the machine "hand" has a more varied job, not a more monotonous one.

REMEDIES AND INCENTIVES

Particular remedies are too diverse to be summarized here. One remedy which will not become general (being mainly limited to luxury and quality products) is the demechanization of production and a return to craftsman status, at a sacrifice of productivity. History will move forward, not backward. Yet remedies exist for some of the troubles, and palliatives for others; and their total effect might suffice to render modern production humanly tolerable, even for those whose work is not a positive human asset.[6] What an analysis like the present can do is to point to the motivations and incentives on which improvement rests.[7]

[5] John A. Hobson's "Work and Wealth" gives him an honorable place among pioneering heretics on this problem.

[6] Preliminary reports on a study in process, sponsored by the National Council of Churches, indicate that workers prevailingly do not feel maladjusted. See "The American Economy and the Lives of the People," by A. Dudley Ward, S. A. Leavy, and Lawrence Z. Freedman (New York: Harper & Brothers, 1954).

[7] One may note that this is what "economic theory" regularly does in the more familiar areas. It does not examine the content of values or

One saving fact is the discovery—comparatively recent
—that if work does violence to the workers' natures, output
suffers. Hence the new art or science of human relations in
business rests on a firm basis of enlightened business interest. And size—which is the enemy, even more than shortsighted financial self-interest—has furthered this remedy by
making possible the employment of specialists in human relations to deal with the problems.[8] Further, in the modern
corporation the professional manager has become, not so
much a capitalist or a representative of the capital-interest,
as an accommodator between the interests of stockholder and
worker, customer and public. And he sees the workers more
continuously than he does the stockholders, while strong
unions make him increasingly sensitive to their pressures.

Not all the indicated defects can be remedied in working hours, though many can be. Even decentralization of
overgrown establishments appears feasible in some cases.
Shorter hours and leisure occupations are part of the indicated program. Perhaps the main thing is tangible evidence
that management is actively interested in the worker and
his problems. To revert to the *motif* of pseudo-individualism, and pseudo-individual—the business corporation—has
rediscovered the actual individual and has gone to work on
the problem of making work tolerable for him. And this is a
matter in which private enterprise has certain advantages
over a collectivist system, especially since unions have more
power in dealing with private employers than they would

techniques of production, but analyzes incentives. The chief difference in
the present area is the indefiniteness of the relation of the employers' incentives to the dollar measure. The defect to which employers' efforts in
this field are vulnerable lies in an admixture of superficial "window
dressing," adulterating or impairing more genuine efforts to understand
and remedy the basic human problems. Another defect is a tendency to
concentrate on adjustment of the worker to the job, to the relative neglect
of adjustment of the job to the requirements of the worker's nature.

[8] In this connection the work of Elton Mayo of Harvard deserves
mention. Professor Roepke suggests Frédéric Le Play (an engineer) as the
pioneer thinker in this field.

have in dealing with a collectivist government. With organized workers ready and able to seize their share of the gains from increased productivity, both sides may be coming to realize that management is working for the workers about as much as the workers for management. And that—with due regard to other interests—is one of the keys to welfare in a free economy.

CHAPTER SEVEN

Economic Welfare in a Free Society: III, Requirements of a Serviceable Economy

Diffused Gains and Costs

This heading covers a heterogeneous mass of cases, over-lapping at least some of the other headings here used and united only by the common fact that the net financial income realizable by private enterprise is an inaccurate measure of total net contribution to economic values.[1] This is due to diffused effects, including costs for which private enterprise does not have to compensate, or gains conferred on parties from whom it cannot collect corresponding compensation. These diffused effects are potentially identifiable, at least in principle, and some are potentially measurable in money terms, though actual measurement is often difficult or virtually impossible. Strictly speaking, all production has some such diffused effects; hence it is wise in practice to stick

[1] Pigou's *Economics of Welfare* is, of course, an outstanding study in this field.

to fairly clear cases in which there is real ground for thinking the diffused effects especially important. This limitation
would presumably apply almost as fully to a collectivist
economy as to one based on private enterprise. It is beside
the point to argue that collectivism would automatically and
accurately weigh all these values and costs. The bureaucratic or political methods which it would have to employ
afford no guarantee of a correct answer.

Under a system of private enterprise, diffused gains may
lead the public to undertake certain kinds of production,
where the privately appropriable gains are too small to attract enterprise. Examples would include the aid often given
by communities to attract primary productive enterprises,
around which secondary and tertiary activities will gather,
or such activities as the Tennessee Valley Authority has undertaken as a supplement to its basic water developments. In
evaluating such policies from a national standpoint, it is always pertinent to ask whether they stimulate production that
would not otherwise come into being, or merely determine
the location of production that would take place somewhere
in any case. Or more broadly, does a given productive activity utilize resources that would otherwise lie idle, or would
they be used for other purposes? In the latter case, would
the alternative uses carry their own diffused gains and costs,
roughly equivalent to those resulting from the activity in
question? [2] Uncompensated costs furnish ground for familiar
kinds of preventive controls; examples include real-estate
zoning and regulation of stream pollution and of a smoke
nuisance.

The indicated conclusion is that while diffused gains and
costs are very important in some cases, it is extremely difficult to substitute economic measurement for political proc-

[2] A case in point is dealt with in J. M. Clark, Eugene L. Grant, and
Maurice M. Kelso, *Report on Secondary or Indirect Benefits of Water-
Use Projects*, U.S. Bureau of Reclamation, June 26, 1952, multigraphed
for limited circulation.

esses and pressures as means of guiding policies based on them. Conservatism is indicated, limiting such policies to fairly clear cases. If kept within such limitations, these policies need not interfere with the legitimate scope and productiveness of private enterprise.

Conservation of Resources

Conservation is a public concern because private incentives tend to stimulate socially improvident utilization, inflicting diffused costs on future generations. But the determination of optimum policy faces difficult and far-reaching questions. Will future generations need a given resource as much as we now need it, or will science have developed substitutes before existing supplies are exhausted? If no account is taken of future substitutes, how should supplies be rationed between present and future? What is the importance that should currently be attached to provision for future needs, as against present utilization, or utilization by the methods that are currently cheapest but may waste part of a nonreproducible resource? Where limitation of present use carries a raising of the present price, should the private operator receive the benefit resulting from a policy publicly imposed for social reasons?

Methods of conservation include mainly public reservation of supplies for future use, and control of methods of present exploitation to prevent waste.[3] Examples include lumber conservation, prevention of soil erosion, and control of methods of extracting oil, coal and other irreplaceable minerals. The upshot is a limitation or modification of current use, for the sake of future gains that are bound to be more or less uncertain, and in some cases extremely so. This

---

[3] In the case of trees, for lumber or soil protection, private planting may be stimulated by financial inducements.

uncertainty is the chief reason for discounting the future in such cases; but there is no reason for supposing that the market rate of interest, which governs such comparisons of values in private production, is a correct measure for these social comparisons. We have to do the best we can; and a collectivist system would face the same kind of uncertainties.

The problems are many and various. In the case of forestry, lumber can be converted into a self-reproducing crop of slow growth; and if forests are so treated, rather than being merely held unproductive, the burden on current development and the limitation on current use need not be a serious matter. In the case of soil conservation much of the benefit accrues fairly quickly, and the need is subject to a minimum of uncertainty. Other kinds of cases are more uncertain, in the light of the possible miracles of modern science. And the motive for conservation is often to escape dependence on imported supplies, which might be cut off in case of war or which might be pre-empted for the use of the producing countries if they industrialize their economies.[4] All-out war, of course, tends to submerge all policies of conservation except those of most immediate necessity, leaving the country to wrestle later with the resulting problems of scarcity—as various countries are now doing, as an aftermath of lavish use during World War II.

Conservation does limit, or burden, current production; vetoing some things that a free-market economy would do. And conservationists can make mistakes. But to abandon all conservation would be a worse mistake, and the pressure of business interests toward limitation of conservation policies needs to be resisted. Reasonable conservation policies leave plenty of scope for the operation of free private enterprise. They present no threat to its essential soundness. This is

---

[4] The Mid-Century Conference on Resources for the Future (Washington, December, 1953) has promoted informed awareness of these problems.

true, in fact, of all the varieties of welfare policy so far considered, if reasonably conceived and administered. We come now to certain policies which, from this standpoint, present greater and more general difficulties.

Maintenance of High and Stable Employment Opportunity

Here I shall venture into the well-worn comparison of a collectivist economy and one relying on private enterprise—as heavily, let us say, as the United States does—with regard to the maintenance of employment opportunity. And I would like to present for discussion the hypothesis that with respect to this problem and the means available for handling it the two kinds of economies have more in common than appears on the surface, and the American economy has available not only a reasonably adequate assortment of methods, but an assortment that corresponds, with or without differences of form, with most of the elements in the policies which a democratic collectivism would use.[5] This is still more true if, in place of a theoretically complete collectivism, one considers a system which, while it may be labeled as "socialistic," defines socialism in terms of a result —democratic social control of the economy—and is pragmatically willing to use a wide variety of means, including private enterprise.[6] The differences between such a system

[5] Since writing the above, I note "Unemployment in Planned and Capitalist Countries" by Alfred R. Oxenfeldt and Ernest van den Haag, *Quarterly Journal of Economics*, February, 1954, pp. 43–60. The authors' conclusions afford considerable support to the general hypothesis expressed above, though with particular differences in the more detailed analysis.

[6] Eduard Heimann has defined socialism in this way, and has spoken of "emerging pragmatic European socialism." See *Goals of Economic Life*, A. D. Ward, ed., 1953, pp. 134, 142, 145. And Barbara Ward has recently described both the "profit motive" and socialist thinking about it as in flux. See "A Fresh Look at the Profit Motive," *The New York Times Magazine*, April 29, 1956. Left-wing socialists stay closer to Marxian doctrines.

and our own are matters of degree. Dangers would remain; chiefly perhaps those of public encroachment on the field of private investment, of unduly burdensome taxes, and of sanctioning a harmful degree of inflationary bias in the economy.

The kind of collectivism I shall envisage, for comparative purposes, will be one that maintains consumers' free choice, workers' free choice of occupation, and progress in the development of new and improved products and methods of production; and which in general undertakes to allow the supplies of particular products to adjust themselves to the market demand for them, while holding total demand equal to, but preferably not in excess of, total product at a desirable level of employment. This last would be construed to afford room (among other things) for desirable and useful turnover of labor (which might be greater in this country than in some others), and includes the irreducible minimum of disciplinary discharge, unavoidable seasonality, and avoidance of any material, chronic inflationary bias, except such as the economy is prepared to counteract by means consistent with its own health.

We are dealing here with economy-wide aggregates. And the problem—in a market economy—arises because the market, instead of tending to correct discrepancies between total supply and demand, as it does in the case of particular commodities, tends within wide limits to make the discrepancies cumulatively self-reinforcing, in the direction either of inflation or contraction. Because causation returns on itself, it is somewhat arbitrary to select any one factor as primary, but we may provisionally give that name to fluctuations of investment. These have a basis in the unavoidable irregularities of technical change and progress; and some such irregularities must be assumed in our progressive collectivist economy, as well as in one of private enterprise. Much the same is true of consumers' durable goods which, like long-lived capital equipment, have the characteristic that a given change in total stock (other than the continuance of a steady rate of increase) calls for an intensified change in current rate of output.[7]

These changes normally go through the stages of pilot plant, full-scale plant and subsequent growth. This last stage may, under private enterprise, be intensified by the Schumpeter effect, of waves of imitation; but it is not clear how much this adds to the growth-waves to which a collective economy would be subject. More important, perhaps, is the delaying of improvements, which occurs under large-scale business, but is likely to be even more characteristic of collectivism, with its freedom from competitive pressure. While some delays are warranted; on balance this is hardly a desirable way to reduce fluctuations in investment.

STABILIZATION OF CONSUMER INCOME

The outstanding secondary effect is a fluctuation of consumers' income resulting in the first instance from fluctuations of employment in the investment industries. If it were not for this, consumer spending would presumably fluctuate little, outside of durables. These fluctuations spread cumulatively through the field of consumer spending, and return to intensify fluctuations in investment, with further effects on consumer income and spending. Perhaps the most strategic starting point for stabilization policy, under either economic system, is mitigation of fluctuations in consumer income and spending, in the face of some fluctuations in investment which it would not be feasible, or even wholly desirable, to eliminate completely.

[7] Theorists may note that I have here attempted to segregate one element in the "principle of acceleration" which is an inescapable mathematical relationship, distinct from the less-determinate relation between changes in "total stock," inventories or capital equipment, and the behavior of demand for the end products of such equipment or for the use values yielded by consumers' durables.

This can be done in various ways. Workers can be kept on part time, with or without full pay, or can be laid off with unemployment pay. Credit for the purchase of consumer durables can be manipulated. A collectivist system can alter its social dividend; or a private-enterprise system can act on the same factor by manipulating consumers' disposable income through alterations in the amount and distribution of tax burdens and transfer payments. One basic problem arises from the undesirability of paying everyone as much for idleness as for full-time work. This is especially awkward where the resumption of full-time work requires a shift of jobs and perhaps a shift of residence—as would often be the case. With freedom to choose occupations, some incentive is called for to bring about these needed shifts, let alone eliciting full output from workers who can get equal pay for less work.

The inescapable logic of this situation, if total consumer income is to be completely stabilized, while idle workers receive less than full-employment income, is that other workers, already employed, should receive more real disposable income for no more work. For this purpose the method of tax manipulation interferes least with a free market system, leaving consumers free to choose what they will buy, and producers free to produce for the resulting demands. It does not require of a system of private enterprise the collective planning of production. But it does require either quick legislative action on taxes, or delegation of authority for tax changes to the executive, both of which are foreign to our normal governmental procedure.

The "built-in" stabilizers of our present system, including both unemployment compensation and the progressive features of our tax structure, have possibly been overemphasized in recent discussion. A study by the Department of Commerce indicates that income after taxes would shrink 85 per cent as much as income before taxes, in a moderate recession, and more in a heavy one, indicating a mitigating effect of 15 per cent or less.[8] Other estimates are higher. The total mitigating effect includes also unemployment compensation and other factors, and has been variously estimated at from less than 40 per cent up to about 50 per cent. Thus it appears to constitute an important but partial stabilizing factor, far short of full stabilization. It should, however, considerably reduce the derived fluctuations in investment.

STABILIZATION OF INVESTMENT

Turning to the question of stabilization of investment itself, a collectivist economy would be in a position to do a good deal of direct scheduling, including especially new construction, but only at the cost of running two alternative risks; of delaying construction after the point at which it became economically desirable, or of building ahead of demand, with the chance that the location and character of the work would prove inappropriate to the demand when this ultimately materialized. The same would be true in greater degree of productive equipment. One thing that has commonly been proposed—that the kind of investment which is public in a private-enterprise economy be made to fluctuate anticyclically to counteract fluctuations in investment for the production of saleable consumer goods—would presumably not be needed if consumer income were sufficiently stabilized, since this would eliminate most of the fluctuations in derived investment (though not all). Long-lived consumer durables, however, might still present some fluctuations. And if consumer spending were not completely stabilized, there would still be a problem of making the kind of investment which is public in a private-enterprise economy fluctuate in a contrary direction.

This would create instability of employment in the in-

[8] U.S. Department of Commerce, "Markets After the Defense Expansion," 1952, p. 79.

dustries affected, which would be no more desirable for
them than the contrary kind of instability which now occurs,
except that unemployment would occur at times when it
would be easier to get other jobs. But the incentive to seek
other jobs, with possible loss of seniority and skilled standing, plus possible change of residence, might be insufficient
if the policy of sustaining consumers' buying power included
very liberal unemployment benefits. To secure desirable mobility in the face of such liberal benefits might require the
authorities to be fairly tough about canceling claims to employment benefits on refusal to accept a "reasonable" job
opening, construing "reasonable" to include openings less
desirable than continued employment in the former job
would be, but fair in terms of what the economy could offer,
in the light of a genuine need for movement. Whether such
toughness would be politically feasible in a democratic "welfare state" may be doubtful; but the difficulty appears to be
one common to collectivist and private-enterprise systems.

A less exacting standard of stabilization of investment is
the goal of stabilizing the construction industry. This, however, presents difficulties similar to those of stabilizing investment as a whole, merely less in degree. Construction is
not a homogeneous industry; and to stabilize it completely
as a whole, in the face of cyclical changes, would create anti-
cyclical changes in particular parts of it, which would give
rise to the same kinds of problems just discussed.

This brief and inadequate survey makes it appear that
we can hardly expect 100 per cent stabilization, and that we
must look to mitigating fluctuations in both main fields, of
investment and consumer income, possibly with greater reliance on the second.[9] Perhaps the greatest distinguishing

[9] Since the above was written, the author notes that big corporations
appear to be laying increasing stress on advance budgeting of capital
outlays, apparently encouraged by the persistence of long-run growth
trends. This may afford sufficient support to consumer income, so long
as realized growth validates the advance programs. If it fails to do so,

characteristic of a collectivist economy, as compared with one relying heavily on private enterprise, would be a greater amount of "disguised underemployment," in which workers keep their jobs but have less to do, or are employed on work of inferior value. Parenthetically, hoarding of labor is a well-established practice in the Soviet system, and it is one form which the "industrial reserve army"—or corps—takes in that system.

INTERNATIONAL ASPECTS

So far this discussion has assumed that employment will be dealt with by internal means, not by the mutually defeating efforts of different countries to distort international trade in the direction of a "favorable balance" and thus export unemployment, or prevent other countries from exporting theirs. Pressures in this direction would be aggravated if one country's policies in support of employment should lead it into price inflation. This international aspect of the problem may be left to other writers better qualified in that field. One awkward feature of the world situation, with respect to this problem, arises from the dominant size of the American economy and the dependence of other countries on our imports for demand for their products, coupled with the fact that this demand of ours for their products is supersensitive to our domestic fluctuations. For our own internal purposes, we might be ready to accept a reduction of our fluctuations to moderate proportions, coupled with unemployment benefits at rates that we could easily afford. But other countries have reason to be alarmed at even moderate fluctuations in the United States. In this matter we probably cannot be expected, and very likely cannot afford, to be as good a neighbor as these countries would wish. Their stabilization poli-

---

private investment-budgeting may prove to have been a first line of defense, needing the backing of a second line, in the shape of public support of consumer income. (Footnote written in May, 1956.)

cies (like our own) will need to be sturdy enough to take care of some disturbances originating outside their boundaries, including (but not limited to) those stemming from the United States.

HOW MUCH CAN WE AFFORD?

The question of what we can afford in this matter brings us back to the dangers mentioned in the opening of this section as resulting from setting our sights for stabilization too high. One danger is that of too much non-self-liquidating public outlay, resulting either in tax burdens injurious to the vigor of private enterprise, or in inflationary deficits. If this is avoided by letting government enter the field of self-liquidating private investment, the result could be to displace an amount of private investment equal to, or greater than, the added public investment created. Excessive transfer payments to consumers, in stabilizing their incomes, would have effects similar to those of other non-self-liquidating public outlays. This could lead—if our sights were set too high—to chronic inflationary excess of demand.

Or the virtual guarantee of jobs might peg the demand side of the labor market at a height that would invite wage demands that would be inflationary from the side of pushing up costs. One incidental difficulty, which may be substantial though temporary, can arise during the expansion of "fringe benefits" in wage bargains, which increase labor costs in a form that does not automatically and immediately constitute "take-home pay," which will increase demand commensurately with the increased cost of goods. This matter of wage costs is one of the inflationary pressures with which our system has not yet learned how to deal.

Policy as to Inflation

One of the large differences between socialistically inclined economies and our own appears to lie in their greater
readiness to accept a condition of chronic inflationary excess
of demand—largely as facilitating "full employment,"—the
inflationary effect being repressed by direct controls of
wages and prices. Our system regards this as unsound and
dangerous, except as a temporary measure in all-out war—
in which emergency all countries accept it. The post-Korea
defense economy has presented an intermediate problem in
which the determination of correct policy has been more difficult than in either full war or full peace, largely because,
unlike the situation in all-out war, the need for defense
promises to be of indefinite duration and cannot be met as a
temporary crisis in which patriotic incentives may, to a considerable extent, replace or supplement normal economic
ones. In peaceful times our purpose—imperfectly realized
—is to control inflation by preventing the occurrence of an
inflationary excess of demand, chiefly through balanced public budgets and control of expansions of private credit.

The reason for this is simple: our economy is dependent
on nice adjustments of cost-price margins to bring about desired production, to allocate resources or to cause goods to
move where they are wanted. The minor maladjustments
inevitable in any controlled system of prices are bound to
grow into serious matters as price-formulas reflecting past
conditions get out of date. Our system depends on a free
market to reward improvements with gains that will be temporary, after which prices would follow the new level of
costs, with a flexibility that controlled prices could hardly
hope to approximate. Wartime controls induced producers
to shift from cheaper to more expensive grades of goods
on which margins were higher. If peacetime controls are to

avoid these and other distortions, they may fix price-cost margins at a higher average level than genuine competition would permit. Goods would still be produced, but there seems to be substance behind the idea that the health and vigor of the system would be impaired.[10]

In discussions of this country's preferred policy inflation and "deflation" are sometimes spoken of as if they were simple opposites, and as if the policies suited to dealing with the one need merely be put in reverse to deal with the other. This does not fully take account of various differences of operation between expansions and contractions of total demand. Expansions act partly on physical volume and employment and partly on money scales of prices and wages, with a progressive shift to more emphasis on the price-wage component as employment rises. Contractions, owing to the "ratchet action" of an economy in which wages and prices resist downward movement, act more predominantly on the physical volume of production and employment.[11] Another difference is that one of the chief available weapons—control of credit—has its main effectiveness in restraining expansion, but is not equally effective to reverse a contraction. As bankers have put it, "You can't push on a string." As a result, a mere reversal of our accepted policies will not return us to our previous position.

[10] It is, however, not true that output will not change, nor resources move, except in response to price changes. Change of demand, without change of price, is often sufficient.

[11] The above statement avoids the tricky term "inflation." In the Keynesian thesis that "true inflation" begins only after "full employment" is reached (*General Theory*, pp. 119, 291, 301, 303), the treatment is such that the reader, if not the author, is likely to confuse two kinds of asymmetry of response to changes in demand: (1) above vs. below "full employment"; (2) upward vs. downward ("ratchet action"). I am assuming ratchet action to apply over all the ranges of employment that concern us for our present purposes. It applies, of course, unequally to different parts of the economy. But even in agriculture, price supports resist declines, while "parity" moves upward with increases in nonfarm prices.

CREDIT POLICY

As a weapon against inflation, restriction of credit suffers from certain limitations. It is working against the "ratchet" action, and hence is likely to have more effect in shrinking employment than in restraining prices or bringing them down if they have risen. There is warranted fear that vigorous use of this weapon would be less likely to level off the economy than to precipitate a recession. As a result of this fear there is reluctance to restrict credit vigorously until the need is clear; and by that time investment is likely to be overexpanded, leaving the economy ready to slip into a recession if the brakes are applied. Skillful management may avoid this danger, but the attempt is likely to mean using credit restriction too gingerly to have full effect in curbing inflationary pressures.

FISCAL POLICY

Fiscal policy is more adapted than credit restriction to working in either direction; but it is obviously much harder to mobilize quickly enough to deal with fluctuations. Against sustained inflationary pressure from the side of demand, it is a mainstay of policy, but it makes increasingly severe demands on the conscientious resolution of legislators as public budgets get heavier. This growing weight of budgets also makes well-nigh inevitable the levying of taxes that are bad from the standpoint of impairing business incentives, and especially of impairing the opportunity of small business units to grow into effective competitors of the larger, established ones. These difficulties are well known, and to discuss them would lead us too far afield. The American economy has, on the whole, shown surprising vitality in resisting them. It is worth noting that the size of current budgets is due mainly to defense outlays rather than to welfare expenditures.

IMPACT OF UNIONS

Neither fiscal policy nor credit control deals with the inflationary push that comes from the side of wage costs. And unless this is successfully dealt with, neither a collectivist economy nor one of private enterprise can be assured against inflation. We must assume the existence of strong unions, though the degrees of their power may vary. We must probably assume, on their part, a philosophy under which wages should rise when demand is strong, because the strength of demand permits increases, and should also rise when demand is weak, as a means of sustaining purchasing power and thus averting recession. Until recently we had to assume, in the United States, rivalry between the AF of L, and the CIO, and Mr. Lewis's comprehensive Local 50, to attract members by promising and securing greater wage gains. (The railroad brotherhoods also enter into the contest to maintain or improve wage differentials between trades.) The merger of the AF of L and CIO may reduce this particular form of interunion rivalry, but this does not mean that union bargaining power is less. Most of all, perhaps, we must assume that union leaders are politicians in their unions, making promises to their constituents and striving mightily to come as near as possible to fulfilling them. These add up to strong pressure to push wages up faster than the approximate 2 per cent annual increase in the productiveness per man hour of the economy as a whole, which may be taken as representing roughly the limit of noninflationary wage increases.

Strategic bargaining power is influenced by such things as the closed shop or union shop, nation-wide bargaining or nation-wide unions bargaining separately with competing employers, and seniority rules. Bargaining leverages become more effective as the nonunion shop diminishes in importance; and they tend to insulate the wage bargain from the effect of any unemployed workers who may be willing to accept less than the established rate. These elements of monopolistic and semimonopolistic power can be modified, but only in the face of political power and pressure which seem sufficient to assure that union bargaining power will not be greatly weakened.

The alternative course lies in the other direction: that of increasing responsibility as union bargaining is increasingly influenced by national leaders who understand the limits of aggregate union power and the dangers of inflation. Mere understanding, without centralized leadership, is not enough. Leaders of particular unions understand well enough that if they refrain, others will gain, inflation will not be avoided, but they will have lost in the contest over wage differentials. A collectivist economy, especially under a labor government, has an advantage in securing responsible co-operation in antiinflation policies; but this is only partially effective in a system which, even if called socialistic, still relies heavily on private enterprise.

The kind of inflation here contemplated is of the "creeping" sort; and the question may be raised: "What is wrong with it?" One obvious answer is that sustained inflation at an average rate of 2 per cent per year would wipe out half the value of savings in about thirty-five years, while at 3 per cent per year it would do the same in about twenty-four years. This is in addition to disparities between unionized industrial trades and other occupations in which salaries rise more slowly.

To sum up, it appears that the problem of inflation is one shared by both kinds of economy we are considering; and that effective safeguards depend heavily on moral elements involving responsible restraint in the use of economic and political power. This is only one matter in which the

successful continuance of a free system, including freedom
to organize, rests on a moral basis, the demands of which
are continuously increasing and becoming more exacting.

Maintenance of Competition

In the United States it is accepted as a commonplace
that a free system of business enterprise rests on the checks
that competition imposes on irresponsible abuse of private
economic power; and that the progressive vigor of such a
system rests on the competitive incentives that serve to combat tendencies to the apathy of undue security. The primary
objective here in view is the protection of the customer in
the obvious matters of output and price in relation to quality
of products.[12] We want to keep the area of directly regulated
public-service industries as small as possible. And it is in
this spirit that we regard the noncompetitive fixing of prices
by private industry as an evil in itself, and refuse to make legality depend upon whether the prices fixed are reasonable.
We do not want government to be forced to make that determination for industry and trade in general.

It is perhaps in our national character that we have multiplied statutes, some aiming to close loopholes, others to re-
lax the law in favor of particular groups; also that controls
have moved from broad and general antimonopoly provisions to increasingly pervasive control of numerous kinds
of trade practices that may be judged to restrict or injure
competition. It is around these latter extensions that the
chief current problems center. The issues involved are:
whether these controls can be effective for their purpose,
and if so, whether they can do it without interfering with the

---

[12] The limitations of competition in relation to the more qualitative
aspects of welfare, and the need of further safeguards, have been indicated in earlier sections of this discussion.

everyday conduct of private business to an extent that may impair its spontaneity and vigor.

Nevertheless, it has so far remained true that the principle of antitrust controls represents the one way of protecting the public interest in these matters and still keeping private enterprise free in its main operations. It is a mainstay of private enterprise, recognized as such and supported "in principle" by the American business community. This is so true that if it did not exist, business would have to invent it for its own protection, economic and political. Business might prefer a too-perfunctory interpretation and enforcement, but if so, it is not likely to get all it wants in this direction.

Clearly, competition is not accepted as a universal reliance in a system that includes public utility controls, agricultural price supports, resale price maintenance, and exemption of labor unions from the antitrust laws. The support of competition, in operation, applies primarily to rivalry of business units in the production and sale of goods. This includes rivalry in the purchase of materials and "subassemblies" and of capital goods generally, and to a less extent in the hiring of labor. It includes some competition among workers in securing jobs and holding them, through qualifications and performance; but not, in the main, in accepting less than the going rate of wages.

Policy clearly goes on the principle that competition, other than between business units, can be unduly severe— which suggests the further question whether there may also be some business conditions in which it may be too severe. This appears to be a fact, and some policies have acted on this principle: witness the NRA Codes, the fair-trade laws, the special treatment of bituminous coal,[13] and the Inter-

[13] In the Appalachian Coal Case (288 U.S. 344; 1933) the Court approved a common sales agency which covered a substantial part of the relevant production, but still had competition to meet from other sources. After the end of NRA, under the Bituminous Coal Act of 1937, schedules

state Commerce Commission's limitation of competition in rates between railroads and trucks. So far our antitrust laws, in the field where they operate, do not appear to have recognized undue severity of competition as a justification for restricting it. A change in this respect would require a reinterpretation of the "rule of reason."

A skeptic might say that where competition comes full strength we want to weaken or eliminate it, and where it is naturally exposed to restriction or extinction we want to preserve and strengthen it. Or we sympathize with shelters for the "little fellows"; but do not want the "big fellows" to have any more shelter than their size makes inevitable. Particularly we do not want them able to grow bigger by unfair or predatory methods which depend on size and bargaining power rather than on productive efficiency. At any rate, it appears that our antitrust policy is to be judged by its effects in the areas of industry and trade, especially in those areas in which dominant size or combined action (always relative to the size of the pertinent market) are easiest to bring about.

BENEFITS OF COMPETITION

What do we want competition to do for us? What benefits do we expect from it? The main economic benefits may be listed under four heads.

1. We expect competition to furnish incentives to increased productive efficiency that are more compelling than the interest a monopoly has in improving its processes. To get the benefit of this incentive, where progressive increase in efficiency depends on expensive research and experi-

---

of minimum prices were laboriously prepared and went into effect in October, 1940. With the armament effort conditions changed, maximum prices were installed by OPA in 1942, and the Bituminous Coal Act was allowed to expire in 1943. In other industries more modest continuations of NRA code protections were struck down under the antitrust laws.

mentation, requires that business units of large size shall still feel this competitive incentive.

2. We expect the rivalry of independent producers to give us an ample variety of types and qualities of products to choose from, including new varieties. This competition in quality implies that the offerings of different producers shall be distinctive; that is, they shall be in some respect unique. And I would contend that this uniqueness is a competitive fact, not a monopolistic one, so long as others are free to imitate or not, whichever seems to them more advantageous.

3. We want the gains from all this to be diffused as widely as possible and as rapidly as consistent with business enterprise having the incentives to the necessary pioneering. As fast as the "state of the arts," or the knowledge of what kinds of products consumers want, become common property, no one can make a special profit by merely equaling this standard. But if he excels it, in productive efficiency or in the quality or attractiveness of his product, he can still make a special profit—for a time, until others catch up and his achievement is in turn absorbed into the "state of the arts." If instead of excelling he falls behind, he will make losses; and unless he can better his position, he may end by being forced out of business.

Gains may be diffused to customers in lower prices, or they may go in paying standard rewards to added capital that is used in making improvements, but historically the greater part of the diffusion has been to workers in higher real wages. And this is as good a way of diffusion as any other, on two conditions. One is that wage increases do not amount to more gain than there is available to diffuse. This would be inflationary. The other is that the structure of wages maintains equity between different occupations, and does not give some an enduringly favored status because the industries that employ them have made more than the average rate of progress. The fulfillment of these conditions would be impaired to just the extent that either employers or workers in a particular industry possessed and exercised the power of a privileged monopoly position.

This indicates the limits of the useful role of "countervailing power," which J. K. Galbraith has recently suggested as a substitute for competition.[14] If this meant that competition were completely displaced, "countervailing power" would take the shape of bilateral monopoly, which Galbraith apparently regards as a response to unilateral monopoly and a rough remedy for it, diffusing its gains at least in part. A more common view regards bilateral monopoly as an aggravation, operating as an unholy alliance in which, if a union grabbed an employer's monopoly gains, the employer could get them back from the customers. But in practice there may be enough competitive pressures or enough resistance to price increases to prevent the employer from recouping his gains in this way; thus imperfect competitive forces may set limits on the gains available for a strong union to grab, even if competition is not strong enough to diffuse all the gains to the customers in the first place.

On the buyer's side, what a strong buyer does is generally to get access to some alternative source of supply and make the most of it as a bargaining leverage, thus bringing to bear competitive alternatives of which weaker buyers would not be able to take advantage. When it acts in this way, "countervailing power" would seem to be, not a substitute for competition so much as a complementary factor, activating competitive alternatives that would otherwise be ineffective, or, if competitive forces are sluggish, bringing about a condition in which sluggish competitive forces are sufficient. Gains may still be diffused, though less completely

[14] See his *American Capitalism: The Concept of Countervailing Power* (Boston: Houghton Mifflin Co., 1952).

and less evenly than active and two-sided competition is supposed to diffuse them.

This diffusion of gains results in keeping the over-all level of profit down to the minimum necessary for healthy incentives; and this is important. But it is important largely for a different reason from the one economists tend to emphasize and which has at times led business men to characterize the economists' ideal as one of "profitless prosperity." A scaling-down of the over-all rate of profit, if it has been unnecessarily high, is a social gain, but if that were all, it would be a strictly limited gain, which could be secured only once. It seems more than likely that its more important effect is on the incentives to progress; because industrialists who are capable of making improvements are placed in a position in which, if they are to renew their profits, they must go on making more improvements in a progressive series. And such a continuing series is bound to outweigh any once-for-all gain; the resulting profits can be absorbed repeatedly, as long as the improvements continue. The mark of effective competition is not absence of differential profits, but their successive creation, erosion and re-creation as one of the incidents of progress.

4. Competition frees the customers, and others who deal with business, from dependence on the good will or benevolence of business for the diffusion of the gains it makes, giving them instead the leverage that comes from a chance to choose between rival offers in a field that is open to all who see a chance to make some net gain. This does not deprive business of all discretion as to price and policy, but it keeps it within the limits that the rival offers set.[15] A

---

[15] One sometimes sees an overstatement of this goal, implying that any margin of discretion in private hands is an improper degree of power, and that impersonal economic forces should determine the result so completely as to eliminate this private "power." This seems to imply that no one should have any discretion—except government officials. The exception exposes the fallacy of the rule.

further incidental benefit is that a "market" may result in which many buyers who do not themselves canvass all the rival offers may get the benefit of others' canvassing in the shape of fairly standardized terms. Obviously, if too many buyers rely on others' canvassing, the benefits may be impaired or even lost. If people are completely negligent in protecting themselves, even efficient antitrust laws may not give them full protection.

LIMITATIONS OF FORMAL THEORETICAL MODELS

While this list of the main benefits expected from competition is one with which most economists would be expected to agree, it differs from the picture that would be derived from the analyses of formal "economic theory." It emphasizes the dynamic factor of progress; and formal theory has regularly subordinated this to the conditions that are necessary to a static equilibrium—so much so that Schumpeter's dynamic theories still stand out as exceptions to the general rule. This formal equilibrium-theory finds its most complete expression in models of "pure and perfect competition," in which the profits and losses inseparable from progress are eliminated. For our present purpose the pertinent question is the bearing these models may have on antitrust enforcement. But "perfect competition," being a hypothetical model, not realizable in practice and one-sided as an "ideal," is not a legitimate standard from which to gauge whether actual competition has been injured.

On one point, however, it has had a salutary effect. Early judicial decisions were too easily satisfied with very small numbers of competitors. Theoretical analysis has at least called attention to the importance of adequately large numbers, and it has rendered a service by raising the problem, though without furnishing a feasible answer. Courts today should not be as easily satisfied on this score as some were three or four decades ago. Nevertheless, what is needed in practice is not the kind of competition called "perfect," but competition consistent with large-sized units where they are necessary to progressive efficiency, with quality-differentiated products and the development of new ones.

SOME SELECTED PROBLEMS

The field of antitrust policy is too large and many-sided to be comprehensively dealt with here. It includes outlawing of outright collusion on output and prices, and prevention of mergers that would substantially restrict competition, while renewed attention is being given to proposals for some kind of restriction of size as such—this last an amazingly involved problem. It includes vertical integration (which can be a form of competition or a means of spreading monopoly), contracts restricting freedom of dealers or suppliers, undue extension of patent rights, organization for foreign trade, and other matters. From this array of perplexing issues, we may single out a few extremely general impacts of the attempt to control trade practices to prevent those that injure or unduly restrict competition.

Here the basic difficulty is that the line of legality cannot be laid down in a statutory blueprint. And if a controlling body such as the Federal Trade Commission were to specify what practices would be regarded as legal, it would be undertaking positive regulation of such practices; and that *would* present a threat to the health of a free private system. It would tend to ossification, and health and progress lie in the other direction, that of keeping the patterns of trading flexible and mobile. But the alternative, of forbidding a given practice, in a given state of facts, without specifying a permissible practice, leaves the law uncertain. A business man cannot be sure, try as he may to keep inside the law and still do business, that he will not be held to have been acting illegally.

This can be an injustice for a sensitive and conscientious

business man—and there are such. It is complicated by the fact that conscientious men may disagree as to whether a given "orderly" trade practice unduly lessens competitive pressures or merely prevents them from becoming destructively chaotic. The resulting uncertainty is presumably a lesser evil, and does not appear likely to impair the vigor of private business in reducing costs or promoting improved products, though part of its time and attention may be diverted to legal defense. What seems more likely to happen is that an attitude would come to prevail in the business community that the law is such that one cannot do business without violating it. And this is not healthy.

We need to develop procedures that embody a kind of "due process" more suited to the economic logic of the kind of cases we are considering. They are cases in which legality hinges on whether a given practice impairs competition. To an economist, this calls for a comparison of the effects of this practice with those of some feasible alternative; but legal procedures do not naturally lend themselves to such comparisons. This involves a real dilemma, since without such comparisons "injury to competition" has no rationally defined meaning, while the making of such comparisons might carry enforcement agencies undesirably close to prescribing the permitted trade practice. While the difficulty cannot be conjured away, it appears that procedures could be better adapted to elicit disclosure and argument on the economic theories that underlie charges of impairment of competition.

Granting that the antitrust laws do not seem to interfere with business practices in such fashion as to impair efficiency, is the shoe on the other foot? Are antitrust policies bound to be ineffectual in preserving enough competitive pressure to keep the economy healthy? The question should be taken seriously, and it may be difficult or impossible to give a permanent and universally valid answer. Business men are not immune to the general dislike of being exposed to the full impact of competition, and they tend to seek shelters from it. But an active and vigilant antitrust policy has a strong preventive effect, ruling out many of the kinds of shelters business would otherwise seek. This effect is probably more important than the results of actual cases, which often appear baffling.

Mr. Thurman Arnold recently voiced the view that a prime reliance is the "cussedness" of American business men, which makes them difficult to regiment or stereotype. This may be a diminishing factor, and it runs counter to another tendency we have noted earlier: for business men to be less single-minded in the pursuit of their immediate individual financial interests and to give more attention to making their enterprises good citizens via a longer-run accommodation among the various interests of the community. Possibly a healthy (but imperfect) system needs both types of personality in the business world!

One of the reasons why a fair number of enterprises is needed in an industry—and it need not be a very great number—is to make it fairly certain that a trade will contain some of the more rambunctious types. A few such can put competitive pressures on the others—if the law is on their side—and can keep things stirred up. If a country wishes to preserve a free market economy, it seems important that it should develop a vigorous antitrust policy before trading practices become too stereotyped and while the business community still contains some competitive rambunctiousness, which can be given a chance to affect the tone of the whole by the competitive pressures it exerts.

The picture, some few aspects of which have been briefly and inadequately sketched here, offers no neat and simple solution. It is loaded with problems and dilemmas. But with the vigilance against abuses which is the proverbial price of freedom, coupled with a realistic tolerance of the genuine necessities of business and of the inevitable imperfections of any feasible *modus vivendi,* it seems that sufficient decentralization of power is possible, with adequate avenues of escape from the abuses of private monopoly, and without substituting a degree of centralized governmental regimentation that would be fatally stifling to private initiative. It seems that American industry has somehow combined the efficiencies of size wih a dynamic drive that includes a good deal of competitive spirit, and it seems probable that the antitrust laws can take a share of the credit. Even though the competition may be directed more to quality, selling costs, and service and less to reducing prices than a theoretical economist would like, still Americans have an amazing amount of products per capita and incomes to purchase them.

Conclusion

As to the compatibility of modern welfare policies with the requirements of a healthy private economy, this survey has revealed some real dangers, greater in some areas than in others, but no conflict that need be irreconcilable. It will take all we can command of technical skill and integrity merely to avoid serious mishandling of the ever more complex and involved economic impacts of governmental operations. And if we are to live up to the requirement that the economy be more consciously directed to social ends than was dreamed of in the philosophy of the "invisible hand," this will call for all the understanding we can muster of what these ends are, putting first the needs of human beings as co-operating members of an economy that can fairly be called "voluntary" and as citizens of a free and self-governing society.

It is a foregone conclusion that, in a society in which

people are free to fulfill these responsibilities well or ill, there will be lamentable shortcomings, judged by any standard of what is fully satisfactory. We may be willing to put up with some shortcomings when we reflect that in a society that is not free the subjects would be held responsible to the rulers, not to the society; and the rulers would be a prey to the proverbial corrupting effects of power that is absolute or irresponsible. But toleration of shortcomings cannot safely spell complacence. Both market action and political action are indispensable but imperfect instruments: things that can be made to work, but cannot be trusted to work well enough automatically to assure the survival of a free society. They need to be used as checks on one another and to supplement one another's weak points. The line between them cannot properly become a fixed one, but needs to be flexibly adaptable to changing conditions and needs, which stem largely from changing industrial techniques and organization. Such flexible adaptability presents a severe and growing challenge; and we shall need to grow if we are to keep abreast of it.

While a free society needs a moral basis, as this presentation has stressed, it appears that this is one side of a two-sided relation of mutual dependence. This kind of morality, being essentially a quality of free individuals in their relations with other free individuals, can be generated and preserved only in a society in which individuals have a wide range of freedom of choice and action. Of this sort is the basic ethic of fidelity to agreements.[16] The requirements of

---

[16] Eugene Lyons, *Assignment in Utopia* (New York: Harcourt, Brace and Company, 1937), p. 513, makes this point by way of contrast with the Soviet habit of agreeing to specific terms before official witnesses, and instantly forgetting them. In the Soviet case, of course, the moral corruption of absolute power is compounded with the deliberate glorification of unmorality: the doctrine that the end justifies any means. In the real or ostensible service of "the revolution" this becomes "revolutionary morality": a new and higher form which has relegated truth, humanity, and other such trifles to the category of "bourgeois superstitions."

socially responsible conduct—economic and political—are far more exacting. There can be no assurance that we shall rise to the challenge they present; but to the extent that we fail, our society will not remain free.

This discussion has pointed to some tendencies and concepts characteristic of academic methods of thought and of the isolation of academic disciplines which appear less than perfectly useful as guides to policy. On this same subject it has been said that if a future generation looks back on this one, "it may be seen that many of our scholars . . . were locked deep within their own categories when they should have been trying to plumb and define the universals of human values that were at stake in the crisis of the twentieth century." [17] Among these categories, we have encountered the concept of the scientific character of economics as consisting of "laws" more precise and determinate than the subject matter they purport to describe. Especially, we have observed this concept applied in the realm of values. We have glanced at the category of "economic welfare" as synonymous with real income of marketable consumers' goods, with consumers' choices taken as final and "interpersonal comparisons" dismissed as not scientifically possible. And we have examined briefly the categories of "pure and perfect competition," which tend to be treated as ideals and which in that capacity are too one-sided to be sure guides to policy.[18] We have found all these categories at times serving to confine thought rather than to equip it.

We must defend the right of free academic inquiry, even though some of it takes these forms. Its job includes exploring what may ultimately prove to have been blind alleys; but

[17] Norman Cousins, in *The Saturday Review*, August 15, 1953, p. 22. The present writer does not follow all of Cousins' argument, and would contend that we need also to consider values that are not universal.
[18] Needless to say, space has not sufficed for adequate presentation of the pros and cons of these categories. That could fill several volumes.

it also includes freedom for those who think the alleys *are* blind, to search for more promising routes. We must speak, and work, for the co-operation between disciplines, and between academic and nonacademic thinking, which may broaden economic perspectives and bring economics into working relation with more realistic concepts of welfare. If there is truth in the saying that war is too important to be left to generals, or that public finance is too important to be left to financiers, there may be some of the same kind of truth in the proposition that economics, where it becomes involved with welfare, is too important to be left at the exclusive mercy of economists.

At least we need to consider whether the money measure, which gave economics an early advantage over other social disciplines in quantitative definiteness, has not become a handicap at the point at which welfare refuses to be ignored. For welfare can be distorted if measured solely with a monetary yardstick, about as badly as if the monetary expression of human values is wholly ignored. The position here contended for is that if we are to talk about welfare at all, we should insist on a conception that can at least claim to be the genuine article, and should accept no monetary substitutes. If that be economic heresy, the right of free inquiry includes the right to such heresies.

One thing the money measure does is to help an academic economist, having formulated a problem, to build a model containing all the factors needed to solve it; thus satisfying his problem-solving "instinct of workmanship." But if problems of welfare are faced in all their imponderable quality and unmanageable complexity, it is clearly out of the question to "solve" them in the same precise fashion. They call not only for knowledge, but for knowledge unified in the service of the highest ends, married to wisdom and tinged with prophetic insight. And since the academic mind at its best is incorrigibly honest, it is bound to report that these Godlike qualities are disquietingly scarce and not too likely to be placed in the seats of power.

What we have to work with is a different array of talents. It includes specialized knowledge of technical matters, animated by professional standards of service; also some talent for social invention, generally conceived from a specialized point of view. All this has to be co-ordinated by nonspecialists. What may be feasible is to follow the specialists' guidance in clear cases; and in the more general work of co-ordination to eke out a scanty endowment of saintly and prophetic virtues with the more limited and ordinary wisdom of common human fellow-feeling, of realization that we are all on board the same vessel, crossing stormy seas, the wisdom of compromise and of checks and balances, all of which may culminate in evolutionary adaptation.

But these are limited gifts. Therefore I shall sternly deny myself the luxury of a peroration envisioning the solution of this complex of problems. Instead, if we do our best and if luck does not turn too strongly against us, we may hope, not to solve our problems, but to evolve with them.

CHAPTER EIGHT

The Ethical Basis of Economic Freedom: I, The Need for an Ethical Basis

The World Struggle Between Free and Totalitarian Systems

I shall start, where so many discussions start nowadays, with the overshadowing fact that the free world is locked in a life-and-death struggle with the world of totalitarian tyranny. And I shall focus on one aspect of this struggle which, while it is too omnipresent to be ignored, may not be sufficiently emphasized, and which explains why this struggle is so crucial for the fate of humanity. I believe that at bottom, back of atom bombs and propaganda, back of the changing tactics of alternate intimidation and ingratiation and the unchanging aim of Communist world dominion, back of attempted comparisons of economic performance, this is a struggle between two irreconcilable ethical systems. And one advantage the Soviets have over us is that their system, be-

This and the following chapter are reproduced with permission from the published version of two lectures sponsored by the Calvin K. Kazanjian Economics Foundation, 1955.

ing laid down by central authority, achieves a unity and conformity which no free system would be willing to try to impose. As an incidental result, what may be called the propaganda version of the Soviet system is much easier to explain to other peoples.[1]

Their actual system is dominated by one supreme end; namely, world-wide Communist revolution. To that end, not only are individuals reduced to the status of mere means, but truth and the feelings of common humanity are expendable as "bourgeois superstitions" whenever they do not serve the supreme end of world revolution, or when they do not appear to serve it, in the eyes of the rulers.

The ethic which we oppose to this one is far less simple because, being the ethic of freedom, it must somehow accommodate a multiplicity of personal ends, while still maintaining the essentials of orderly co-operation which any society must have if it is to survive. It is a commonplace that freedom unrestrained can destroy itself in the anarchy of conflicting purposes, of parasitic and predatory activities. These must be restrained. A free system is one that does this with a minimum of coercion and a maximum of reliance on voluntary action, including the voluntary assumption of the obligations that go with working together. Freedom will survive to just the extent that we learn that these obligations are a part of it, and take some trouble to find out what obligations our kind of society calls for, if it is to go on working.

Freedom is something I want for myself, because it is an essential feature of my conception of the dignity and self-

[1] This contrast was well illustrated by an interchange between Mr. Akintola, a member of the Nigerian Assembly, and Mr. Hugh Gaitskell at the Milan conference on the future of freedom (see *The New York Times*, September 17, 1955, p. 6). Mr. Akintola said he understood what the Soviets stood for and wanted a formula that would do the same for Western democracy. Mr. Gaitskell said it meant that each country must develop for itself the forms that suited it. A Westerner may be skeptical as to whether Mr. Akintola understood what Soviet rule would actually bring about, or merely what Soviet propagandists promised.

realization without which life loses its chief meaning. If I want to live in a free society, that means I also want freedom for others, I am conceding the same claim to them. From this it follows that the basis of any system of generalized freedom is the ethics of humane respect—Albert Schweitzer calls it "reverence"—for our fellow human beings as individuals. Only on such a basis can society be safe for freedom, or freedom safe for the society.[2]

In each of its spheres freedom carries its appropriate complement of obligations. First comes freedom of the mind: freedom of thought and belief, and freedom to know what others think—which means that these others must have freedom to speak and to publish. The major responsibility that goes with this is the responsibility of truth and sincerity, plus the tolerance and temperance that goes with respect for the sincerity of others, who may hold different views. Those who falsify, or conceal their real aims in public discussion, are abusing this right, and have forfeited it morally; though legally it may be necessary to extend to these abuses the equal protections of the first amendment. John Milton would be revolted at many of the degenerate forms of present-day publications that find undeserved shelter behind the arguments of his *Areopagitica*.

Next comes freedom of political action, with its many-sided array of moral problems. It is natural, and within limits proper, to use political methods to promote private interests—others being free to do the same, and the authorities having the task of trying to fuse these divergent private interests into a common public interest, or at least to compro-

[2] George F. Kennan recently put this in the following telling words: "Freedom . . . lies in acceptance of that system of restraints most closely in tune with our own nature and with the order of the world, most conducive to the dignity of our relationship to others and to the self-respect and humility with which we contrive to accept ourselves." He contended that any attempt to find freedom through avoiding social obligations resulted invariably in some new enslavement. *The New York Times*, September 18, 1955.

mise them. At some point political promotion of private interests becomes an abuse; but the limits are difficult to define and impossible to identify in any simple formula. Where the market fails to protect substantial interests, the political forum is bound to be resorted to, for better or for worse.

This brings us to the sphere of economic action. Here it is a commonplace that humane regard for our fellows does not organize the supplying of New York City with food and clothing. For that we depend heavily on hard-headed types of self-interest. True, but such self-interest would not supply New York City either, unless it were operating in an effective harness. Conditions on the waterfront bear witness that when the harness slips, the supply service is jeopardized. Most problems of economics boil down at bottom to the question, "What kind of framework and harness does it require to make the pursuit of private self-interest not only safe for the society, but constructively serviceable?" Constructively serviceable the system has been, to an amazing extent, despite all that can truly be said about pathological sectors like the New York waterfront.

For the United States, our duty at home is clearly to maintain this constructive serviceability, regardless of the fact that our prosperity makes us an object of envy. The purely technical features of our economy have become models to be imitated, even by countries that have no desire to imitate precisely our private business institutions. The combination has placed our system, in the eyes of the Soviets, on an uncomfortable eminence as the foremost enemy to be discredited and isolated. In combating this effort, it is our further duty—also our interest—to see to it that our relations with other countries are constructively serviceable to them, with due regard to the ways in which their situations differ from ours.

If the new attitude of Moscow really means that the Soviets give up armed conquest and, as Khrushchev has recently stressed, confidently expect to displace our system in a non-shooting rivalry of economic performance,[3] this implies a contest for the minds of the still-free parts of the world. In this contest total communism will be opposed, not by its obsolete antithesis of total individualism, but by what can probably best be called a balanced economic system, including a sector of private enterprise with enough size, freedom and vigor to give a tone to the whole.[4] And such a balanced system, in whatever specific form, will stand or fall by a double test: not only by whether it can organize the productive powers which modern science makes possible, but whether it can direct them to meet the rapidly rising standards of human welfare of which science and education are making all people increasingly aware.

All varieties of economic system must meet this test if they are to survive—that necessity is their one most basic common factor. Our system, being somewhat democratic, is under more immediate need than the Soviets'; but even dictatorships are not wholly exempt. To meet the shifting requirements of times of change and strain calls for flexibility, and flexibility calls for realization that the specific forms needed to meet this test vary with time, place, and circumstance: with techniques, knowledge, and traditions or attitudes. It should go without saying—but does not always seem to—that for different countries, in widely different economic and social situations, this test does not call for a carbon copy of any one system, our own or any other. For the countries we choose to call "underdeveloped," the test is vastly harder to meet than for countries that have already

[3] Statement reported in *The New York Times*, September 18, 1955. "Non-shooting rivalry" does not automatically preclude methods of boring from within.

[4] This terminological point seems important. To call ours a "mixed system" is to give up half the semantic battle at the start. "Mixed system" seems more appropriate to describe systems in which limited enclaves of modern industrialism have been inserted in preindustrial societies, without real assimilation.

assimilated modern industry, and have wider margins above
the bare necessities. Even for these most favored nations, the
answer is not easy. To find it, in our case, will require all the
constructive forces we can muster, including ethical ones.

And if a balanced system is to win the struggle for the
mind of the world, it not only needs to keep pace in practice
with developing ideas of the welfare an enlightened people
want from their economy, but it also needs an articulate and
convincing philosophy which will explain these features as
natural and integral parts of it, not as things that somehow
happen in spite of the inherent nature of the system. To
frame such a philosophy is not an easy task. More than one
self-appointed emissary of our economy abroad has failed to
understand all this, and has expounded the American system
in terms of a one-sided individualism which this country has
long since outgrown. In its most extreme form this individualistic theory is more than one hundred years out of date; it
was vulnerable to the counterblast which Karl Marx
launched in the mid-nineteenth century. Both theories were
one-sided—that of Marx more violently so—but it is too late
to answer it by a return to the classical individualistic theory.
A reply to Communism, if it is to be successful, must include
elements that classical individualism neglected, as well as
those it emphasized, and must build them into a better-
balanced synthesis.

Classical Individualism, as Practice and as Theory

Because we shall be using this classical individualism
only as a point of departure, it may be legitimate to present
it in an oversimplified capsule, as the philosophy under
which a society, interested in the multiplication of goods for
the use of all, could safely entrust this to individuals, to each
of whom the making of goods was a mere means to the mak-

ing of private profit. Adam Smith's philosophy centered in
the belief that the competitive market could transform the
pursuit of profit into an incentive to the making of more
plentiful goods, in which the masses would share, and reducing profits to the smallest amount that would serve as an
adequate stimulus. This was in harmony with the spirit of
the Enlightenment of the eighteenth century, and represented an advance over the more hard-boiled and undemocratic attitudes of the preceding period. And it left an enduring legacy in its standard of what constitutes good
performance for an economy. Whether or not subsequent
economies live up to this criterion, they will be judged by it.

Meanwhile, the actual factory system—rudimentary by
our present standards—bore little resemblance to Utopia. It
multiplied and cheapened a few familiar products, especially
textiles, which were able to find a market, even though the
wages of the factory workers were too low to enable them to
buy plentifully. The humane liberal thinkers of the period
deplored the low wages, but saw them as a result of supply
and demand, which could be remedied only if the workers
were to restrict their own rate of increase. This was seen as
their primary ethical duty in the economic field. On this issue the classical economics was closer to the present facts of
the "underdeveloped" countries than is the modern Western
economics, which is the thinking of developed countries that
have escaped from the bondage of overpopulation.

To Karl Marx, on the other hand, this poverty was the
inevitable result of the profit system, which was bound by
its inherent nature to keep wages down to bare subsistence,
and which contained seeds of decay rooted in this defect.[5]
Down to 1955, the official Soviet picture of the current state
of the Western economies was the picture as Marx saw it in

---

[5] Current Soviet spokesmen disclaim the view that the breakdown
of capitalism is automatic. Possibly that would leave them too little to do
to bring about its downfall—still regarded as inevitable.

the mid-nineteenth century, hardened into Soviet dogma, superior to factual evidence. If the facts did not agree with the dogma, the facts were guilty of heresy, and must be purged before being reported—as Eugene Varga learned some years ago, when he described too objectively the wartime record and postwar state of our economy. In October, 1955, a new line of objectivity was announced, recognizing Western technical achievements, and condemning the older stereotype.[6] But Mr. Matskevich, as spokesman for the visiting Russian agricultural delegation, found himself not wholly free to report the facts as he saw them.

Americans know that the Marxian dogma does not describe their economy. But neither does the opposite theory of the free market as a perfect and all-sufficient mechanism for the production of needed goods and services.[7] It is time we looked at this theory in sufficient detail to identify both its strong points and its limitations. The theory rested on a system of law, for which a remarkable rationale was elaborated by Bentham. Under this, the law was supposed to prevent people from using their persons or property in ways that would injure others, leaving them free to pursue their own interests in any other way. Then, since no one can coerce me into furnishing him goods and services, he can secure them from me only by offering me an equivalent in exchange.

To assure that it will be an equivalent, the system relies on the principle that individuals know their own interests and will look out for them better and more vigilantly than others would do on their behalf. Add competition, and the mechanism becomes complete (in theory), able not only to

[6] See *The New York Times*, October 12, 1955, citing an editorial in *Kommunist*. Only time will tell whether this new objectivity will be transmitted to the Russian people, who have absorbed the older stereotype.

[7] This theory, like its opposite number, is a stereotype useful to the extent that one realizes its prerequisites and their incomplete resemblance to reality.

utilize self-interest but—in the eyes of some over-enthusi-
astic adherents—able to dispense with any other motives, in
the realm of everyday economic dealings. Adam Smith, who
wrote on moral sentiments, said that it is not from the benevolence of the grocer that one expects one's next meal. He
had little regard for those who profess to trade for the public
good, and added that few words need be employed in dis-
suading them from this affectation. This attitude contains,
of course, a deal of truth. And it has become so deeply em-
bedded in our mores that nowadays if a business man does
do something from motives of public interest, he generally
takes pains to explain that he is really doing it because it is
"good business."

But the mechanism which this theory describes is far
from being as perfect as the early theorists conceived it,
viewing it as they did in its rudimentary stages. For one
thing, it is limited to marketable goods and services; and a
growingly important number of the products of our developing system take the shape of diffused effects, often unexpected and unintended, which are not bought and sold in
markets. Outstanding examples are the things the system
does to health, employment opportunity, and social morale.
Some of these unintended by-products are welcome, some
unwelcome, and many are not yet understood. The unwelcome ones and those we do not understand create problems
that call for fresh adjustments. It is in this sense that Veblen
remarked that "invention is the mother of necessity."

In the light of these considerations it becomes evident
that the theory sets an impossible task for its basic institution, the law. To put it in a nutshell, law cannot completely
prevent individuals from doing things that unfavorably affect the interests of others—not without fatally hamstringing
their freedom and opportunity to do anything constructive
and creative. And where the capacity of the law ends, ethical
obligation begins.

The law itself has changed its character profoundly since the classical period which we are examining. It was, or conceived itself, as primarily a system of rights which were the same for all. In this characteristic it took justified pride. And it was this characteristic that Anatole France satirized when he said that the law, in the majesty of its equality, alike forbids rich and poor to sleep on park benches. In contrast to this, modern law has become a highly differentiated structure of rights and duties growing out of the differentiated roles which different individuals and groups play in our complexly specialized society. But even with this growing specialization, law cannot provide for everything.

Again, the classical theory presupposes competition, and competition of a healthy and constructive sort; and this does not maintain itself automatically; as Adam Smith saw, and remarked in his famous passage about the tendency of members of the same trade to conspire against the public—a passage which has probably been cited in more antitrust cases than any other single bit of evidence. The theory depends also on the ability of the buyers to select goods competently; and this encounters serious and increasing difficulties in an economy in which applied science is multiplying synthetic substitutes, and in which the effect of new products on health has become a matter for scientific specialists and beyond the ken of the man in the street. Finally, the original theory took no account of the internal problems of great private organizations, corporate and other, or of their external power, which goes far beyond the power of the small units that existed when this theory was formulated.

To sum up, in a modern economy it has become impossible to trust an "invisible hand" to turn crude self-interest into an efficient engine for meeting every social need. We must have a sensitive awareness of what our social needs are, and what the economic machine is doing to them; and we must work with conscious purpose to make the economy meet these needs.

Social Objectives and the Obligations They Involve

In this setting, it becomes important to ask what we want our economic system to do for us. But this question is not complete without asking another: namely, what consequences follow from the kinds of means which the economy necessarily uses? The answers to these questions will reveal many specific areas in which an effective sense of responsibility is a necessity, if the system is to go on working in tolerable fashion.

1. First come the most obvious objects of desire: marketable goods and services. We want these in ample amounts. And we have found a way to get them: namely, via the economy and efficiency of mass production. This means big corporate units; and it also means big labor unions, for reasons it is not necessary to elaborate here. The idea that this kind of mass unit should become the mainstay of our productive organization was one that Adam Smith, for example, did not entertain: he did not think companies could be efficient enough.[8] In order to be efficient, both internally and in their dealings with one another, they must attain a workable level of integrity, voluntary co-operation, and loyalty. These are the most obvious moral requirements of efficient mass production. Business corporations have not always enjoyed even tolerable levels of internal integrity; in fact, in the decades following the Civil War a corporation was too often an inviting object for plunder by any group that could gain control. A management that is determined to check waste and dishonesty can accomplish this fairly

[8] See *Wealth of Nations*, Modern Library Edition, pp. 712–15.

well by using a system of forms and filing routines that records and traces every transaction. But this also becomes so burdensome that real efficiency is seriously hampered, government paper work being a stock example. If the big organization is to be flexibly efficient, it must be able to trust its employees and agents, without watching their every move. It can afford to allow them perquisites, but these must stop somewhere short of plunder.

Unions have the same problem in their field, highlighted recently by the uncovering of evidence of gross abuses in a few of the union welfare funds. In that connection it is worth noting that welfare funds are a recent form of union activity; and they illustrate what is probably one of the most general principles applying to ethical standards; namely, that in a new activity, bringing people into new relationships, appropriate ethical standards take time to develop. The lines of responsibility may not be well defined at first, or the obligations focused and formulated. It may take a series of abuses to reveal what the necessary requirements are. This applies where the new activity does not in itself have any strong ethical purpose. Where it does, there is an opposite kind of danger; namely, that the original zeal may wear itself out and the original purpose be subtly altered under pressure or overlaid with a mass of routine activity. In such cases eternal vigilance is the price of maintaining intact the original purpose and vigor of an organization. It is good for it to be challenged sufficiently to force it to renew its sense of purpose; but the everyday pressures may erode it instead.

2. We also want to move forward; and this dynamic factor involves problems of its own. It means that neither methods nor products remain the same; and the adjustments we make to them are continually needing to be overhauled. Jobs change their character, particular skills lose their value, more efficient methods may displace workers from particular jobs or particular industries. And for the consumer, new

products are remaking his way of life, sometimes insensibly, often in unexpected ways, and sometimes at a spectacular and bewildering rate. Is the remaking for better or for worse? Who can say with certainty? All we know is that these elements of change raise problems and affect human values in ways that no automatic "invisible hand" can be trusted to take care of.

In remaking our way of life new goods act in partnership with the increase of leisure, which is one form in which people are choosing to take a substantial part of the gains from increased productivity. The leisure activities which increased goods make possible occupy an increasing fraction of our time: an increasing portion of our lives. Accordingly, it becomes increasingly important whether these activities are of an elevating or a degrading sort. Commercial agencies and their propaganda take the initiative in offering us the means of these activities; and they bear some responsibility for the directions in which they tend to steer us, over and above the obvious responsibility to avoid definitely false and misleading statements. Whether they realize it or not, they are agencies of education; trustees for the evolution of our culture. But they will be guided by our responses: if these give evidence that we respond more readily to degrading stimuli than to elevating ones, the degrading ones will be the most profitable and more of them will be produced. In this sense the ethical obligation to recognize and combat degenerative tendencies and influences rests on everyone. If city housing is hopelessly sordid, and if facilities for healthy recreation do not exist or are inadequate, then leisure time may become more of a danger than a benefit. The more of it people have on their hands—especially young people— the more destructive will be the effects of these deficiencies in their environment.

3. A third need is that the material gains from rising productivity be widely diffused. This is not merely some-

thing that humane philosophers want; it is a practical necessity for the working of our kind of system. Mass production requires the mass market. It is a necessity that Karl Marx believed the system would not meet, and this was one of the chief reasons why he expected it to break down. But the system has met this need, to a surprising extent, especially in the last half century, which has witnessed an outstanding reduction in the inequality of incomes. Still more surprising, perhaps, is the fact that the major part of the equalization shows in incomes before direct taxes: progressive personal taxation is apparently less important than other causes.[9]

This phenomenon is easy to announce and bafflingly difficult to interpret, registering as it does all the currents and crosscurrents of half a century of rapid and interlocking changes. Perhaps the chief discount that needs to be applied to the bare figures arises from the fact that much household production has moved out of the household and into the realm of money earning and spending, where it shows in the figures, as it did not show before. And many housewives have followed it out into the employment market. To the extent that this is a mere shift, the increased dollar incomes do not represent clear gain. To this extent the increase in the total of wage and salary incomes may be misleading.

Much of the change, however, must represent a change in the differential structure of wages and salaries. Among the causes at work are: minimum wage laws, increased supply of white-collar workers and of academically and techni-

[9] Cf. Simon Kuznets, "Economic Growth and Income Inequality," *American Economic Review*, March, 1955, pp. 1–28, especially p. 4; also his *Shares of Upper Income Groups in Income and Savings* (National Bureau of Economic Research, 1953), especially p. xxxvii. For a skeptical scrutiny of the data, see Lampman, "Recent Changes in Income Inequality," *American Economic Review*, June, 1954, pp. 251–68. The forces at work may include some slight indirect effects of progressive taxation, in the escape from income into capital gains and the concentration of high incomes on tax-free securities. The mores of plowed-back corporate earnings and stabilized dividends, product increasing faster than capital, and price inflation, all have played their part.

cally trained workers, and the growth and increased power of labor unions. But along with this, and complementary to it, has been the adoption and increasing acceptance among employers of the idea of the "economy of high wages," as a positive working philosophy. For the country as a whole, high wages may be merely "good business," in the sense that money paid out as wages brings back increased demands for goods. But when Henry Ford, for example, initiated his once-famous minimum wage of five dollars a day— hitherto unheard of—he could not have expected that all the increased wages would be spent for Ford cars. More directly, perhaps, he was seeking good workers for his assembly lines. But he was also helping push the high-wage idea into general acceptance, carrying with it the idea that high wages are necessary to the success of our modern mass-production economy as a whole.

With the growth of collective bargaining the forces acting on the relative rewards in different occupations have changed their character. Unions struggle to protect customary differentials or to change them in their own favor, and their primary leverages may be a mixture of supply and demand and sheer bargaining power; but claims of fairness are used to gain public support. And while a compromise adjustment may represent no clear meeting of minds among the trades affected, it is at least less likely to be quickly upset if it does not rouse deep feelings of injustice on one side or another. The trend of such adjustments seems to be coming nearer to embodying a rough sense of equity, neither unanimous nor infallible, but working on balance in the general direction of reduced inequality.

4. Another desire is for something called "security." This covers a considerable assortment of different matters, physical, financial and psychological; but for the moment we may focus on the group of institutions that includes insurance against industrial accidents and illnesses, unemploy-

ment and old age. Here the revolution that has taken place in the current century has established the principle and practice of a minimum provision by collective responsibility, in place of the former practice of leaving it entirely to the individual to provide his own protection—if he could and would spare enough from the demands of current consumption, and if he could and would put the resulting protection in the form of insurance that would meet these various contingencies. The present system is so firmly established, and taken so much as a matter of course, that it is not easy to realize that within the memory of middle-aged persons the method of socially assured provision ran counter to strongly entrenched moral conceptions of the way in which these contingencies should be met. They were regarded as things the individual should handle on his own responsibility; anything else was undermining the basic virtue of personal self-reliance.

This attitude was gradually worn away by the combined operation of a number of factors. One was the obstinate fact that adequate provision was not made by individuals. The quantitative magnitude of the problem was driven home convincingly by the statistics that were becoming available, inadequate as these were. The human impact of the economic casualties was brought home by the experience of pioneering social workers, and the dollar cost of the wreckage appeared in the budgets for relief, while the public conscience gradually came to reject any method that carried such an indiscriminate stigma of charity. Ultimately, the ideas governing policy shifted their center of gravity; the moral luxury of blaming individuals for not meeting these needs came to seem less satisfying than seeing to it that the needs were met, at least to the extent of a basic provision.

In the case of industrial accidents the new developments encountered obstacles in the old-fashioned individualistic law of liability. The doctrines of this older law are not so much unjust as reflecting conditions of a time before the advent of modern mass production.[10] They embodied a theory of personal blameworthy responsibility, with the claimant for damages bearing the burden of proof. The change that has taken place embodied a different theory; namely, that accidents are one of the costs of industry, to be borne by the industry like other costs. One of the practical considerations is: if the burden falls on the worker, he will not generally insure against it; and, considering his situation, the urgency of present needs and the natural human tendency to take the chance that "this won't happen to me," it is not realistic to expect him to insure. But if substantial liability is laid on the employer as representative of the industry, he can and will insure.

As to whether this system of "social security" tends in its over-all effect to undermine individuals' responsibility and habits of providing for their own needs, the general verdict of informed persons seems to be that the provision so far made is not liberal enough to take away the individual's incentive to provide more, and that the chief effect is to bring adequate provision within reach, if the individual adds what he can to the provision already made, whereas under the older system, really adequate provision was out of reach.

[10] The basic concept was that the burden lay where it fell—that is, on the injured individual—unless he could establish a claim for damages against someone else. To do this, he had to show that the other party was to blame, and also that he was not himself responsible through contributory negligence. The employer had a duty to provide a reasonably safe work place, but the worker assumed the ordinary and inherent risks of the industry. Even if the employer failed to provide a safe work place and the worker knew it but still took the job, he could be held to have assumed the risk of the employer's negligence. If the negligence in the case were that of a fellow servant of the injured worker, the injured man still had his claim, but it was against the fellow servant instead of the employer. And the fellow servant was, of course, typically no more able to pay adequate damages than the original worker was to bear the cost of his injury directly. The results of this system can easily be imagined. Compensation was received in too few cases, when it did come the amounts were capricious, and the claimant was too often victimized by unscrupulous lawyers.

This security floor could not be attained until the newer ethical ideas underlying the social method of providing security had succeeded in making their way into acceptance and pushing aside the taboos which the older individualistic ideas had imposed. This is not the only instance in which the spirit of the present age has shown itself skeptical of inherited principles which, in the name of morality, would condemn many persons to suffering and disaster and which, when forced to recognize the necessity of providing for essential needs, would attach the stigma of "charity" to the provision.

The change in the ethical attitude toward unemployment is typical, and it is related to shifts in the prevailing picture of the causes responsible for it. The two extreme opposite views might be: "Anybody can always get a job if he really wants one, therefore being unemployed is one's own fault"; and, on the other side, "The man who loses his job in a modern recession or depression is the innocent victim of a social malady that he could do nothing to prevent." The first view is one for which there was some warrant in the days, more than a century ago, when the country was expanding at top speed into the resources of a seemingly limitless frontier. But when industrial crises began to appear, this view could no longer be held wholeheartedly except by the unthinking; and it seems to have vanished for good in the great depression of the thirties.

It remains true that when workers are to be laid off, the question whether one is a good or a poor worker is likely to have something to do with whether one is kept on the force or not. However, in the impersonal grindings of the great industrial machine other considerations can enter—an employer who was forced to close down may have had about the usual proportion of superior workers, and when other employers are taking on no new hands, these workers may not readily find a new employer. Those who are out of work at any time will, by and large and on the average, be poorer workers than those who are employed; but the question whether there shall be 2.5 million or 3.5 million out of work at any given time depends on forces quite different from the qualities of the workers. In recognition of this, the prevailing emphasis has shifted from an individualistic view to one laying heavy emphasis on social causes.

It should go without saying that it is not safe to wipe out all individualistic requirements and incentives. The unemployed worker has a duty to make a real search for a job, to take a reasonable job if offered, and to meet such reasonable standards of performance as the employer may set. But it is one thing to say that such standards must be met in order to qualify for unemployment benefits and a very different thing to say that unemployment benefits themselves must not be permitted, on the ground that they undermine the individualistic virtue of self-reliance.

One may approach this matter from the standpoint of the principle that it is a healthy thing to have to encounter challenges, provided one has a reasonable chance, if one does one's best, of being able to meet the challenge and surmount it. The responsibility to get a job and keep it is a challenge. If jobs are guaranteed to everyone, be their performance good, bad or indifferent, the challenge ceases to be a challenge; its value as a spur to performance is lost. But if it is a statistically foregone conclusion that so many millions are doomed to fail regardless of their merit, then the value of the challenge as a spur to performance is lost for an opposite reason.[11] This leads up to the next thing we want from our economic system: namely, ample and reasonably stable opportunity for employment.

5. Not only do we want such opportunity; today's ethical standards hold that this is a responsibility of the eco-

[11] Actually, it is likely to be reversed, leading the worker to limit his performance for fear of working himself out of a job.

nomic order, or of the community as a whole, and that its record in this matter is one criterion by which an economic system can properly be judged. The means available for this purpose raise plenty of problems, but they are not the problems that primarily concern us here. Suffice it that a good deal can be done to mitigate fluctuations and inadequacies of aggregate demand, by policies that are becoming increasingly understood and accepted, though no one knows exactly how effective these policies can be. From what has just been said, it follows that there can be no claim of an unconditional guarantee of jobs for all, regardless of performance. The individual has reciprocal responsibilities in the case. The precise definition of these reciprocal responsibilities is something that needs to be left adjustable in the light of experience. It belongs to the creative process of evolving adaptation, and cannot safely be rigidified.

If this is true of the obligations to be assumed by the public and by the worker himself, it is even more true of the obligations that the private employer can be expected to assume. He can handle most technical improvements so as to shift workers, not discharge them, and can offer aging workers jobs suited to their powers. But he cannot go on producing goods for which there is no demand—that is his basic limitation. He can find ways of mitigating seasonal fluctuations—this is perhaps the type of unstable employment most nearly within his control and with respect to which it is highly desirable that he be given all feasible incentives to achieve greater stability. But in a general business recession he cannot be expected to do much to stem the tide. He can do something toward sustaining employment by working to stock, to a limited extent, and usually at some slight risk of finding that the goods he has produced and held for a time are not precisely suited to the preferences of the market when the time comes to dispose of them. In a growing industry capital outlays may be made in dull times, necessarily in anticipation of a future revival of demand, and at some risk of obsolescence. Payrolls may be sustained—but only within rather narrow limits—rather than slashed to the fullest amount that the interests of economy might indicate.

But if business cannot be counted on to do much toward successful combating of a pronounced recession, once it is under way, there is much that it can do under more favorable conditions, when demand is sufficiently active and the question is one of policies that may tend to keep it that way. Business may not succeed in increasing its investment in dull times; but when the prospects warrant expectations of fairly continuous growth, large and strong businesses may take the lead in scheduling and maintaining a steady flow of investment, thereby helping growth to remain steady. Something of this sort seems to have been happening in the past few years, the chief reservation being whether particular programs presuppose an expansion in key industries that is greater than demand can continue to keep up with. For example, automobile production was overexpanded in late 1955, and accumulated inventories forced curtailment in early 1956.

An example of what business can do by organized effort in a recognized emergency is the reconversion campaign of the Committee for Economic Development at the end of World War II. Here there was an adequate backlog of potential demand; but its realization depended on a task of rapid remobilization that could have stumbled seriously if it had waited for the demand to materialize. The Committee's nation-wide drive did much to assure that reconversion would not stumble. This phase once past, the Committee shifted to an important work of study and education appropriate to the task of good business citizenship for the longer pull.

But permanent and complete stabilization is not a feasible standard for a single employer in a competitive system.

Competition, as an active process of business rivalry, implies that some enterprises will succeed in expanding at the expense of less successful rivals—which in turn implies that the less successful rivals will shrink, at least temporarily. If the proportions of a market held by different producers remain the same for a considerable time, the industry is likely to find this fact being used as evidence against it in an antitrust action. And if an employer were to make a contract with labor, guaranteeing a completely stable volume of employment, the antitrust authorities might logically be quite curious over the answer to the question: "By just what means do you expect to be assured of being able to fulfill this contract?"

This has a bearing on the vexed problem of the "guaranteed annual wage," which is high on the list of problems calling for economic statesmanship. Such a guarantee is feasible only to the extent that it is feasible for individual employers to guarantee stability of operation and employment; and an absolute guarantee of this sort seems inconsistent with a system of private enterprise. If the argument is used that wages should be on the same basis with dividends, and that dividends are maintained during recessions—for awhile—I am sure that the workers would not want to accept the full implications of this idea, since dividends are, in the last analysis, contingent on earnings; and to put wages on the same basis would expose the workers to contingencies that they are surely not ready to accept. And if the guarantee were to be applied to selected categories of permanent employees, this would sharpen differences of status among the workers, raising problems that seem to need more thorough discussion than they have so far received.

Nevertheless, the way in which the impact of fluctuation now falls on the workers is not satisfactory, and the possibility of change deserves serious consideration, in the light of what private enterprise can assimilate.

6. Another crucially important value, which is not a marketable product and is not automatically taken care of by a system of "free exchange," consists of the rights of labor on the job: rights with regard to discipline, transfer, and discharge and all the human relations that are bound up with the status of employment in modern large establishments. In this realm the past generation has witnessed a tremendous transformation, in which the arbitrary powers which the employer and his agents used to take for granted as inherent and right have been modified and subjected to procedures of review. The established ethics of business have had to make room for this transformation which is, in principle, thoroughly justifiable. It should go without saying that it cannot properly go to the extent of wiping out the employer's necessary powers of discipline, as it might do if the power were simply transferred from an arbitrary employer to an equally arbitrary union, if the power of unions became supreme and if it were exercised irresponsibly. Here, obviously, is an area of problems in which a vital necessity is a sense of responsibility on each side for the essential and legitimate requirements of the other.

By and large, it seems likely that the gains that unionism has made in this area are greater and more important than such gains in wages as unions can properly be credited with; that is, gains that would not have taken place without the power and pressure of unions in collective bargaining. This, of course, can not be proved; it is merely a judgment. The record of collective bargaining shows instances of irresponsible and arbitrary action in this realm, including "wildcat" strikes in which the members have refused to follow their leaders' counsels of moderation and responsibility; but the best and most responsible unions and employers have, by and large, made a good record in the equitable adjustment of these important human rights. In this area our system has done better than might have been expected in adjusting itself to protect the intangible human by-products of modern business enterprise; and it has done it by reason of a willingness to undertake an enlightened and evolutionary adjustment of traditional ethical standards inherited from the period of old-fashioned individualism.

7. Another value, which represents perhaps the largest single "blind spot" in traditional economic theory and practice, consists of the quality of activity involved in work itself as a value in its own right. The oldest and simplest view was that work is a "disutility," incurred for the sake of the goods it brings. A more discriminating view included the possibility that work, in moderation, might be in itself a positive value but held that, since it is rewarded, it is bound to be carried past that point. And to a type of theory which is interested primarily in "marginal adjustments"—in this case the adjustment of the length of the working day—it makes no difference whether or not the earlier hours are desirable in themselves or the opposite.

Actually, it does make a difference, which on any objective estimate is far more important than the additional marketable products which we receive from the latest additions to our output of marketable goods. Even Adam Smith had a sense of this problem—witness the famous passage in which he excoriated the effects of subdivided and monotonous labor on the mental and social development of the workers. This was in a section in which he was urging public education as an offsetting factor. Another escape consists of increased leisure. But such offsets are not enough; and an age of modern psychology cannot remain satisfied with such an implied defeatist attitude toward the human impact of work-activity itself.

Fortunately, the effect of modern methods of production is by no means as unrelievedly bad as Adam Smith pictured it. The monotonous job is precisely the job which the machine stands ready to take over; and this often leaves the worker with a job that is more responsible and more varied. The process will probably always fall short of the ideal, which might be defined as the well-rounded development of the worker's faculties, in jobs that call for their adequate exercise, in a setting that includes healthy human relationships. But with increasing time and energy available for leisure activities, the remaining one-sidedness of work may be compensated for—always provided that people in general learn to use their growing leisure for healthful types of activity. The industrial side of this two-sided problem may be one of the most important items on the agenda of a modern business system, which has gone far enough to reduce the urgency of the problems arising from the mere scarcity of tangible products. For our present purpose, the problem is: what motives may be enlisted, and what devices of organization employed, to make this an effective purpose of industry, to an extent commensurate with its importance? To this problem we will turn in the following chapter.

8. Finally, one of the things that is needed from modern industry is that it should be a "good citizen" in its local community. This becomes especially important as the size of single establishments makes them substantial factors, and sometimes dominant ones, in the total volume of employment in a town and in its civic planning as to public centers, parks, schools, and commercial and residential areas, not to mention taxes. The duties of industry in these respects are a matter of some delicacy, since these are mostly matters to be democratically handled by the citizens at large, and the citizens include employees of the industry—usually a minority —plus local tradesmen, professional men, teachers, and others, who are independent in their economic status but nevertheless vitally affected by the decisions made by the industry, without which the town would not have its existing size and character. The industry must be co-operative, but not dictatorial, while it still has its own necessary interests

to protect, since if it cannot survive, the effect on the community may be nearly as bad as the effect on the industry itself. The industry needs good public relations locally, as well as in its wider relations, which may be national in scope. The mutuality of this relationship is illustrated by the fact that localities often grant an industry temporary tax concessions as an inducement to it to locate there. The town can afford this—within limits—because the tax-paying capacity of other interests in the town will be increased if it acquires a new industry.

This problem arises in one of its most difficult forms when strictly business considerations urge that a firm should close down some or all of its local activities and shift them elsewhere. This is a matter for the solution of which no simple formula can be prescribed, and certainly no hard-and-fast legal obligation. Should the industry accept reduced earnings for the sake of the local interests affected, or would this merely mean perpetuating an uneconomic national distribution of productive resources and activities, in which case it would probably only postpone the evil day? If the difficulty arises from the competition of lower-paid labor elsewhere, is this something that nation-wide collective bargaining may be expected to equalize in a reasonable time, and if so, can the enterprise afford to wait? To what extent is the disadvantage offset by differences in productivity; and if it is not so offset, or if it is due to local factors of higher cost, should the difference be equalized by a reduction in the local wage scale? Such an adjustment would encounter resistance from a national labor union, which may have been forced to accept regional differentials in wage scales but hopes to be able ultimately to iron them out. The only single rule that can be laid down is that the parties involved should deal with the problem in a spirit of equitable adjustment, accepting changes that appear inevitable, but standing ready to share the burdens and easing their impact on the interests immediately affected, so far as may be feasible without perpetuating an adjustment that will ultimately prove untenable.

The reader will recognize that I have been speaking in general terms of a problem that is of very specific concern to numerous industrial centers in New England and New York.

9. Policies of sustaining employment via sustaining demand and policies fostering the increase of wages may either or both of them lead to price inflation; and price inflation may dilute or even neutralize the beneficial effects of the policies. The possible increase in real incomes is limited to the aggregate increase in the per capita productivity of the economy as a whole, which in this country has a well-established upward trend of about 2 per cent per year. Any greater increase in total money incomes is bound to be neutralized by inflation; any greater increase for particular groups is at the expense of other groups; and with wages constituting as large a fraction as they now do of the total "disposable income" of the economy, the scope for further gains at the expense of other groups is too small to be a substantial factor. The members of the community cannot all gain 10 per cent a year by forcing their money incomes up at that rate; and if many can and do make such money gains, the resulting inflation will prove to be the most inequitable of all possible ways of redistributing income. Any groups that have this kind of economic power are under an obligation to exercise it within the limits set by these inescapable facts.

Other community interests include health, conservation of natural resources, and the public defense. Beyond all these stand the requirements of making our economy a good citizen of the world. In all these matters there is a general obligation to give loyal support to any public requirements that may be set, plus a willingness to go beyond the minimum which the letter of the law may set.

Conclusion

To sum up, even old-fashioned individualism required an ethical basis; and the requirements have multiplied enormously in what one newspaper man has called "the era of vastness and complexity through which our civilization is dog-paddling." [12] Big organization, both in industry and labor, carries responsibility for its internal integrity and its external power. Industry has responsibilities—in which we all share—for what it does to its products, to the quality of our activities in leisure and in work, for equitable distribution of incomes, for security, for employment opportunity, for avoiding inflation, and for good citizenship generally, in taking care of the ramifying effects and social by-products of industry. These ramifying effects create problems: something generally needs to be done about them if industry is to be self-sustaining for society in the large, and if it is to justify itself, as a contributor to social welfare, rather than a parasite preying upon it.

The something that needs to be done often takes the shape of "passing a law." But before the law is passed, there must have been some understanding of the problem and some discussion of possible remedies. The first obligation of the good economic citizen is to have some such understanding—enough to make him aware of what is going on and why. Then after the law is passed, it must be administered; and this calls for a more active sort of understanding and compliance, coupled with criticism and pressure for amendment where this is warranted, but not mere stubborn resistance to any change in traditional methods of doing and thinking. But there are many of these problems for the solution of which we have no formula ready—certainly none

[12] Gladwin Hill in "Test Pilot," *The New York Times Magazine*, September 18, 1955, p. 56.

ready to be crystallized into a legal obligation. Here what is needed is a creative process of experimental exploration, by the joint efforts of men of good will.

In the struggle for the mind of the still-free world there is no need to tell foreign peoples—especially those of underdeveloped countries—that our technology can produce goods—they know that. What they may not so fully understand is the extent to which a business system can not only promote this technology but place it at the service of widely diffused human welfare. Indeed, there is no reason why the underdeveloped countries should understand this. They are being ceaselessly told the opposite by the most formidable propaganda engine in history. And their contacts with the Western business system may not have been of a sort calculated to furnish automatic refutation of this hostile propaganda. In its relations with them, Western business may have lent itself at worst to a picture of exploitation, or at best to one of paternalism with a "colonialist" flavor.

Still less could these peoples be expected to understand the conditions that are necessary to the best results of which economic freedom is capable—something of which we ourselves are only gropingly half-conscious. As for the adaptations called for by the varying conditions of different countries and peoples, these represent an area the very existence of which is hardly realized by many, and which is in the early stages of exploration. All of this goes to make up what may be the most formidable challenge which our economy has to meet in the fateful second half of the twentieth century.

Suppose we do not meet it? Suppose that groups with power fail to exercise it responsibly? Suppose that a recrudescence of narrow self-interest puts an end to further voluntary social adaptation? Our economy would not forthwith collapse or hand itself over to a neofascist dictatorship. But there would be an increase in the number of abuses for which coercive controls would appear to be the only effective remedy, and the remaining voluntary elements in our system would survive more and more precariously. The health of a voluntaristic system would have begun to go downhill, because it had reached the limits of its capacity, not for production but for voluntary social adaptation.

I do not expect that freedom will succumb to these degenerative forces. And the chief reason is the amount of adapting our system has done, the amount of change it has assimilated, in the past century, and especially in the past half century. With all due humility for our shortcomings, the record argues that our society possesses the kinds of aptitudes and resources that are needed if we are to bend, rather than break, under the pressures of new conditions.[13] In the next chapter I shall look at the question of what some of these aptitudes and resources are.

[13] A notable study in this field is: *Social Responsibilities of the Businessman* by Howard R. Bowen, with commentary by F. Ernest Johnson, 1953.

CHAPTER NINE

The Ethical Basis of Economic
Freedom: II, Resources Available
for a Responsible Economy—
Agencies and Motivations

Introduction

In the preceding chapter we looked at the setting of the
problem in the world struggle between free and totalitarian
societies, viewing this in its aspect as a struggle between irreconcilable ethical systems. I attempted to indicate the nature of the ethics of freedom and defined the challenge it
now faces, raising the question whether an economy of mass
production and applied science, evolved out of nineteenth-
century individualism, can adapt itself to meet twentieth-
century standards of welfare by methods that retain the essentials of its free and voluntary character.

We looked at the classical conception of individualism,
in which a competitive-market economy was superimposed
on a legal foundation derived from Bentham, and the com-

bination was pictured as an automatic mechanism for turning the pursuit of private gain into an engine for multiplying marketable goods for all. We looked at the prerequisites and limitations of this theory, and we decided—or I think we did —that even basic individualism required a moral foundation; and further that some of the most important products of industry are not marketable goods, but unintended and often unexpected by-products in the way of effects on social welfare—on health, security, and morale—the burdens of technical innovation, and the distribution of the benefits of plenty.

To handle these by-products in a reasonably satisfactory way has called for something in addition to the mechanisms of free exchange operating under motives of strictly private self-interest. In place of an "invisible hand," cheating our selfish strivings and turning them to our own good in spite of ourselves, there is required a capacity for social adaptation and the handling of economic activities with a conscious eye to promoting the common welfare. This social adaptation is not less important than our capacity for material production. In this chapter we shall be looking at some of the resources on which this capacity for social adaptation depends.

The Darker Side: Discouraging Features of the Picture

If one makes this kind of a survey with an eye open for shortcomings, it is too terribly easy to become discouraged. People seem altogether too generally absorbed in dangerously narrow group interests. Where their private interests are concerned, they display a frightening capacity for persuading themselves that "what is good for me is good for the country." Sheer corruption crops up too frequently; the opportunities for it appear to multiply with the growth of organizations, and there never seem to be quite enough people who combine inherent integrity with the executive talents necessary to man the posts of responsibility. And it appears impossible to make honesty the best policy by paying every incumbent of such positions more than he would be able to steal or graft.

Men of honesty and of average or above-average intelligence show a discouraging lack of imaginative thinking and a tendency to resort to clichés in place of thought, when they encounter novel situations. Politics tends to make the party organization an end instead of a means; and the party, instead of knowing what it stands for, often seems to be asking to be told what aims it should espouse—that is, what ostensible aims will promote its real aim of winning the next political contest. If a politician has ideas of the public good which he wants to serve, he must pay for the opportunity by serving also the narrower interests of the pressure groups on whose support he depends for his continuance in office. An aroused public may sometimes support the passage of a much-needed measure—after which it generally turns its attention to other things, leaving the execution of the measure at the mercy of the many contingencies that beset officialdom. Vigilance in any one direction is not unceasing. Statistics of crime and juvenile delinquency are not consoling reading for members of a society that depends on progress in its moral standards if it is to justify its claim to survival.

Why indulge in such concentration on the dark side of the picture? Because that side exists and represents the obstacles with which the positive forces have to contend. It is not helpful to close one's eyes to them. But neither is it helpful to accept these obstacles as insuperable. When one is tempted to yield to this kind of defeatism, perhaps the best antidote is to take a glance backward and gauge the distance we have come in a generation, or two, or three. There has been an amount of social adjustment that is truly surprising to anyone who can remember where we were fifty years ago. And this did not happen by itself. Back of it lie stubborn selfish battles and grudging settlements; also perception of needs and seeking of remedies, learning by mistakes, persisting after defeats, and learning tolerance and the art of compromise. Unlike the French Bourbons, we have learned some things and forgotten others. With all its defects, this adds up to a great creative adaptation.

Is it great enough to save us from shipwreck? Of that there can be no guarantee, and the challenge is endless. But the record affords the standing proof of the existence of the constructive forces that brought it about and that stand ready to deal with fresh problems. These forces we shall examine. But first a word of warning against two widespread misconceptions. The fact that I have encountered them is my excuse for venturing farther into the realm of ethical theory than may be safe for a mere economist.

What Economic Ethics Is Not: Two Opposite Misconceptions

When one suggests any degree of reliance on motives of an ethical or moral character in economic dealings, someone is sure to say, "You are proposing to substitute altruism for self-interest, and that is hopelessly visionary. It is contrary to human nature." I am not proposing this, nor is there any need to renounce self-interest. But this may explain my allergy to the use of the term "altruism." It seems misleading in suggesting an "either-or" relation: if one is interested in others, that is something outside one's self and distinct from it, and one acts for the interests of others instead of for one's own interest. And if one substitutes others for one's self, in one's thinking and acting, that may further seem to imply that one is committing the impertinence of trying to do in their behalf the kind of thinking which only they can properly do for themselves. This last may perhaps be dismissed as a perversion of altruism, perpetrated by someone incapable of really putting himself in another's place. One who does enter into another's feelings will not be guilty of this kind of officious meddling.

All of which may have been put in a nutshell by the child who, after church, asked his mother, "What am I here for?" She replied, "To help others." He pondered and then, with childhood's fatally direct logic, asked, "What are the others here for?"

For ordinary economic conduct, a less ambitious starting point—even if only a starting point—would be the relations we actually have with other persons, including many we never see, and the attempt to conduct those relations so that they will be useful and constructive for those whose lives they affect. That is a pertinent standard for economic dealings; and it is not contrary to human nature. In fact there is ample ground for holding that a world of utter self-interest, excluding all consideration of others, would be fully as contrary to human nature as a world of "altruism"; since it would place everyone in a merciless competitive struggle in which he would find every man's hand against him. His security would be shattered, not only in the economic sense, but in the much more basic psychological sense. He would have no group on which he could count for fellow feeling and moral support, let alone financial. Few personalities are strong enough to stand the kind of strain which such a world would inflict.

In place of altruism, the more pertinent conception for our purposes seems to begin with reciprocity in a broader sense than that of mere bargaining—in the sense rather of wanting all one's relations to be mutually serviceable in the fullest sense, including a feeling of responsibility for the diffused and unintended by-products as well as the direct objects of exchange transactions. This is an extension of the widespread virtue of honesty—of wanting to pay one's way. In some degree or other, it is a very common virtue.

Most people go further than this. Very basic in their natures is the impulse to identify themselves as members of a group, whose particular group interests they adopt. Or one may identify one's self with wider interests. These may expand both in space and in time. As to time, a valid perspective extends beyond the present generation both backward and forward, regarding it as a link between generations past and generations yet unborn. In any case this kind of widened identification of the self is something quite different in its implications from caring for others instead of one's self, as altruism is sometimes taken to imply.

But conceding that the name "altruism" designates something that really exists, and disregarding reservations about the connotations of the term; if an individual wants to serve all humanity, he still has a primary obligation to the sector of humanity closest to him—himself and his family. Or if a business man's main motive in his business is to make it a service to society, still he will not succeed in this altruistic purpose unless his business survives and stays solvent. And he may have to devote much time and strenuous effort to seeing that it does stay solvent.

Those who urge that we cannot depend on altruism sometimes put forward as a substitute the conception called "enlightened self-interest." This is eminently sensible—so sensible that it is not easy to identify the point at which it can go astray. It is quite true that the supply of the higher ethical motives is limited, and it is the part of prudence not to put more burdens on them than they can bear.[1] Self-interest is bound to be a major economic motive, for reasons

---

[1] Sir Dennis Robertson has given notable expression to this theme: see *National Policy for Economic Welfare at Home and Abroad*, R. Lekachman, ed., *op. cit.*, pp. 1–6.

to which Adam Smith gave classic expression. Unenlightened self-interest can be socially disastrous, and enlightenment can transform it into a powerful constructive force. We need all of this that we can get. But the concept is misused whenever it is carried to the point of claiming that it does away with the need for genuinely ethical standards. This implies that we shall get good enough results if we consider the interests of others only insofar as we can thereby get more out of them for ourselves. This means treating others as mere means to the ends of self; and this is contrary to the basic ethics of a free and humane society, as already laid down.

But the term "enlightened" really means something more than this kind of calculating shrewdness in utilizing others as means to one's ends. Self-interest is not really enlightened unless it is also enlarged until it identifies itself, to some extent at least, with the interests of others. And once this enlargement has taken place, it can never treat others as mere means. Enlightenment is an invaluable way of approaching this kind of enlargement, but it is not complete unless the enlargement has taken place. Then what we are doing to others concerns us because it concerns them, and we care what we do to them, wanting it to be constructive. And if "enlightenment" goes this far, it has become ethical. It has gone beyond the idea that "what's good for me is good for the community" and has accepted at least some part of the idea that "what's good for the community is good for me"; or that my economic relationships cannot be healthy unless they are part of a healthy community. If a business man has gone this far, but still wants to insist that his regard for community interests is merely "good business," I have no quarrel with him. He has broadened his conception of "good business" until it has become a moral one; that is sufficient. But if he has not gone this far, and if his enlightened self-interest is mere farsighted shrewdness, one can be sure that at some point or other the shrewdness will not be farsighted enough and trouble will result.

Available Means and Agencies

THE BASIS IN HUMAN NATURE

The whole character of our problem stems from the fact that man is a two-sided creature. He is an individual, making many personal decisions which, we are forced to assume, are not precisely dictated by external forces, no matter how much he may be conditioned or influenced by his environment. But he is also a social animal. He wants to "belong" and to stand well and to deserve to stand well with some group of which he is a member. In some degree or other he identifies himself with the group. In fact, for various purposes, he identifies certain of his purposes with the various particular purposes of a large number of groups: a business establishment, a trade union, a professional association, a church, a boy-scout unit, or a bridge club. This identification with a group is moral, as far as it goes. To the extent that the group is not in any essential conflict with other groups in the society, this kind of attitude may be sufficient.

The trouble is that the groups with which people identify themselves most strongly, and whose purposes they adopt most fully, are relatively small and homogeneous groups with common interests—one's kin, one's craft or union, or one's profession. Where group interests conflict, it is a fairly exceptional individual who will fail to side with his group, whatever the interests on the other side may be. The largest group with which most people identify themselves very strongly is their nation. The trouble here is that their strongest patriotic feeling is likely to be reserved for crises when their nation is in conflict with some other nation. But on internal economic issues they seldom think nationally. For example, the tariff is proverbially a "local issue." Even when an individual thinks he is trying to see what the over-all national interest is, within which all the conflicting group interests are comprehended, it is remarkable how highly it turns out to be correlated with the interest of his industry, his occupation, or his section. Therefore these conflicts remain conflicts.

A recent illustration of the mental habit of putting small groups first appeared in the shape of a story—presumably apocryphal—of two Boston Brahmins talking about an acquaintance. One said, "So-and-so has become very prominent lately." To which the other replied, "Only nationally." One wonders whether there may be something similar back of the uneasiness or suspicion with which professors are frequently viewed nowadays. Is it because, instead of thinking in terms of a particular group interest, they persist in thinking nationally—or worse yet, internationally?

What is to be done about this difficulty of group bias? There is, of course, no panacea for it, but a fair amount of experimenting is being done in bringing members of different groups together, looking for the best way of doing this, under the best conditions. In general, the most promising method seems to involve rather extended and informal association, promoting understanding appreciation of one another's circumstances and of the basis of one another's sincere beliefs.

Another trait of human nature, which supports the impulse to identify self with wider interests, is the impulse to seek the meanings of things. At the most primitive level things have meaning for man as they serve his personal ends. But he does not stop there. Sooner or later he is bound to ask what he himself means. And he finds this meaning—if he finds it at all—in a relationship to something larger than himself; something with ends larger than his personal ones.

This search for meaning is extremely unlikely to be satisfied with identification with the interests of any limited and particularistic group. It seeks identification with some really comprehensive objective.

The ultimate search for meaning, and the ultimate answer to the search, may be religious. But at the economic level the search may be satisfied if the individual feels that he understands the way in which his personal activities fit into the life of his society—the society of which he is aware. Or, if his way of life is a highly traditional one, it may not be necessary for him to "understand" it in an intellectual sense; it is enough if he fits into it in a way that he accepts. It is in this sense that observers of the impact of the modern commercial-industrial society on the life patterns of primitive peoples say that it destroys those people's sense of the meaning of their old way of life, before it overwhelms that way of life completely. They are faced with a more powerful scheme of things, into which their gods and their customs do not fit. They become uprooted peoples.

It has been said that in the homelands of the Industrial Revolution its coming had a similar uprooting effect on the common man, though not with the same catastrophic suddenness and completeness, and without the added shock of subjugation by a racially alien culture. As we have seen, the philosophy of classical individualism furnished a partial rationalization of the way in which people fitted into the new order. In England this philosophy appealed to intellectuals, "gentlemen," and independent business men, and that was sufficient for the moment, since other classes did not count politically at the time when the craft economy was being uprooted. But as the common man gained education and the vote, it became clear that the question of his place in the new scheme of things included a deal of unfinished business.

In this country the individualistic philosophy was more widely accepted from the start, but was combined with spontaneous mutual aid in frontier communities. There were conflicts, especially between the frontier-agricultural culture and the commercial-financial culture that trod on its heels. But both were variant individualisms. The prevailing sense of the common man's meaning in the scheme of things needed enlarging, rather than rebuilding from the ground up.

There are other traits of human nature which play an important part, if a less fundamental one, in the business of social adjustment. In a society that teems with organizations of all sorts, people are daily being asked to be members of committees or boards, or officers of this or that organization; and this means that they are being asked to assume the role of representative, or trustee, for the interests expressed in that particular organization. And it is quite surprising how readily people respond to such demands, and how well, by and large, they fulfill the responsibilities. Not always and not perfectly, of course. We have already seen how persons in control of corporations were able, especially in the early and unregenerate days, to use them for personal plunder. But as the customs and standards of an age of organization develop, the grosser betrayals become more exceptional, and the acceptance of representative roles becomes increasingly the prevalent pattern.

Another widespread human trait, of a reinforcing sort, is the trait whereby things we do for ulterior motives come to command our interest in themselves.[2] The worker's techniques may be a means to earn wages; but if he is given a fair chance, he will become interested in competent workmanship for its own sake, and the same is true of the business man's interest in production as such. But this trait may reinforce undesirable as well as desirable activities. The game of sharp trading, or of getting something for nothing, is itself an interesting game. The political party machine can be-

[2] I take this to be the trait underlying what Veblen called "the instinct of workmanship."

come an end in itself, to the detriment of the public ends it
might serve. But if people are persuaded that their job includes socially useful things, they do seem to have a way of
becoming interested in these, too.[3]

The term that seems to come nearest to summing up all
the things we have been discussing is responsibility, partly
for the reason that it is a two-sided concept. On the one side
it describes an individual attitude toward the decisions a
person makes for himself. This implies, first, that he does
have some margin of discretion in deciding how to act, and,
secondly, that he voluntarily exercises that discretion with
due regard to the other interests affected by his actions. And
I hope we have decided by this time that this is not wholly
"contrary to human nature." But there is another side, suggested by the idea of people being "held responsible," suggesting pressure from outside. For our present purpose, this
does not mean formal legal requirements, but rather those
more general and elastic requirements imposed by "a decent
respect to the opinions of mankind."

LAW OR FORMAL STATE CONTROL

In a free society law cannot work unless it has the common morality of the people behind it. This comes about
fairly naturally in the slow evolution of the common law.
For our present purpose, the special problems arise when
law is changed by the more rapid course of legislation. Here
the duties of a good citizen include supporting needed new
measures, watching their administration (usually through
some private organization), and conforming to the existing
law because it is the law, even if he disapproves of some
features of it and is working to change them. In this country
we seem to have these qualities sufficiently—for most purposes. There are few prejudices so ingrained as to make nul-

[3] The psychologists have a word for it; they speak of internalizing
social standards.

lification of law a real threat—the color line being one of them.

One of our chief shortcomings arises, as we have seen, because the public pays attention to one issue at a time, and between times leaves them to the processes of administration. But in these periods when the administrative agency is out of the limelight of public interest, various things can happen, since administrative agencies are no more immune than anything else to the laws of change. In a given case there may be an initial creative period when able and dedicated persons are giving the agency its distinctive character. This may be followed by a period of preoccupation with routine administration, subject to continuous pressure from the private interests directly affected, and the character of its operations may be unobtrusively altered. Or the story may take a different course. Here the public needs the services of dependable civic agencies who will watch what is happening and inform or arouse the public in case of need.

THE MAINTENANCE OF COMPETITION

The attitude of business toward competition is a most interesting mixture, and becomes more interesting the more one looks at it. Of course, there are different attitudes in different industries, and among different individuals in any given industry. Therefore, in venturing a few generalizations, I am only too keenly aware of oversimplifying. To expect business men willingly to support competition is to put them to a very stern test, because competition generally hurts somebody. Probably few business men actually enjoy the pressures of their rivals' competition on them, though to a few, who have a well-founded confidence in their capacity to come out successful, the pressure of rivalry may be felt as a welcome and invigorating challenge. On the other hand, few business men would resist the temptation to gain some business by a competitive move of their own, if they saw an opportunity. Accordingly, one may conjecture that if American business were left to its own devices, it would probably seek to mitigate competition by informal understandings, then discover that these were not binding, and then substitute various methods of enforcement—in short, business in America would become cartellized, to an extent not too different from what prevails in Europe.

But this is conjecture; and in making it I am deliberately leaning over backward to avoid claiming that it is due to some unique merit of ours that American business is not cartellized. My surmise may be wrong. There may be enough competitively minded mavericks, plus enough people interested in keeping the doors of opportunity open for entering any trade, to prevent cartellization. In any case, the conjecture is academic, since American business has not been left free to drift into this course. It has been made forcibly aware that public opinion objects to the ending of competition, especially, of course, if it is done by big units, for which the voters do not have the same fellow feeling they have for the worker, the small trader, and the one-family farmer. For these latter, the voters are prepared to make concessions. In the light of this attitude, business recognizes that the maintenance of competition is one of its own necessary safeguards, and it supports the general policy of the antitrust laws. If they were to expire tomorrow, part of the support for re-enactment would come from business.

This, of course, does not mean that it would automatically give the laws such perfect obedience that they would be self-enforcing. That is a different matter. The frontier of control today consists of difficult decisions on the competitive or anti-competitive effect of a great variety of trade practices; and any given company is extremely unlikely to see eye to eye with the Federal Trade Commission or the Department of Justice as to particular practices of its own which these enforcing agencies may call in question. It is not necessary that it should, so long as business in general supports not only the laws but their enforcement. On this score, business would undoubtedly welcome softening amendments or constructions of the law where rigorous construction and enforcement would hamper what business regards as legitimate operations, or might even work real hardship—as can happen under the Robinson-Patman Act. But there appear to be vigilant watchdogs in Congress in case proposed amendments should amount to emasculation. And it remains true that business can be counted on to support this body of law as a whole, hardships and all, even if particular provisions are criticized. This attitude may in the main be "enlightened self-interest"; but mixed with this there appears to be a genuine belief in competition which is sturdy enough to withstand considerable strain of the sort just indicated. One of the major responsibilities of the business community is to keep this general belief alive. Otherwise, competition might not last long, and then private enterprise would give way to regimentation, with unforeseeable effects on freedom in areas other than the economic.

THE GROWTH OF PROFESSIONS

No account of the enlargement of human motives in economic life could go far without having to deal with the increasing number and permeating influence of people engaged in those special callings we designate as "professions." What is a profession? In the first place, it is a calling requiring special training, of the sort that is had in special institutions. And this has several results. Primarily, perhaps, it means that the professional man knows more than the purchaser of his services about the technical requirements of his job and his product. Therefore the market rule of *caveat emptor*—let the buyer look out for himself if he can—is peculiarly out of place. The professional man gives his customer advice with a peculiar authority, and as a result he assumes responsibility for the quality of his service and for suiting it to the recipient's needs. The recipient becomes a client instead of a customer in the commercial sense. The professional adviser assumes an obligation, not only to render good and conscientious service, but to do it within a framework of socially approved standards and regulations which are set for him.

He is licensed to pursue his calling, after examination, and the license certifies to his competence. Not only that, but the requiring of a license is in itself a recognition of the need for a more expert scrutiny of his qualifications than the client himself is competent to make, and it fortifies the professional man's responsibility for the sincerity of his own workmanship. This may or may not be further fortified by the taking of a solemn oath, such as the Hippocratic oath which medical students take on graduation. This is further backed up by the possibility of being deprived of one's license as a penalty for malpractice, this penalty being administered by the organization representing one's professional peers, by whom one is thus held responsible. There may be a formal code of ethical practice, and there is sure to be an informal one, growing out of the *esprit de corps* which results from all these factors. The formal code may, among other things, frown on advertising, this being unnecessary to enable a good professional man to secure as much business as he can properly handle. The informal code, as is natural, is a somewhat two-sided affair, concerned with the interests of the members of the profession itself, as well as with their public responsibilities. And indeed, the line is sometimes thin between sustaining the quality of service which gives the profession its place of honor, and sustaining its reputation by being slow to criticize or even by covering up shortcomings.

Is business a profession? Obviously it does not possess the full quota of characteristics that mark a full-fledged profession, and it is unlikely ever to possess them completely. And it does not seem desirable that it should. Entry into business needs to be freer than entry into professions, and a general requirement of a license to practice business would restrict this proper freedom. But business has gone part way. More and more business executives have been through graduate schools of business, and there is more and more recognition of responsibilities beyond those which the market automatically enforces. A further significant factor is that business is increasingly putting particular activities in charge of professionally trained people, who carry genuine professional standards into their work. This is one of the ways in which the effect of professional standards is spreading.

BIG BUSINESS: ITS EVOLVING CHARACTER

The characteristic behavior of corporate enterprise has shown remarkable changes during, let us say, the ninety years since the Civil War. In general, it has evolved from a state in which corporations were too frequently plundered by those in control, or followed a course of buccaneering toward their rivals and those with whom they had dealings. From this, in successive business generations, it has developed standards of internal integrity and of responsible management in respect to the other interests concerned. There is no time to tell this story, or trace in detail the course of this development, but its character might be faintly suggested by a fragmentary list of outstanding names, starting with notorious post-Civil-War buccaneers. Such a series might include Daniel Drew, Jim Fiske, Jay Gould, three successive generations of Rockefellers, Elbert Gary, E. H. Harriman and Averill Harriman, three generations of Fords, E. A. Filene, Henry Dennison, Owen Young, Ralph Flanders, Paul Hoffman, Chester I. Barnard, and in my own state of Connecticut, Herman Steinkraus. Without detailing the qualities of each individual in this list—something that would call for extended study—the evolution which it represents should be obvious, from picturesque piracy to notable and constructive economic citizenship and statesmanship.

One feature of corporate big business is that it acquires longer time perspectives, and its policies are framed accordingly. Thus the tactics of the typical "fly-by-night" concern find no place in the policies of an organization that looks to continued existence even beyond the lifetimes of the present controlling officials. In such a long-term perspective the need for good public relations is more and more felt. Corporate business must still consider profits, and it has an obligation to do as well by its equity investors as it reasonably can. But when economic theorists describe business as "maximizing profits," they are indulging in an impossible and unrealistic degree of precision. The farther a firm's policies extend into the future, the less certain can it be just what policy will precisely "maximize profits." The company is more likely to be consciously concerned with reasonably assured survival as a paramount aim, and, beyond this, to formulate its governing policies in terms of some such concept as "sound business," usually contributory to healthy growth. From this standpoint, it would seldom be sound business for a strongly established company to follow the policy that would squeeze the maximum of profits out of the market in any given year. Longer-run advantage lies with less grasping policies. This general fact becomes more certain with lengthening perspectives, even as they reduce the precision of specific forecasts.

Where there is this margin of uncertainty as to precisely what policy would "maximize profits," there is room for management to give the benefit of the doubt to policies that represent good economic citizenship. And it seems that an increasing number of managements are giving increasing weight to this kind of consideration.

As already noted, some of the most delicate problems for big business center around the obligation to maintain competition, and to maintain it at a healthy and constructive level. Here the special problems of size include the fact that tactics that carry no threat to extinguish or weaken competition when practiced by small concerns may come to involve such a threat when backed by the added power that comes with great size. A case in point is price discrimination, which may, under varying circumstances, be either one of the means of keeping price competition alive and active or one of the ways of extinguishing it. Equally interesting is the case of a concern that has developed an important new product in which it has, temporarily but inevitably, a monopoly. The principle on which our system rests is that such monopolies are proper incidents of progress, but that they should give way, after a reasonable time, to a condition in which others are free to imitate and to compete. And what happens during this transition is extremely important. The possessor of such a monopoly may be under an obligation, difficult to define legally in terms of specific practices, to lean over backward in avoiding practices that would deny others a full opportunity to enter and compete.[4]

Even a large concern must watch its volume of sales. If customers prefer a rival's product, and sales shrink, that is a condition urgently calling for a remedy. For a multi-product firm—nowadays the type—an important aim is to have a sufficiently diversified output to give the firm as a whole fair assurance of survival and growth, even though single products are exposed to the vicissitudes of competitive innovation. This implies that there is room for give and take. If the shares of the different members remain too closely uni-

[4] This appears to be the economic effect of Judge Learned Hand's decision in the Alcoa case of 1945, in which none of the obvious exclusionary practices were charged, but vigorous expansion was held to have exclusionary effect. U.S. vs. Aluminum Co. of Amer., 148 F. 2nd, 416, 430, 431.

form for too long, suspicion will arise that the members are deliberately "sharing the market."

To revert to the general position of management, it appears to be becoming less a single-minded representative of equity stockholders, than an accommodator—I have elsewhere called it a "battered buffer"—between a list of interests including equity stockholders, customers, workers, and the community. And it is not self-evident that the equity stockholders always have paramount weight. It is not wholly meaningless that the dealings with workers and customers go on daily, while the stockholders make their contacts with management at the time of stockholders' meetings.

Management has an interest in the day-to-day morale of the workers, in addition to its interest in the more obvious issues involved in disputes or in negotiations over the periodic renewal of a collective bargain. If the workers are disaffected or maladjusted, output suffers. And so a progressive management may feel it worth while to engage personnel men with a professional background, to probe into these problems and bring about improvements.

Needless to say, not all business corporations are sprouting wings. And even in the most progressive ones, plenty of problems remain, and always will. What has been sketched is a direction of movement and a few of the factors of organization and motivation that lie back of it. Given favorable conditions, these factors may be expected to carry on beyond the point already reached, raising the general level of practice to which reputable concerns are expected to conform. If we do not go forward, we shall go back, since the problems do not stand still, but multiply and evolve; and we need to keep moving in order not to fall behind.

SMALL BUSINESS

Small business has problems different from those of big business; but small business itself includes wide varieties of firms and conditions. Some rate as small firms merely because others in the industry are so much larger. Actually, they may be quite large; and in terms of some of the problems of social adaptation these large "small firms" exhibit more kinship with big business than with really small business. For really small concerns, matters of social impact, friction, and adaptation take place more by way of personal contacts and with much less need of formal administrative machinery or specialized departments to deal with welfare problems. Then there is the "very small" business, typified by the one-family retail or service establishment, which is too small for efficiency and too small for competent study of the techniques and methods by which it might attain such efficiency as its small size permits. Some help might be given by special agencies—public, private, or co-operative—but handicaps of high cost seem certain to remain. The nature of these handicaps seems equally certain to remain controversial.

Are they due to the superior efficiency of the larger and more modern types of distribution, such as chain stores and supermarkets, or to discriminatory price-favors in the buying of their supplies, which they are able to exact through sheer bargaining power and pressure? If their advantages are chiefly or largely based on extra-favorable prices, then there is color to the claim that the very small dealers might equitably be given protection against this kind of competitive advantage, which does not represent actual operating efficiency. And perhaps the most baffling thing about this group of cases is that both elements appear to enter in: both operating efficiency and bargaining advantage, and it does not seem possible to disentangle them and determine how much each element amounts to.

In the "fair trade" laws the issue is whether a manufacturer selling branded goods in competition with similar branded goods should be allowed to set the dealers' margin on his brand, or whether this should be set by dealers' competition. Manufacturers who set resale prices want to allow the dealers a margin sufficient to interest "regular" dealers in pushing the goods, and they want to protect the resale price from being discredited as unreasonably high by price-cutters who may use this brand as a "leader." Here is a complex of problems in which sound and equitable standards are not exactly obvious and simple. At present, the force of dealers' competition appears to be breaking down fixed margins.

ORGANIZED LABOR AND COLLECTIVE BARGAINING

Labor unions have a dual character. In their internal relations they are social groups in the broad sense: groups in which their members find the satisfactions of "belonging," together with many activities that involve no conflict with other groups; but in their external bargaining relations, they are perhaps the most purely combative of our major groups. Here some of the most difficult problems arise from their growth from a status of underdogs to their present truly commanding degree of power, strengthened by exemption from the antitrust laws. Here, as with big business, some of the tactics that were relatively harmless when organizations included only a minority of workers, even in a given trade, and there was competition with strong and unorganized sectors, change their character as organization becomes more nearly all-inclusive in its trades, and carry fresh responsibilities. Problems corresponding to those of business monopoly exist. The policy of "more, without limit" becomes a different matter when power exists to push gains in money terms beyond the economy's increase in physical productivity and bring on inflation, or, as a possible alternative, unemployment, depending on the condition of the market.

It is only natural that unions differ widely in the extent to which they recognize the responsibilities that go with their present power. A union is, in its internal structure, a political body, to which the principles of political ethics apply, with the added complication that the promises on the basis of which leaders must seek and hold the support of their members are concerned not so much with adjustments between the interests of the members themselves as with gains to be secured from outside interests. This weakens one of the natural checks on the making of unsound and irresponsible promises. But in actual negotiation the union cannot, without serious consequences, stand irreconcilably for more than the industry can concede and still survive in reasonable vigor. This limit is an elastic and indefinite one and is sometimes exceeded; but in general, to an increasing extent, it is recognized in actual negotiations.

One factor tending toward improvement in this respect is the increasing use of competent economic analysis by qualified experts on the staffs of the better unions. This makes for realism and responsibility. A special feature which has appeared in the garment trades consists of assistance rendered by the union itself to small employers who are in difficulties and who therefore cannot easily meet the standards the union is trying to establish for the trade as a whole. Such employers are aided in improving their efficiency. Here the union has an interest in removing from the market a demoralizing factor which would otherwise tend to undermine standards for the workers. But it is significant when an interest of this sort is promoted in ways that are constructive rather than destructive, supporting efficiency rather than simply protecting inefficiency.

Conclusion

This brief survey is obviously fragmentary and represents only a sampling of an enormous area of problems; and

it is frankly focussed on the search for hopefully constructive factors. This may be justified by the fact that it is with
these constructive factors that the hope must rest for a successful future for a free economy. As earlier noted, it is easy
to become discouraged if one concentrates on the limitations
and shortcomings of the materials an evolving society has to
work with in meeting its changing needs for adjustment, the
slowness of current progress, and its many setbacks. One
may need to seek refuge from such discouragement by looking back and observing the distance we have traveled in the
course of recent history, as a suggestion of what may be
possible in the decades that are ahead.

The millennium will not come tomorrow. What we face
is a gradual development. But it is interesting that democratic socialists, as well as advocates of a humanized private
enterprise, are nowadays recognizing that their millennium
will not come tomorrow, but involves a long and gradual
process of creative adaptation in which the status of the individual as an individual needs to be sedulously preserved.
Their theory and program and that of enlightened private
enterprise are coming closer to one another. Under either
view present performance is far from ideal, and the feasible
next steps may not appear brilliant. But the difficulties are
reason for effort, not discouragement. If, in any of the major
fields that have been touched on in this survey, defeatism
should win and complete corruption, or irresponsible self-
interest, should become the rule, it is only too clear that our
society would be threatened—its feet would be feet of clay.
We have the chance to prove that they are not.

To sum up, the chief aim of these two chapters has been
to point out various ways in which the performance of a free
system—which we prize far beyond its strictly material
gifts—has rested in the past and must rest increasingly in the
future on moral elements that go far beyond the cruder concepts of undiluted and irresponsible self-interest. To repeat,

the message our society has for the parts of the world which are threatened by Communism is that, given the necessary conditions and attitudes, the productive power of modern industry can not only be achieved but can be directed to the welfare of humanity in general, under a system that does not surrender freedom to a totalitarian dictatorship, or to any other system of unlimited regimentation.

CHAPTER TEN

The Interpenetration
of Politics and Economics

Two Levels of Interpenetration of Politics and Economics

This chapter centers around the thesis—possibly obvious—that the march of historical fact has broken down the older conceptions of the boundaries between the fields of economics and government—government in both its political and its administrative aspects—and that each discipline, and practice, enters inevitably into the field of the other. I shall be trying to give this thesis content by examining some of the leading forms which this interpenetration takes. In the field of what may, for lack of a better term, be called "official" government, economic processes determine the structure of economic interests and the conflicting economic forces which shape political issues and measures. The resulting economic tasks of government determine its administrative form. This in turn has cut us off from older and

Adapted by permission from *Freedom and Control in Modern Society*, Morroe Berger, Theodore Abel, and Charles H. Page, eds. (New York: D. Van Nostrand Company, 1954), pp. 192–205.

simpler forms and ideas of democracy, and puts new and
difficult obstacles in the way of achieving and protecting the
substance of popular government under any form. Government in turn increasingly shapes the course of economic affairs, leaving economics to face some problems as to what
its "economic laws" are supposed to be and to do.

Less obvious, perhaps, but not less important, is the
combination of political and economic characteristics in the
nominally private bodies that carry on economic affairs.
This dual nature turns out to be an indispensable key to an
adequate understanding of their motivation and behavior.

Many of us would like Jeffersonian democracy—especially if we could combine it with the material conveniences
of a mechanical age. But these conveniences spell industrialism, and industrialism is incompatible with the simple,
agriculturally based economy which was the most appropriate foundation for Jeffersonian democracy. This, perhaps, is
our story in the proverbial nutshell. And so it comes about
that we live in a society of organized pressure groups, of
commission government, public utility regulation, antitrust
action, farm price supports, social security, supervision of
collective bargaining, and the kind of regional planning involved in the Tennessee Valley Authority. We live in what
is variously thought of as the welfare state, the transfer-
payment state, the Santa Claus state, or the grab-bag state.
The principles of government cannot be understood as independent of the economic tasks the electorate assigns it to
perform. And while some of these tasks may be needless ex-
crescences, many of them are not optional, given the modern
economy and an educated electorate.

From the other side, an economist seeking to analyze the
forces that determine economic action is more and more
forced to recognize these governmental interventions as factors in the complex of determinants. Insofar as he studies
conditions in some chosen field, he necessarily encounters

regulatory laws and their execution. After examining their economic consequences, he may suggest modifications. This much contact with governmental matters he can hardly avoid. If he tries to avoid them, while engaging in pure theoretical analysis, he usually takes refuge in analyzing, or speculating about, what *would* happen if government were willing to keep its hands off. As to the relevance of such analyses, no short and simple statement can be adequate; but it clearly presents a problem in an interventionist society.

At the nominally private level, trade unions and large business corporations not only are affected by the actions of official government, they exhibit governmental qualities in their own structure and motivation. What are students to do about this? As to economists, if they can gain sufficient understanding for their purposes by simply assuming that these organizations follow their organizational self-interest (defined in some meaningful fashion), then they may perhaps be content to ask no questions about the internal arrangements that bring about this result. They would merely be debarred from representing their theoretical system as a deduction from the assumed pursuit of *individual* self-interest. They are instead assuming that individuals act as faithful representatives of the collective interests of an organized group. Actually, the assumption that organizations act as "economic men" needs to be supplemented before theory can fill certain gaps in its scheme of explanation of business behavior.

As to political scientists, it would seem that before they could conclude that there is no problem here for them, they would need to ask one further question—namely, "Are these units constrained to act in their collective interest by outside pressures—whether of competition, supply and demand, or the power of bargaining adversaries—which leave them substantially no alternative? Or does their economic behavior depend on how well or how ill their internal quasi-political and administrative organization operates to make them represent the interests of their members?" This last appears to be the case, besides which the organization introduces other material elements of motivation.

This second level of interpenetration—the quasi-political character of private economic units—may be fully as significant as the more obvious relations between private economic activities and formal or official government. It may also be more difficult for the existing disciplines to deal with—both for political science and for economics. So far as economics is concerned, the difficulty may be greatest in some of the theoretical sectors, which naturally tend to lag furthest behind the development of historical facts and institutions. The student in touch with collective bargaining can recognize the political character of unions more readily than the wage theorist can assimilate this into his theoretical models. It is no accident that wage theory is at present in a sort of doldrums.

The Older View: Distinct Fields of Government and Economics

We may take our point of departure in the period—now more than a century past—when "economic laws" were considered as something "independent of human institutions," representing supreme forces by which government action was limited and to which it was bound, in some sense, to conform. These laws were rooted in the basic and inevitable tendencies of individual behavior, including the tendency of population to multiply—regarded as a biological constant—and the drive for the pursuit of individual self-interest. These tendencies were most clearly seen in the behavior of markets that were left free; but they also took effect in resisting or thwarting the attempts of government to interfere, either evading or nullifying them or causing them to lead to unintended and self-defeating results.

Under this theory the activities of government were kept within a simple and modest scope. First, and most fundamental for the economy, came the maintenance of the basic framework of personal freedom, property rights, enforcement of contracts, and maintenance of justice, on which the operation of the free market depended. Public defense was, of course, also rated as basic. The relation of church and state we may leave to one side, our concern being economic. Next came a rather limited range of fairly obvious public works and some further things for which, for various reasons, the market omitted to afford the necessary conditions and incentives. Public education may have been regarded in this light at first, but later came to be included as part of the basic framework. Later also, the piecemeal control of particular abuses was added, each case bearing its own burden of proof in the face of the general prima facie presumption in favor of nonintervention. Finally, there were actions beyond these limits; and especially regulatory actions. These were invariably held to be mistakes, bound to bring their appropriate penalties under the action of economic law. "Government," in this context, meant what has here been called official government. The more subtle forms of interpenetration, arising from governmental qualities in nominally private organizations, had not worked their way into the integral structure of the economy sufficiently to command recognition.

Actually, the recognized boundaries of governmental action were never as sharp as this stereotype represents them. There was progressive enlargement of the scope of governmental action approved by liberal economists; an enlargement that appears rapid in the light of historical hindsight, although at the time it might have appeared gradual and grudgingly reluctant. Piecemeal controls of particular abuses and shortcomings grew apace. Some of these have already been listed. But the main stream of economic life was not diverted.

More disturbing was a series of developments in the field of labor. Safety-appliance acts were easily assimilated; but employers' liability for industrial accidents and the limiting of hours of labor interfered with the free labor contract; and it was only after long resistance that judges accepted them, with the explanation that "the heart of the contract"—work and wages—was still intact and subject to free bargaining. The final transition to social insurance amounted to compulsory and socialized provision for a large range of personal needs, for which it had been supposed to be the individual's responsibility to make his own provision. The transition was resisted on this ground, as well as on account of being an importation from autocratic-militaristic Germany. The minimum wage was a further encroachment, but left bargaining free above the minimum, and was justified— following the Webbs's argument—as eliminating "parasitic" trades or employers. Even after its adoption, the main stream of production, purchase and sale, qualities and prices, was still subject to accustomed forces. The law that directly determined these matters was still economic, not political. But a change was coming.

Partial Reversal of Relation of Economic and Political Forces

At present the "heart of the contract" has unmistakably been invaded. Not only provision for old age and unemployment, and minimum wages, but farm prices and production, rates of interest, and foreign exchange are subject to public action, along with, for example, the extraction of crude petroleum (with effects on its price). And contractual wages are—or were before World War II—determined mainly by a process known as "free collective bargaining," the term "free" signifying mainly that official government forbears to interfere and leaves the outcome to the informal quasi-governmental organs that have come into existence in this field. Of this, more later.

For present purposes, the essential point is that there has been, to a considerable extent, a reversal of the classical relation between "economic law" and political action. When Ricardian economics was at the height of its prestige, "economic law" was supposed, by economists and a good many others, to be an effective force determining the main features of the actual course of economic events, while political government (once a few questions like the corn laws were settled) made gestures, largely ineffectual, in the direction of its ideas of what was good and desirable. Economic law, to be thus effective, did not have to be understood by the agents who automatically fulfilled the destiny it appointed for them.

Now, on the whole, it may be nearer the very complex truth to say that there are large areas within which agencies of government, plus nominally private agencies of an essentially governmental character, determine what actually happens and are able within fairly wide margins to disregard or neutralize the forces of "supply and demand." The converse of this is that the economists' brand of economic law, no longer an all-pervasive and automatically effective force, is reduced to a body of normative theory, trying not too effectually to sit in judgment on the acts and policies of the agencies that wield the power and to determine whether these acts and policies are sound, or what sound policy would be. To the extent that this is true, economic law does not become effective except as it is understood and deliberately followed by agencies that have the power, if they choose, to act otherwise.

This last seems clearly true of money wages, farm prices, and other prices that are genuinely "administered"; and of trade practices, insofar as they are controlled by unified action, either of public or private agencies. Of course, the general level of real wages may still be limited by over-all productivity, beyond anything collective bargaining can do; and the effects of price changes on consumer demand are still not arbitrarily controllable. Discretionary power acts within some kind of limits which are difficult or impossible to determine with anything like precision. And these limits are not universally identical, but depend on the social and political temper of each people, which is far less uniform than the calculus of self-interest as economists have employed it.

This is, of course, only one side of the story. The other side, as noted at the beginning of this chapter, is the impact of economic interests and forces on government.

Government as Controller and Controlled

There is nothing new about the idea that the kind of government a country can have is a function of its economic and social system. Jefferson long ago stressed the importance of a simple and largely agricultural economy as a base for the kind of democracy he sought. And today Wilhelm Roepke ascribes the political sickness of modern civilization to "massism," and speaks in that connection of the "politicalization of economic processes." He wants a simple, small-scale, decentralized economy, and thinks of Switzerland as a satisfactory example.[1] But, given the modern urban mass economy, this road to political salvation appears closed. Our

[1] W. Roepke, *The Social Crisis of Our Time* (Chicago, University of Chicago Press, 1950), and review by Frank Munk, *American Economic Review*, December, 1951, pp. 962–4.

government rests on a base of sharply differentiated economic groups, with urban labor far outnumbering the farm population and carrying corresponding weight. The business interest, outnumbered in voting strength, must try to maintain its political influence by other means. The government must strike some sort of balance among all these interests, according to a complex of criteria in which the prevalent sense of justice and the common interest plays some part in enabling minority groups to get the support they need from other groups if measures in their interest are to go through. This element is probably at its strongest where nation-wide public opinion is brought to bear directly on a problem. In the kinds of deliberations that take place in the proverbial "smoke-filled rooms," minorities can buy support by the time-tried method of logrolling. And always, a solidly organized minority, which will vote more or less as a unit, carries more weight than more numerous but unorganized groups, whose votes will scatter.

The issues these groups raise for political action arise out of the way in which our economic life is organized, and the needs and inequities each group feels. Many of these are rooted in the character of our complex mass economy, which is only to a limited extent automatically self-adjusting. As these issues become more numerous and differentiated, government perforce becomes more specialized and complicated. And as the subject matter becomes more technical, administrative agencies proliferate, and popular control of government becomes more remote and more difficult. Here lies one of the most powerful ways in which the character of the economic base affects the structure and functioning of government.

To take one major example, one of the principles which we have accepted as an essential of representative government, as we conceive it, is the separation of powers. But the specialized and technical character of the subject matter of the regulatory activities has made inevitable the growth of commissions, specialized to different subject matter and acting under such indefinite mandates that they may be compelled to create the content of these mandates (a legislative function), put them into effect (executive), and settle disputed cases (judicial). Courts tend increasingly to accept a commission's verdict on the economic evidence as final, limiting review to more strictly legal matters. The Federal Trade Commission prosecutes cases before itself as a quasi-judicial tribunal, and has not wholly overcome the drawbacks arising from this dual personality.

More serious, however, is the inability of the public, or even Congress, to watch continuously and effectively all these various baskets in which the governmental eggs are distributed. The public can concentrate its attention on only a few things at a time; and after the original setting-up of a commission, or one of the rare major revisions of its mandate which arouses real interest, public attention turns elsewhere. A twofold danger results.[2] An original vigorous sense of public mission may decline, with time and changing personnel, into the morale of bureaucratic survival and routine operation. And while public attention is intermittent, the activities and pressures of the interested parties are continuous and may wear down the purpose of the agencies while the public is looking the other way. Thus the democratic character of government may be impaired as a result of the multitude and technical quality of the tasks imposed on it by the character of the modern mass economy. This is one of the serious problems of the interaction of government and the economic subject matter with which it is forced to deal.

[2] This point has been forcibly developed by Walton H. Hamilton; see "The Law, the Economy, and Moral Values," in *Goals of Economic Life*, pp. 248, 267–70.

The Dilemma of Normative Economics

From the other side, what of the problems of an economics whose theories have become largely theories of what is sound and economically correct, rather than of the forces determining actual events? Economics, in the capacity of science, is not supposed to carry the full responsibility for policy recommendations—that is a task for persons who must weigh both economic and political considerations. They must weight the economists' testimony in the light of what the "people" want and whether suggested measures are administrable. The next question is: Should economists take this into consideration in advance and accept the idea that it is poor advice that flies in the face of the political machinery through which policies will be reshaped and carried out? If so, would this amount to accepting political standards and resigning their proper special function as economists? Or if not, would this mean that their analysis, with its policy implications, would be doomed to impracticality and ineffectiveness? This is a real dilemma. In one form, under the Truman Administration, it beset the operations of the President's Council of Economic Advisers—that important experiment in the utilization of expert economic diagnosis to guide the comprehensive economic policy that current economic conditions impose upon government.

Economists outside government can escape the obvious impact of this dilemma and should be free to let their analyses lead where they will. But difficulties remain. For example, concepts involved in the pure theory of perfect and imperfect competition, adopted for intellectual reasons, are imperfectly adapted to serve as guides to antitrust policy and other policies to which these theories may have relevance. Such theoretical analysis may point to so many defects in competitive practice that, if government were to attempt to deal with them all, both government and business would be overloaded—as indeed they may be already. Furthermore, some of these "imperfections" are really virtues, since theoretical "perfect competition" is defined with reference to a single objective—reducing prices to cost at the optimum scale of production, given existing techniques. This leaves out the more important conditions of progress in methods and in products.

Economists need to retain a sense of the relative importance of the issues on which their analyses impinge and of the relative availability of official and unofficial ways of dealing with them. At less theoretical levels their most essential service is rendered by unsparingly objective critical analysis both of conditions and of the economic effects of governmental policies. Some may have a talent for devising remedies. But when they do this, they become something more than economists, and assume a responsibility for considering political and administrative feasibility on their own account or for collaborating with those who will bring these considerations to bear.

Collective Bargaining as a Quasi-Political Activity

So far we have been looking at the relation between economics and official government. Turning to the second level of interpenetration—the governmental character of nominally private bodies—we may look first at collective bargaining, starting with its impact on wages. Economists naturally want a theory of the forces determining wages. Their inherited theory—that of marginal productivity—is a theory of competitive equilibrium; and its relevance is obviously called in question by modern forms of collective bargaining. And attempts to develop the so-called "bargain theory" into an adequate substitute have not so far had convincing success. I should like to explore the hypothesis that the source of the difficulty lies in the attempt to treat unions as economic bargaining units of the traditional sort, rather than recognizing their political character.

Theorists feel obliged to assume, as a basis for a theory, that a bargaining unit is trying to maximize something; but they have so far failed to identify just what it is that unions try to maximize, or ought to try to maximize. Increased money wage rates may be closer than any other single objective to the actual aim of most union bargaining about wages. But is that a rational objective, if pursued without regard to effects on prices or employment? As to prices, a union may concede that increased money wage rates in excess of the average increase in physical productivity for the economy as a whole tend to be neutralized in the aggregate by increased prices. But a single union may still gain if it outstrips the others, or may lose if it falls behind them. And it may judge that its own self-restraint will not stop the general procession.

A disregard for the effects on employment may be rationalized via the theory that higher wages make for increased employment, through increasing the diffused variety of purchasing power; or it may simply rest on recognition that no one really knows enough to generalize confidently about the effect of wages on employment, so they might as well concentrate on the thing they can see and measure. Or in cases in which it may appear fairly certain that employment would suffer from the level of money wage rates that is being demanded, the demands may still represent "economic rationality" for those workers whose seniority protects them from being laid off. These may also be the most influential group in determining union policy. But at this point we clearly enter into considerations that are matters of internal union politics.

Or if an annual wage is demanded in a given industry, is

this done in the light of the probability that, if granted in this particular industry, it would be bound to be confined to workers who have been employed for a minimum term? If so, how many of the union members who are invited to support the demand do so with recognition of this probability? Again, this is a matter of internal union politics. Or is the demand a bargaining maneuver, with intent to settle for some less sweeping gain in out-of-work provisions or other "fringe benefits"? If granted, would it perhaps make the industry adopt a more hospitable attitude toward efforts of government to stabilize employment? Once more, a question of political implications.

One pioneer theorist in this field has pictured a union balancing the probable cost of a strike against the probable wage gain the union might hope to secure by striking, beyond what it could secure without a strike.[3] On the basis of such a weighing of probabilities it is supposedly determined whether the employer or the workers will "have to yield," or whether both are interested in concessions. Such a theory has a certain rationality, but it would appear to be different from the rationality displayed in the fairly numerous cases of long and costly strikes for a trifling wage gain above what was available without striking. It seems likely that there are imponderables here, presumably related to prestige or the demonstrating of power, or both, which cannot be summarily dismissed as irrational, but which do not possess the kind of rationality assumed in economists' theoretical models. On the whole, it appears to be rather a variety of political rationality, or political motivation, rational or otherwise.

It appears that one falls far short of understanding unions if one approaches them via the assumption that each is an economic bargaining unit, with a quantitatively defined objective which it pursues single-mindedly and undertakes

[3] See F. Zeuthen, *Problems of Monopoly and Economic Warfare* (London: Routledge, 1930), Chapter IV, especially pp. 111–21.

to maximize, after the fashion familiar in the models of economic theory. As a key to the interpretation of union behavior, this leaves too much unexplained, and in some respects is too wide of the mark.

Suppose one tries instead the hypothesis that the union is primarily a political entity? At once things that have baffled the economic model begin to fall into place. True, it is notably different from the more familiar kinds of political entities, but the main elements are there. Officers are elected, and to get elected they make promises or point to a past record; having made promises, they must deliver as much as possible and find scapegoats to blame for any shortages. They must claim credit for all gains made, whether or not these gains would have come if the union had not existed. It is not gains made, but gains won by union action, that constitute the record on the basis of which the union makes its appeal for new members, and for old members to continue their support, and on which the union official makes his appeal to his constituents. Employers who volunteered a wage increase have at times found that the increase the union would have demanded in any case has simply been added to their voluntary concession. If they had made the increase unilaterally, without giving the union a chance to pass on it and to do some bargaining about it, they might have been found guilty of an unfair labor practice.

Unions are considered less democratic than towns or states, as is natural for an entity which specializes in combative external relations; but by way of compensation, the divergences and conflicts of interest within the membership, while decidedly in evidence, are nowhere near so strongly marked as in the population of a city or a state. But the most notable distinguishing feature of the union as a political entity is the dominance of external relations in its scheme of activities and interests. With all its internal social, educational, civic, and benefit activities and interests, it is still like a state whose economic revenue is determined by the terms of a trade treaty periodically negotiated with a powerful neighbor state. Its very subsistence centers in the arts of negotiation, normally peaceful but with the possibility of war always in the background.

It is, of course, a limited war. It is as if there were an international law, more powerful than actual international law has ever been, regulating the tactics of combat and protecting the rights of the parties to resume trading with one another after one of their temporary stoppages of intercourse. This code does not, of course, prevent all violence. But if union and employer are pictured in the guise of sovereign states, negotiating with one another, they operate within a federal league or union which has effective judicial machinery for interpreting and enforcing the treaties that are made. And the best of these treaties are of constitution-making character, defining the rights of the parties, not only in money terms, but in terms of the human rights involved in the standing relationships entered into, in which the worker undertakes performance and subjects himself to discipline, but acquires protections against arbitrary action by foreman or boss. Such a development was needed in place of older absolute rights of dismissal, and employers have adjusted themselves to it; but in the process many an employer must have felt as if he had been compelled by *force majeure* to grant rights of extraterritoriality in an area over which his sovereignty had previously been absolute.

In fact it seems probable that it is in this realm, of human rights and the jurisprudence that centers around them, that the most important gains of unionism are found: more important even than wage gains. Much of the increase in real wages would presumably have come without the compelling force of unions—no one can tell how much. But this body of human rights pertaining to the employment relation, and of private jurisprudence to interpret and enforce it, is the peculiar creation of collective bargaining.

In the foregoing, we have seen the essential political factors at work, though in the distinctive forms peculiar to collective bargaining. Elections and appeals to the electorate, executive government or leadership, diplomacy and treaties, constitution-making and jurisprudence—all have played their part; and the resulting structure exercises, within its scope of action, a genuine authority over individual union members. The result, as far as it goes, tends to support the hypothesis that, to understand the motivations that take effect in collective bargaining, the character of unions as political bodies must be taken into account.

The Character of the Business Unit

The business unit does not present such a striking array of political characteristics as do trade unions, but it will repay a brief examination from this standpoint. It is possible for economic theory to proceed on the deceptively simple assumption that all business units seek to maximize their profits. This has considerable relevance. Also, as already noted, it by-passes the question how and to what extent a large corporate organization comes to act as if it were a single unified personality, leaving this question to the students of management and industrial organization. They have dealt with it, both practically and theoretically, and have been known to express the view that in developing the principles of administrative organization, they were ahead of the political scientists. Economists, under the heading of the "theory of the firm," are making beginnings with analysis of how the different classes of members in a great corporate team go about the task of gearing their functions, perspectives, and activities together. In studies of corporate organization—but not in general economic theory—they have envisaged divergences of interest among management, directors, and stockholders.

A case could be made for further departures from the simple assumption of maximizing profit, on the ground that this is too limited a theory of motivation to account for all the significant facts of corporate behavior. Management may be conceived as hammering out an accommodation among the interests of investors, customers, workers, the government, and local communities. It may be shortsighted, or may look far ahead, or may adopt conceptions of sound practice that imply a long time-perspective to justify them. Survival, prestige, physical growth, and public relations all enter the picture; and at times the continuity of the business itself seems to become an impersonal end in its own right. For a struggling business unit, immediate necessities may dominate policy; it is the strong and well-established enterprises that have sufficient margin of discretion in policy to be able to give weight to considerations further removed from immediate profit. But these stronger enterprises may be more important than the weaker, struggling units in determining the behavior of an industry as a whole.

Conclusion

We have been looking at a few of the ways in which government is determined by its economic setting and the economic tasks it is called on to perform, and at the dilemma of economics as government increasingly takes command as a determining force in the economic realm. We have also looked at the ways in which economic bargaining units themselves present features and problems that pertain to the science of government. We have been raising problems

rather than undertaking to settle them, but this cursory in-
spection points to certain conclusions as to the spheres of
study of political science and economics.

Political scientists hardly need to be told that, as government becomes more frankly a vehicle through which groups
may directly promote their particular economic interests, the
strains on political and administrative machinery are enormously increased and the democratic character of government seriously compromised. Economists may not be fully
aware of the way in which they have, in their various fields,
been making their adjustment, with more or less success, to
the extension of government's controlling functions. In the
Keynesian economics, theory has been in the van of this adjustment; in other areas it has lagged, especially in the
theory of wages. And in unions and large business corporations we have seen a fruitful field for joint study by economics and political science, both being equally well advised
to beware of trying to apply their ready-made models to this
material, since it has its own unique qualities and requires
fresh study and interpretation from both its political and its
economic angles. For better or for worse, the two aspects
are interwoven.

CHAPTER ELEVEN

Free Enterprise
and a Planned Economy

Should Man Try to Shape His Destiny?

I shall assume that it is not the function of the church to
take a position on economic questions on which reasonable
and qualified students may differ; but that it is a part of its
function to promote examination of such questions in a setting of general principles that can be squared with Christian
ethics, aiding individual Christians to clarify their own attitudes on these questions. The dominant consideration is that
the economic system is an instrumentality, not a fetish. As
such, it should be our servant, not our master; and it should
be judged by the degree to which it contributes to ends that
the people as a whole can properly approve.

"Planned economy" is a fusion of two ideas. "Planning"
defines a process, the forward-looking process of choosing

Reprinted by permission from *The Christian Demand for Social
Justice*, Bishop William Scarlett, ed. Copyright, 1949, by the New American Library of World Literature, Inc. This chapter was based on a paper
read at a conference sponsored by the Joint Commission on Social Reconstruction of the Protestant Episcopal Church, January 31, 1948.

objectives and devising means to attain them. "Economy" defines the character and scope of the subject matter to which this process is to be applied; it is planning for the economy as a whole, which under modern conditions is world-wide. It means that in this realm of life man is seeking to shape his destiny.

This has not always been regarded as within either his competence or his rights. The idea that the gods disapproved of radical forward-looking advances in the means of attaining his ends is as old as the story of Prometheus; and the related story of Adam's fall from primitive innocence extends a similar idea to the choice of ends—the knowledge of good and evil. Ambition on man's part to control his total destiny has long been regarded as a presumptuous attempt to enter realms reserved for higher powers. Adam Smith's early philosophy, as expressed in his "Theory of Moral Sentiments," is perhaps the last great semisecular embodiment of this idea. In his system man's efforts to gain his particular and immediate objectives are, for his own good, overruled by a beneficent nature, in order that they may work to "the good of the species." This idea has been dwindling, with the gradual evolution of secular utilitarianism, starting with the philosophy of Bentham.

But the idea is not extinct. I note an article in *Life* describing science, and man's accompanying faith in himself, as the Devil's five-hundred-year plan for destroying the world, accelerated to a three-hundred-year schedule and now nearing fruition.[1] And I suspect C. S. Lewis of thinking that the incipient "science of man," which foreshadows a great extension of "planning," is a form of Promethean sacrilege and part of the Devil's three-hundred-year plan for man's spiritual, if not his physical, destruction. There has been a long history of such protests against the process of extension of secular thinking and action into areas formerly

---

[1] Article by Whittaker Chambers, *Life*, February, 1948.

thought to belong exclusively to religion; and I will not presume to forecast the fixing of final boundaries.

Our present topic, however, is the economy, and that is clearly a secular matter. Here, if man is not to be trusted to get what he wants, it is mainly because his objectives are selfish, particularistic, and conflicting. The world is in deadly danger because powers of gaining such objectives have outstripped both the checks devised by Adam Smith's beneficent "nature" and our capacity to organize consciously for comprehensive objectives. I am tempted to suggest that, if there is a conscious purpose outside ourselves, guiding the history of the partly-human race, it would seem to have been "planning," for at least two centuries past, that about the middle of the twentieth century the race should face three necessities—three "challenges," in Toynbee's terms:

1. As between countries, men must learn to keep the peace, or they will perish physically.

2. The people of single countries must learn to work together well enough to keep complicated and vulnerable economic systems going tolerably well, or go to smash.

3. They must do both things of their own free will, by voluntary co-operation, or else by conquest and submission to force. And the latter might mean spiritual death for a Western people, if their immovable devotion to the dignity of the individual is subjected to the irresistibly shattering assault of modern totalitarianism. They are, one fears, temperamentally incapable of that spiritual recourse which requires them to "love" the enemy who is crushing them. The passive resistance of a Gandhi, or the kind of inner defense which the Jews have opposed to centuries of oppression, appear hardly attainable by the prevailing Western mentality. And totalitarian "brain-washing" has its ways of beating down or brushing aside such attempts to preserve the inner integrity of a subjugated people.

What Do We Want of Our Economy?

While many objectives are controversial, a few that seem to command general assent can be listed. First, we want to preserve our country, and what we judge to be the essential values of our system. Looming large among these values is a high degree of personal freedom, and scope for its exercise. This has economic implications, but is not coextensive with business freedom. In the economic field the notes composing the dominant chord have been freedom and self-interest— which do not always produce harmony—with competition as the third note, on which harmony mainly depended through automatically harnessing self-interest to the general good. This passed for sound economics in the nineteenth century, though not unchallenged. Further, the philosophy of unrestrained pursuit of individual interest had its share of responsibility in promoting the unmoral concept and practice of democracy in the political field. I believe this has never been good politics; and the corresponding economic philosophy can no longer claim to be adequate economics. Emphasis needs now to rest on a different chord: freedom, good will, responsibility. The system that Americans are justified in wanting to preserve is one that contains these elements and affords them a chance to develop.

This system, with these essential values, we want to defend against attack from without. We want to do this by the best and most effective means. The necessity of including national armed forces among these means is a concession to the primitive state of international relations and our inability, so far, to work out better and more effective means; toward these we must continue to strive with our best efforts and abilities, in the face of discouraging natural obstacles and deliberate and baffling opposition. But that is outside the scope of this paper, except as one of the essentials of defense is a sound domestic economy.

We want an adequate and well-distributed supply of material goods and services. We want freedom of thought, speech, political activity and personal life, consistent with social order and safety. We want economic freedom too, but with larger qualifications. We want reasonable protection against insecurities, recognizing that some degree of uncertainty or insecurity is inseparable from freedom. We want opportunity for useful and self-sustaining employment to be open to all on meeting reasonable requirements. We want a system that recognizes the dignity and worth of the individual and affords him economic relations, and human relations within his economic relations, which are consistent with his worth and dignity. We want individuals who recognize the duties and responsibilities that go with their rights. As to dealing with defects and seeking for improvement, most of us want a system of orderly and evolutionary change, which draws support from its roots in the past, without being bound by the past in meeting the challenge of the present and the needs of the future. As against violent revolution or adoption of whole-cloth contrived systems, we think such evolutionary change is more likely to be both sound and humane, economizing coercion and avoiding a ruthless sacrifice of individuals to the impersonal requirements of a system. The highest product of a system is a people made up of the highest type of socially civilized individuals.

What Are the Real Alternatives?

Some think that only two systems are possible: thorough-going *laissez faire* or complete collectivism. I shall contend that for this country no very close approach to ei-

ther of these extremes is thinkable and that all our pertinent
alternatives lie somewhere in the mid-range.

Absolute *laissez faire* or free enterprise is a myth; the
nearest approach to it involves a good deal of control. One
definition of free enterprise is a system of controls, in accord
with people's sense of right, to which they have become so
acclimated that they do not think of them as "controls." Another definition is: a system of controls mainly negative, telling people what they must not do, and leaving them free to
choose within the limits thus set. Such a system has elastic
limits, which may change with time. But it would, as a minimum, leave a majority of the work of creating economic
goods in private hands—to the extent of what to produce
and how much, at what price, and whom to employ on what
terms. In most of these matters, except perhaps quantity produced and price, controls setting some minimum standards
are accepted as consistent with free enterprise.

Planning implies that someone, somewhere, has power
to act in pursuance of the plans, or else the plan is mere advice or pious wish. One plans what one administers. Business
men plan for their enterprises; government plans its policies
with a view to probable results; but under private enterprise
no one plans the economy as a whole. A planned *economy*
implies power to administer the economy as a whole, or
power of control sufficient to determine the quantitative outcome to a roughly equivalent extent. On the other hand,
planning need not include complete power to dictate the
outcome—as every general knows when he plans a battle, or
every farmer when he plans a crop. There are always conditioning factors one does not control. Business plans subject
to the market, which it does not control. A planned economy
would exert some conscious control of total amount of demand but not dictate its precise directions. In any economic
planning we need contemplate, output of consumers' goods
will be planned subject to demand arising from consumers'

free choice; and wages and the allocation of employment will be planned subject to individuals' free choice of occu- pations. In these matters, planning will include inducements, not commands.

Private Enterprise

The system of private enterprise displaced the medieval system of relatively static techniques and custom-sanctified status, with a system of rapidly changing techniques, in which status (with the possible exception of the landed aris- tocracy) was at the mercy of unmitigated competition. It had its theory, that competition made business the servant of the people in their capacity as consumers—roughly true as to physical supply, though advertising is a good deal more than an obedient servant, and standards of taste, ideals and morals are shaped by agencies we have little reason to trust for such social leadership. In these early days of dominant individualism the people, in their capacity as workers, were not so well served—to put it mildly.

The subsequent story has been, first, one of development of piecemeal controls to deal with particular abuses and blind spots of the system. These controls business has learned to assimilate, and for present purposes we may pass them over. Second, more pregnant for our purpose, is the fact that along with these piecemeal controls the history of the system has been the story of various methods of escape from the extremer rigors of competition—some generally approved and others not—until our system can no longer fairly be characterized as a competitive one, following eco- nomic laws tending to a definable competitive equilibrium; rather, it has become an indeterminate economy of organ- ized groups, in which competitive forces act on the "busi- ness" sector, but spottily and unevenly.

It is indeterminate because these groups now have more power than was contemplated by the original theory of *laissez faire*. These rival powers of business, labor, agriculture and others threaten the free system, bringing it face to face with the alternative of coercion or chaos, if the existing powers are used irresponsibly and without limit. It is perhaps a minor matter that they have ruined the determinate accuracy of those formulas with which economists defined the results which economic adjustments naturally tend to bring about, and which were called "economic principles." They have brought to the fore one overshadowing economic principle that had little recognition in the nineteenth century: the principle that the degree of freedom that can persist is determined and measured by the degree of responsibility with which group economic power is exercised. This may be a moral principle, but I believe it is also a statement of objective cause and effect, having as much claim to scientific standing as many traditional "economic laws." Irresponsible self-interest can no longer be accepted as a satisfactory basis for an economic system by people who know what is happening in the world they live in.

In the third place, in this setting we face the most currently-emphasized defect of the system of private enterprise—its failure to afford assured opportunity for employment to all who properly qualify.[2] This is the problem that will give the dominant character to the continuing evolution of the system in the next decade or two—assuming that it develops by evolution rather than by catastrophic change, and that we are not caught in another great war. Ink has also been spilled, especially in British economic journals, over the issue of equality in distribution of incomes. In terms of income after taxes, this does not appear to be a dominant

[2] Written in 1948. This problem has become less urgent as of 1956, but it has not disappeared.

present issue, in Britain or the United States, except for really low incomes that have fallen behind the rise of prices.

We have, of course, the system of social insurance; and if employment is maintained at a high average level, this can take care of the residue. If unemployment gets large, the fiscal burden of adequate social insurance will be too great, and the demand for work in place of doles will probably force a change, even one that risks forcing the abandonment of the system of private enterprise by imposing unaccustomed burdens and requirements in such amounts and at such speed as to exceed its powers of acclimatization. The question is whether private enterprise, plus public policies consistent with its continuance, can turn in a good enough performance to maintain itself after the combination of temporary postwar stimuli have exhausted their effect.[3]

In the twenties we thought that credit policies aiming at stabilization, under the Federal Reserve System, were sufficient. We were disillusioned. Competitive flexibility of prices and wages is still thought, by a dwindling minority of economists, to be a sufficient anti-depression stabilizer. Since 1929, policy has, on the whole, been moving mainly in the opposite direction—toward stabilized wages and prices, and measures sustaining purchasing power. If these measures should prove insufficient to prevent another major depression, we shall be driven to go further, into measures to which private business has not acclimated itself, and which contain numerous possibilities of disappointing their advocates' expectations. The mildest are attempted stimuli, to which the response of business is uncertain. The ones that are more positive in their effect come under the lesser degrees of planning.

[3] Since this was written, in 1948, the Korean War and subsequent defense spending have prolonged this type of stimulus, and an early and drastic reduction appears unlikely.

Degrees of Planning

1. Totalitarian control. This plans and directs not only the economy, but all other activities, including expression and, so far as possible, thought. Such control is inconsistent with democracy, since it negates the independent judgment of the citizen, on which democracy rests.

2. Complete economic collectivism. This need not extinguish personal liberties of thought, expression, political action, etc., but it would put obvious difficulties, for example, in the way of the preservation of a free press, since the press would consist either of government organs or cooperatives. Government as the sole employer would have opportunity to tyrannize over the citizen through its power over his job; and this would need to be guarded against by decentralization of hiring and firing, strict prohibition of any kind of blacklist, and a firmly established spirit of "eternal vigilance" with power to take action against abuses. It seems just possible that our British cousins might be able to preserve personal liberty under these conditions. Our larger and less coherent population would make it harder for us; so would our keener spirit of competition and determination to gain the immediate end. Personal freedom and freedom of business enterprise are not the same, and propaganda that confuses them should not be taken seriously. But complete collectivism would be a threat to personal freedom; and this seems to be the strongest single reason against adopting it at this time.

It could, if it would, provide substantially full employment. This would be due partly to planned and regularized capital outlays, including residential construction; and more, perhaps, to control of the distribution of income and of incentives to saving; but most of all because output need not stop when profits turn into losses. In short, it would be due, not mainly to planning per se—plans will miscarry even under such a system—but more to unified ownership and operation of industry. And a good enough result could probably be secured by less drastic means.

3. Mixed systems. These may be of two main varieties. First, predominantly collective, but with private enterprise in special sectors for special reasons (bearing the burden of proof); for example, in small-scale trade, agriculture, newspapers, magazines and publishing generally. This would take into the collective area the industries that are primarily responsible for the fluctuations of capital outlays, which in turn are the main cause of general business ups and downs. This would be especially true if housing were included in the collective sector.

Second, those predominantly private but with government enterprise or co-operatives taking a considerable part in producing marketable goods and services, either displacing or competing with private enterprise in these sectors. These might include further extensions in the field of banking—already entered by government on a large scale—also natural monopolies, or other monopolies or imperfectly competitive industries where "yardstick" competition is sought as a regulator; or they might include industries selected mainly because the government is attempting to bring about an adequate and stable flow of capital outlays and finds it impossible to produce a sufficient effect without actually administering the capital outlays in a fair-sized sector of the field. In that case, industries would be selected involving large capital outlays of sorts that lend themselves to controlled timing. The socialized sector might exert regulatory effect over the private sector, either for expansion or, more positively, for restriction of booms, by limitation of basic supplies. The nature of this effect is highly conjectural.

4. A regimented economy, where nominal ownership and operation remains in private hands, but where policies

are positively dictated, so that production, investment, and employment can be planned with some approach to the certainty that would characterize public operation. A totalitarian society could do this; whether a democratic one could do it successfully is a question open to considerable doubt.

5. Private economy with public or collective planning and management of aggregate demand. This might be called a "compensated economy" (Walter Lippmann's phrase, I think), especially where the emphasis is on stabilizing fluctuations, though the term might be equally appropriate for an economy that undertakes to compensate for an unbalance that chronically fails to spend all the income a prosperous people would make in active times, and therefore chronically fails to employ its resources fully. It would also, in principle, include the opposite kind of compensation—action to neutralize an excess of aggregate demand over supply, such as is responsible for the demand side of inflationary pressures when they occur. This represents the general kind of planning with which we shall probably be experimenting within the next decade. It is advocated as planning not to displace private enterprise but to preserve it by making it work.

The operation of this grade of planning is crammed with technical questions of feasibility, about which the specialists are busily disputing. What seems fairly established is, first, that policies coming under this category can have a good deal of stabilizing effect, but are far from being able to guarantee perfect stability. Second, they can do something to raise the long-run average level of production and employment, if it needs raising, but are far from being able to guarantee "full employment" without going beyond the limits of this type of program. Third, they can restrict demand—that is, they are technically capable of restricting it—if it is found to have reached unhealthy "boom" proportions, and thus they can have some effect in reducing inflationary pressures; but it seems virtually certain that this alone will not be sufficient to prevent price inflation without also checking employment substantially short of what would be regarded as a satisfactory level.

One new thing that has been added is the unprecedented power of organized labor. And while "new era" predictions are at a heavy discount, it seems highly probable that this has introduced a long-run inflationary bias into the price system. In that case, the problem is to keep this inflationary bias within tolerable bounds, which for this purpose might tentatively be defined as a long-run upward trend in the general price level at an average rate of 2 per cent per year, or possibly a little more—enough so that the real basic rate of interest would be reduced, by the shrinking buying power of the principal, to a nominal amount, but would not be turned into a minus quantity. Whether an inflationary tendency can be kept within this limit by this type of policy, no one can predict with certainty.

Real Reasons, and False Ones, for Preferring to Maintain Private Enterprise

1. FALSE REASONS

(a) Uncontrolled private enterprise is the ultimate, correct system. This hardly needs disproof.

(b) It is in accord with human nature, because it builds on self-interest. Answer: it has done so too exclusively, and that phase of its development has outlived its usefulness. Under present conditions no system built wholly on individual selfishness can long survive. In fact, I doubt if the system could have survived to the present date if it had been based as exclusively on self-interest as some theories represented. Human nature has little-exploited capacities for responding to a sense of collective purpose. This is obvious in wartime, and needs to be extended to the crises of peace. It is obvious within trade unions, and needs to be extended to more comprehensive units.

(c) Business freedom is identical with personal freedom. This is implied more often than stated; and the foregoing discussion indicates why it is not true.

(d) Free choice of private buyers is always a truer guide to what is wanted or needed than is a governmental decision. Demonstrably false in many cases, despite the perversions to which governmental decisions are subject.

(e) Private enterprise is subject to impersonal economic law, which works correct results. Answer: under present conditions results are largely indeterminate and far from correct. Business has a margin of discretion as to prices; wages are set, not so much by economic law as by power politics and diplomacy, with mass coercion in reserve in an increasing share of cases.

2. REASONS PARTLY TRUE

(a) Private enterprise is more efficient. True in part, as to ends that are well represented by market demand, not as to others. The efficiency is often misdirected; and unemployment and restrictions on output represent major failures.

(b) Private enterprise is more progressive and freer from bureaucratic tyranny, stagnation, and red tape. True only as a matter of degree, and of diminishing degree; but the difference is still of great importance.

(c) Private enterprise rewards talent and capable service. Answer: Sometimes it rewards talent too liberally, by socially valid standards, and sometimes it rewards talent that is misdirected.

3. REASONS OF GREATER VALIDITY

(a) It is wanted, not only by business interests and agriculture, but prevailingly (in this country) by organized la-

bor. Why? Perhaps because organized labor feels it is better
able to maintain its power and freedom, and can make
business serve its interests better, than it could under collectivism. This is valid, in that we need free and strong
unions as part of a balanced social structure; but it is obviously subject to serious abuse. Dictation over society as a
whole by monopolistic special interests is an evil, whether
they be the interests of capital or of labor.

(b) Finally, private enterprise as it now exists is an
evolving thing and affords a basis for further evolutionary
change of the most flexible sort available, with the most
nearly voluntary methods of adjustment of conflicting interests and changing rights. This seems the most cogent reason
for wanting it to continue. It represents an opportunity,
which private enterprise may or may not be able to live
up to.

Prevalent attitudes among average business men have,
rather naturally, a one-sided emphasis on this matter. They
want government to establish a "favorable climate" for
business, and construe this largely in terms of letting business alone to work out its own problems, in the sincere belief
that this will lead to a better record of performance. It may
be true that such a policy would produce quicker revival
from depressions than did the improvised "planning" of the
New Deal; and it may, through long-run investment programs, make a real contribution toward forestalling or preventing such fluctuations. But the idea that its performance
will be good enough to meet the tests of the coming generation—this is an act of faith.

An honorable exception should be made of the leaders
of the Committee for Economic Development. They recognize that a "favorable climate" includes some positive action
on the part of government, beyond the "let alone" policy;
and they are working, explicitly or implicitly, toward a fa-

vorable climate within business for the reception of such policies and adjustment to them. For this matter is two-sided;
the climate needs to be favorable on both sides of the fence;
and the success of governmental policies can be seriously affected by the business climate in which they are received.

What It Takes to Make Planned Demand Work

Planning has to be done in a setting of powerful organized groups, exerting political as well as economic pressures;
and more than likely to pervert it to the protection and promotion of particular interests, in ways calculated to defeat
any rational purposes of planning for the economy as a
whole. This area of problems includes matters on which
qualified students, observers, and participants differ widely
and persistently as to the effectiveness of particular kinds of
measures. The problems are technical. There are certain automatic mechanisms that can be set up—chiefly to mitigate
the cumulative effects of disturbances, and thus reduce the
amplitude of business cycles. But for really substantial results, and especially as an antidote for a chronic shortage of
employment, if it should materialize, it is necessary to rely
on measures, the extent and timing of which would need
to be skilfully managed by the executive arm of government.

It should be guided by standards set up by Congress; but
for effective action, these need to be flexible enough to leave
much-increased executive discretion in the carrying-out of
policy, as well as in initiating programs for congressional
action. Relations between the executive and Congress need
to be not only closer but more constructive. What is called
for is a considerable change in the *de facto* concept and operation of representative government in this country, not because we prefer a different concept on political grounds, but

because it is necessary if government is to be capable of doing the job that has to be done.

In addition, there will be need for as much willing private co-operation as possible. Here we seem to be in the area of things that cannot be guaranteed to work, but which can perhaps be made to work if most of those concerned enlist wholeheartedly in the effort. There is no point or realism in stipulating as a condition that all should co-operate in trying to make things work, since there are always many noncomplying individualists, and in addition there is a revolutionary minority whose moral attitude toward the existing order is that of war, in which everything is fair. This minority can be depended on to sabotage the effort to make things work by nonrevolutionary means, whenever it seems that sabotage can gain something for the cause of revolution. Attempts to make things work must reckon with this handicap. That revolutionary wing which owes allegiance to a foreign power was on our side during the war, when that power was our ally; but it will not be on our side under present international conditions. The rest of us must furnish enough good will to make up for this element of disunity.

I have said that a "favorable climate" is two-sided; government affording a favorable climate for private interests, and private interests a favorable climate for governmental policies. One way to ensure that this requirement will not be met is for each to set a standard of perfection—for the other: for government to be imbued with the idea that any and every imperfection it can find in business must be rectified by public action; and for business men to feel that, because some government policies appear to them mistaken, and some features of administration faulty, that absolves them from all obligation for constructive co-operation with the government in what it is trying to accomplish. Presumably each is bound to be more keenly aware of the other's imperfections than of his own, but he can make a virtue of being willing to concede something for the sake of the common interest in co-operation. The alternative consists of quarreling over the past; and we are still in a crisis in which, if we do too much of that, we shall lose the future.

For the present, the danger is the reverse of the one I have been considering: not unemployment but inflation.[4] We are planning, for some years ahead, to finance a foreign demand for our goods which will, at least for the immediate future, definitely aggravate the inflationary pressures we are already experiencing. Grasping policies as to profits and wages could make this worse; responsible policies could mitigate it. Since the success or failure of the Marshall Plan in enabling Western Europe to save its freedom may hang on a pretty close contest, any handicap to this program might be serious. Added inflation in this country, reducing the buying power of the dollars we send Europe, would be a handicap. If, as some apprehend, inflation should get out of hand, and then bring about a revulsion and heavy depression, it is possible that people would feel that they could not afford the cost of the Marshall Plan, and would let it lapse. This would be a world calamity. It will probably not happen—if we do have a depression, a continued Marshall Plan would be a good form of first aid to our own economy—but if depression got severe enough, the sheer fiscal burden might come to seem prohibitive. So it is doubly important that we should succeed in avoiding a really heavy depression within the next five years, and an uncontrolled inflation now. And this is as much a moral as an economic problem.

In the case of inflation, it is partly a matter of restraint in the use of power to raise costs and prices, and partly one of willingness to submit to necessary governmental controls. One of the strong arguments against the use of direct price controls where the situation really calls for them is the argu-

[4] Though this was published in 1949, its relevance in 1956 is altered rather than destroyed.

ment that they would lead to black-market operations and injustice between those who comply and those who do not. Granting that some black-market operations are inevitable, the question whether controls can work well enough to be better than no controls, or whether they will be crippled by too much noncompliance, is clearly a moral question, of the relative prevalence of such moral standards and loyalty as lead to compliance. During the war, allocations and price controls worked well enough to be vastly better than none. If they cannot do so now, it is partly a matter of the citizens' weariness in well-doing, partly a matter of failure to be convinced of the need—that this is a real continuance of the war emergency—and partly a matter of cynical and organized opposition by interested parties. In this and other problems of "planning," the necessary popular attitude hinges partly on clarifying the need for action and partly on willingness to act in the common interest when the need is clear. Without this combination of clarification and willingness, the prospect for survival of freedom is not good. With it, a free system has a fair chance to survive the critical postwar generation.

CHAPTER TWELVE

The Relation of Western Economic Thought to the World Struggle

Introduction: What Is Our Proper Contribution?

In Chapters 5–7 it was argued at some length that a "balanced" economic system can develop productive efficiency and place it at the service of the welfare of the people at large, while maintaining the essentials of a free and voluntary system. In Chapter 8 it was contended that some variety of "balanced" system, and not dogmatic *laissez faire*, is the

In this chapter use is made, with permission, of fragments (freely modified) from "Problems in the Study of Economic Growth" (mimeographed) National Bureau of Economic Research, 1949; and from discussion of papers on "Economic Thought and its Application and Methodology in the East," *American Economic Review Supplement*, Vol. XLVI (May, 1956), pp. 416–18. Other source material includes papers and discussions by H. B. Chenery, W. H. Nicholls, E. E. Hagen, W. Malenboum, W. E. Moore, B. F. Hoselitz, G. B. Baldwin, W. H. Knowles, and S. Rottenberg, in the same publication, Vol. XLV (May, 1955), pp. 40–79, 156–96. Also "Processes and Problems of Industrialization in Under-Developed Countries," United Nations, Department of Economic and Social Affairs, 1955.

pertinent answer to Communism in the struggle for the minds of the uncommitted areas of the world. Our duty to these areas, it was contended, includes developing the capacities of our own system in the form best adapted to our own conditions, furnishing material resources for the world struggle and also showing what a "balanced" system can do; but with no implication that our particular form of "balanced" system would be found best suited to countries whose conditions and cultures differ widely from ours.

This leaves our positive contribution bafflingly vague; and this vagueness is a handicap in a contest with an adversary whose goal is anything but vague. We urge democracy and a strong private sector of the economy on peoples, most of whom hardly possess the education that we regard as prerequisite to democracy, or the human resources, obvious and less obvious, that are necessary to a vigorous private enterprise. Aside from material and technical aid, can we offer nothing more positive in the realm of ideas? If we can—and I believe it is possible—it will not be in the shape of specific rules, and it will not be a one-way transaction. Rather, it must rest on a mutual desire to understand one another's problems and accomplishments. If such mutual understanding is really sought, it appears highly likely that it could reveal common elements of aims and attitudes, more basic than the admittedly wide differences; and that it would further reveal the real irreconcilable cleavage to lie between totalitarian autocracy and all systems dedicated to the welfare of the people, with freedom for them to pursue it as their understandings and capacities make possible. More simply, it is the cleavage that divides systems according as they do or do not value freedom and place people ahead of ideologies, or world conquest.

The most acute and difficult problems of the "underdeveloped countries" center in their efforts to transform their economic way of life and increase their productivity, in a planned and guided undertaking. They are definitely committed to this transformation, taking as their model the techniques of the industrially developed countries, but not necessarily their institutions for developing, utilizing, and harnessing these techniques. There are compelling reasons why they should not entrust as much of their industrial development to private enterprise as the West typically does; and within their sector of private business they may not be in a position to rely, as heavily as this country attempts to do, on the incentives and controls of a free competitive market.

To many Americans, it may appear self-evident that reliance on private business, with the help of which this country has made such a spectacular record in productivity and speed of growth, is the proper prescription for other countries aiming to use the same techniques. But this reckons without the necessary preconditions. The actual case is by no means so simple; the differences are far-reaching and profound, and the common elements need some identifying and defining. So long as there is in each country a sector of private enterprise, the economics of private enterprise constitutes an element common to all of the countries, within the scope that is allowed to it, and with emphasis on the dynamics of growth rather than on static equilibrium. But this scope is delimited in two ways: by the branches of production entrusted to it, and by the values, affected by these branches of production, which may be safeguarded by welfare regulations or in other ways not dependent on a "free market." This leads to something more basic than the economic laws of the behavior of the private-enterprise sector: namely, the need to articulate this sector—to integrate it so far as possible—into the requirements of a healthy community; so that it may be serviceable to valid community ends, and not run wild to community detriment, as could so easily happen.

This integration is a goal which, with differences of

specification, the modern "balanced" Western economy and the underdeveloped countries have in common—if they can manage to realize it in the face of imperfect understanding and hostile propaganda. It is rooted in the common necessities of an enlightened concept of the community and of human welfare. But they work toward it from different starting points and from different directions, and may never reach an identical terminus. Nevertheless, the variant possible termini—so far as one may usefully speculate about them—differ far less than the routes by which they are approached, for reasons that will appear presently.

To illustrate this proposition by a strong case, we may shift for the moment to increased industrial output as the goal, regardless of the ends it serves. It is hardly thinkable that this country and other leaders in the industrial revolution could have carried out their trail-blazing developments of the nineteenth century without predominant reliance on private enterprise. And it is equally unthinkable that Russia should have made such rapid gains in industrial output as it has made in the past thirty-five years (mainly but not solely by way of catching up with existing techniques) if it had relied on private enterprise to the same extent that we did. We may inquire later whether the Russian situation required the kind of complete collectivization, including agriculture, that was actually pursued. Our examination of certain typical problems of underdeveloped countries will strongly suggest that an accelerated industrialization which, along the way, benefits the people at large, including the peasants, requires something intermediate in terms both of extent of collective operation and speed of industrial growth.

The countries we lump as "underdeveloped" are actually, of course, widely diverse. Some are underpopulated in relation to modern potentialities, some overpopulated. They range from primitive peoples to old and great civilizations. They extend over both hemispheres, and their economic systems range from modified private enterprise to an evolutionary, pragmatic type of near-socialism. I shall be speaking here mainly of Eastern and overpopulated countries.

Their problems are those involved in the dynamics of growth, but these problems are faced in conditions of peculiar difficulty, as compared with the Western countries in which modern techniques, and the institutions and attitudes that go with them, have developed indigenously. So far, their rates of growth have, frequently or typically, failed to equal those of the Western countries with which they are trying to catch up. The discrepancy, which has generated so much potentially explosive unrest, has in many cases not begun to diminish, or has increased. They want to move faster. Toward an understanding of this problem, it may be helpful to examine a few—a very few—of the more general features of economic growth as it presents itself under differing conditions. This is an area in which systematic Western thinking is in its early and tentative stages, though it is being ably and vigorously pushed.

Growth vs. Progress

It stands to reason that what is wanted is not mere quantitative growth, but growth of a kind that will be accepted as desirable, by the best standards available. Where the process carries with it changes in what people want, influencing the accepted standards themselves, it involves peculiarly subtle and difficult problems as to whether the changes in standards are beneficial or the opposite. Such changes are implicit in the transplanting of Western methods to Eastern countries; and they add complications to the essentially simple immediate aim of raising the material level of the impoverished masses, which is hardly a controversial matter.

This aim may, of course, be defeated by unrestricted growth of population. Modern medicine, reducing death rates, has moved ahead of the reduction of birth rates which naturally results from urban life, resulting in increased population pressure of a peculiar severity. Deliberate means of limiting birth rates face difficulties, including religious obstacles; but in varying degree the importance of birth control is accepted, and moves are being made toward the necessary means. Even from the standpoint of military power, a large population is an asset only if it is consistent with a sizable margin above the bare necessities of life, available for military uses, and with a will to use the surplus in this way. From this standpoint, the countries we are considering would hardly be strengthened by additional increases in population.

Progress implies increased real income per capita (or more accurately, per adult consuming unit), but there are deductions to be made before reckoning the residue of clear gain. In modern urban life we work and pay for things that are free goods in a more primitive and rural setting, or we pay high for things that come cheap under simpler conditions. People move to rural areas to escape urban congestion, and they bring urban congestion with them. They spend less time at work and more time moving back and forth between work place and residence. And community conditions in the city itself are not improved by this withdrawal and segregation. If there is a net increase of leisure time, it is an index of opportunity rather than of realized benefit; and a considerable fraction of it is bound to be misused, under the pressure of the commercialized agencies that minister to it. It may be impossible to weigh the benefits against the deteriorations, but some admixture of deteriorations is undeniable, by any conceivable standard that could be seriously employed.

We spend labor removing vitamins from foodstuffs, and more labor supplying the man-made deficiency. Doctors treat urban infections and the stomach ulcers that come from the strains of modern life. Physical suffering is reduced, diseases and childbirth are less dangerous—yet this is coming to be styled the "age of anxiety."

There are a variety of ways in which an economy can expand to the detriment of subsequent generations. It can mine its soil or exhaust nonreproducible resources in general. Or it can suffer erosion of its imponderable resources, including the basis of social and moral coherence, which is nowadays more in need of conscious conservation than it has ever been before, as a foundation for a social and economic system that will work without the coercions of unmoral tyranny. This is a problem that the uncommitted East and the West have in common, though in radically different forms. In the East, with its conflict between preindustrial and industrial cultures and the need for coexistence between them, the problem is far more difficult than in the West—or perhaps its difficulties are merely more clearly evident. In either case, it is a major part of the world-wide crisis of a free society.

In Toynbee's terms, we are facing one of those "challenges" which a civilization is either barely able to meet, or just not able. If a free society survives, it will be because, on pain of perishing, we have been driven, in fear and anguish, to make a major advance in the art and structure of civilized life. If we fail—and failure is an ever-present threat—there will presumably follow an age as dark as that which followed the downfall of Rome; though we might hope it would be shorter. Even if the race did not go back to stone axes, the new scientifically implemented barbarism would witness the destruction of centuries of slow, costly, and imperfect progress in freedom, truth, integrity, and humanity, after which the process would have to begin again. For avoiding this calamity, much will depend on whether the uncommitted peoples choose to conduct their economic modernization in ways that do not open the door to totalitarian tyranny.

Stages and Conditions of Growth: Tangible Products

In comparing Western and Eastern problems, we may start with a look at the actual course of growth in the West, compared with the conditions the East faces, first as to tangibles and then as to intangibles, and later look into the relevance of Western systematic economic thinking. Such a comparison reveals both similarities and notable differences. Perhaps the clearest similarity is that the growth of industry requires growth in the rest of the economy. Even in England, the exemplar of the "industrial revolution," the way was prepared by growth of trade and finance, and more immediately by an "agricultural revolution" which, while it created social problems, afforded surpluses, facilitating the industrial revolution which followed on its heels. Commerce grew from a matter of luxuries to a regional exchange of staple materials, and it also furnished initial sources of capital. Later, of course, industry became able to furnish capital resources for expansion out of its own earnings.

Another sector, always a part of the picture, is the "tertiary" sector, in Colin Clark's classification, including personal, professional, and governmental services. As industrialization matures, there may come a stage—as in this country—in which, while manufacturing continues to increase, this tertiary sector displaces it as the most notably expanding part of the economy. A displacement of domestic service by mechanized household equipment, which has taken place in this country, is far more than made up for by expansions of commercialized services and services rendered by government beyond its traditional basic functions.

This expansion of tertiary services means, among other things, that they are rendered to the many rather than to the few, as the many become able to afford them; and the methods involved change correspondingly.

Government has played a part in developing basic means of communication; and even in the late handicraft stage it fostered the transplanting of manufacturing techniques. More important, perhaps, was the way in which, in the more nearly spontaneous Western growth, the necessary conditions of demand and supply grew alongside one another. Supply of resources—labor, capital, enterprise, and techniques—had to be matched by demand for the products as growth proceeded. In the deliberately fostered and speeded-up process envisaged for the underdeveloped countries, there is much more chance for the parts to grow disproportionately. Investment for anticipated future demand must play a larger and more strategically essential part; and it is a more risky matter when undertaken in the early stages represented by the underdeveloped countries. This points to more publicly fostered investment, with more conscious planning. But if these countries install basic facilities suited to the goal they hope to reach, they may find they have built beyond demand, and have misapplied scarce and precious capital resources.

This brings us to one major difficulty; namely, that an impoverished agriculture does not afford mass demand for the products of modern manufacturing. Unless productivity increases, the rural sector cannot produce enough to feed the growing industrial and commercial cities without keeping the peasant undernourished. The first use such a peasant will make of any small increase in his income, if it is left to his choice, will be to eat better, and the cities will suffer. In order to meet their needs on a voluntary basis, the cities must not merely offer him manufactured products; he must have a large enough surplus to be willing to part with some portion of it in exchange. Thus increased rural productivity appears even more necessary to an underdeveloped and over-populated country than it was for the Western industrial revolution. This appears to be a basic dilemma, limiting the speed of industrial growth.

The Soviets faced this dilemma and met it by enforced collectivization of agriculture. As a means of increasing farm productivity, this was not successful enough to solve the dilemma by voluntary exchange. Moreover, industry was concentrating on military power, and offered the peasant little in the way of consumer products. Thus enforced collectivization was not so much a means of increasing productivity, as a means of forcing the peasant to part with more of his product than he would have done voluntarily, substituting the exactions of the state for those of his former landlord. This was a part of the method of securing the capital resources for rapid industrialization by enforced privation for the masses, for an entire generation. This model is surely one the uncommitted countries would not wish to imitate.

Stages and Conditions of Growth: Incentives, Loyalties, and Forms of Security

It is often said that industrialization of underdeveloped countries suffers from insufficient qualified labor and entrepreneurial talent. In the case of labor, the difficulty includes not only lack of the mechanical types of skills—training can remedy that—but also lack of ready response to wage incentives and acceptance of the attitudes that go with it. A frequent complaint is of an inelastic standard of living, such that increased rates of pay result in less work being done. Back of this lies the fact that the worker clings to his roots in the rural kinship-community from which he came, where his wife and family may remain, and to which he may return. He has not fully accepted the mores of urban industry as a substitute for his former status. In the prestige ratings of the rural kinship-society, industrial labor may hold low rank, or the ratings of factory productivity may upset the relative standings of the young man and his elders.

In the case of entrepreneurial talent, a frequent comment is that those who have the education and resources also have leisure-class standards, and that for those who do seek profits, quick gains in commerce or speculative activities tend to outbid the opportunities available in manufacturing. These last involve heavy investments, committed for a long term and subject to large risks, while the available market can offer no more than a slow and moderate return, which may not appear commensurate with the risks: the burdens of restrictive governmental measures borrowed from Western practice, plus exposure (in some cases) to the contingencies of Oriental arbitrariness, including possible confiscation of successful ventures. The recent United Nations report on this group of problems notes that these conditions lead some Eastern capitalists to prefer investment in more stable and developed countries.[1] These are clearly phases of conflict or coexistence between industrial requirements and preindustrial cultures.

This fact is even clearer when we look at changing forms of individual security and of the sense of community that underlies them. In the Western experience there was a long interval—too long—after the preindustrial forms of obligation and security had lost their power, and before safeguards suited to modern industry had developed. It was in this interregnum that the evils and abuses flourished which were the basis of the Marxian assault on "capitalism." Such an

[1] "Processes and Problems of Industrialization in Under-Developed Countries," United Nations, Department of Economic and Social Affairs, 1955, pp. 23–4.

interregnum the uncommitted countries cannot afford. They must develop industrial forms of community and security, and must articulate them somehow with surviving rural kinship-forms. They must find how to offer urban workers safeguards of security that will be adequate, but not prohibitively burdensome to the employer.

Meanwhile, the rural kinship-units have been weakened as a result of contacts with the world of markets. Products are sold at fluctuating world-market prices, while local handicrafts may be threatened with displacement by Western factory products, without waiting for the growth of domestic industries. Cottage industry may coexist with the factory, though handicapped by low productivity and likely to be unable to pay wages much above the level of the impoverished peasant.

In this contest of culture-patterns some observers foresee a fairly quick transition, in which the preindustrial pattern will give way to the pattern of the modern industrial era. On the other hand, the authors of the United Nations report lean toward the expectation of a rather prolonged period of coexistence, with all the stresses of adjustment which this implies. This appears the more probable view, when one considers all the changes involved in any quick displacement of preindustrial patterns. The masses must become ambitious for manufactured products; and to make this feasible, agricultural productivity must be raised substantially, and the gains must be protected against being wiped out by growth of population. In business enterprises, the drive for efficiency must lead to the giving of positions by the test of performance rather than by kinship, at least sufficiently to prevent nepotism from seriously impairing productive efficiency. Prestige-patterns must be adjusted; the *esprit* of industrial entrepreneurship as distinct from commercial or speculative entrepreneurship must somehow be built up. This means that capital and enterprise must learn to work for long-run gains

at modest rates, under competitive disciplines or some substitute. These are only a few of the far-reaching adaptations
that would have to take place.

The picture raises two questions. First, can all these
changes be made quickly? It seems doubtful. Second, if they
could be made quickly, would it be desirable? Or would it
be too great and sudden a shock to the traditional founda-
tions of loyalty, morals and social coherence? Is it not safer
to follow a more gradual course of evolutionary adaptation,
conserving much of the distinctive social mores of each community, rather than allowing them to be uprooted by what is,
after all, an alien pattern? Continuity of development, and a
sense of that continunity, are precious; and a rupture of it
carries grave dangers. All of which urges that the Western
pattern should not abruptly displace indigenous mores.

In the matter of the race between increasing population
and agricultural productivity, it appears that some of the
Eastern countries have succeeded in improving cultivation
enough to increase total yield faster than population has increased. This suggests two questions. First, how was it done?
It was done not by unadulterated *laissez faire* and not by
Soviet-type collectivized farming, but by methods involving
purposive leadership, stimulation, and guidance. Second,
does this improvement merely push back temporarily the
limit on per capita output of food, which must ultimately
be encountered if population goes on increasing? Here is
the crucial question: increasing how fast and for how long?
In such quantitative terms, we can hardly expect a definitive
answer at this time. But the conclusion is inescapable that
present rates of increase cannot go on without end: the logic
of geometric increase is as inexorable as it was in Malthus's
time, even at much slower rates than he contemplated.

Has the West an Exportable Economic Ideology?

Let us turn now from the lessons of experience to the more technical matters of systematic economic analysis and theory. It is at least as true here as in the more general cultural matters we have been examining, that when the East imports Western techniques and economic mechanisms, it imports also some version of the forms of economic analysis that go with them. And the resulting problem is: How importable are these intellectual structures? To what extent and with what modifications are they applicable to the different Eastern conditions that have just been suggested? They are inevitably simplified formulas. Their usefulness depends on their success in selecting crucial factors for interpretation. If they serve as effective interpreters of factors that are crucial under Western conditions, will they serve equally well in an Eastern setting?

The question is intriguingly complicated by the fact that the interpretation of modern industrial methods is offered in two kinds of ideological package, one bearing Communist labels and the other the labels associated with private business enterprise. And from the standpoint of planned and rapid industrialization, imitating or adapting existing techniques, the Communist package—that is, its propaganda version—possesses clearly discernible advantages, backed by the record of Russia's greatly increased industrial output. The record in fact is marred by unpalatable features, a few of which we have examined; and Eastern leaders appear to understand this well enough to prevent uncritical swallowing of Communist propaganda. But they may hope to put the planned techniques to better uses, and they may not all be fully aware of the extent to which the sacrificing of the present generation is necessary to the Russian-type speed of industrialization.

They may not be fully alert to the nature of Communist infiltration and the kind of colonialism it has to offer, camouflaged under the ostensible espousing of "national independence." Western business enterprise, on the other hand, is associated in the minds of these leaders and their peoples with the kinds of "colonialism" which various of these countries have experienced, and their resentment against it may be more vivid than their suspicion of what may lie beneath the camouflage of Communist propaganda. From the Western standpoint, these represent handicaps, but not necessarily insuperable ones.

Both competing ideologies stress material goods; and some Eastern philosophies are inhospitable to this material emphasis. However, this also does not appear to be an insuperable obstacle. The most extreme example is apparently the Hinayana form of Indian Buddhism, which holds that the remedy for a scarcity of means to satisfy wants is to reduce the wants—ideally to eliminate them, and with them the individual personality. But Professor Millikan found only one prominent Indian economist who took this anti-economic theory seriously enough to regard the need for food as largely a matter of habit. The prevalent concept of welfare among Indian economists did not seem to differ basically from Western concepts.[2]

If there is a remaining difference in working philosophies of value, it seems likely to stem from the Western attitude which accepts activities directed to the gratification of wants as positive values in themselves (if they are in harmony with man's nature). Starting with this attitude, a West-

[2] Max Millikan, "Economic Thought and Its Application and Methodology in India," *American Economic Review Supplement*, Vol. XLVI, No. 2, May, 1956, pp. 399, 402–3. J. K. Mehta, in a volume entitled "Advanced Economic Theory" (Delhi, 1948), has combined the philosophy of extinguishing wants with a normal Western utility-disutility economics, regarded as inevitable (and apparently in some sense serviceable) for the vast majority of mankind, who have not attained the highest spiritual level.

erner welcomes the idea that wants are insatiable and that for every want that is satisfied another takes its place in the borderland of conscious desire. He would—quite logically— reject the idea that this makes the whole process self-defeating, as it would be under a logic in which these efforts are all "disutilities." The extinction of unsatisfied desire is not his aim. Whether this Western activism will be fully assimilated in the East, along with other features of Western thinking, one can only speculate. A tempering of its more extreme Western manifestations might have some advantages.

Turning to analysis of behavior and its causes, one may conjecture that oversimplified formulas are more readily exportable than the understanding of surrounding conditions and necessary qualifications. This effect probably varies among importing countries; Japanese economists have been said to be more inclined than others to categorize economic ideas in terms of "schools." One American observer reports that the more conservative Japanese economists tend to lead an intellectual double life, keeping their classroom theory uncontaminated by their practical activities, while the doctrinaire Marxists show much less of this split personality.[3]

It is assuming a good deal to suppose that our Western theories, in the forms in which we have succeeded in expressing them, contain all the elements that are most essential as guides to the modernization of Eastern economies, even if this application is limited to the private business sectors of these economies. As to that, it seems that a large amount of humility is in order. Somebody—the exporter or the importer—needs to ask more searching questions than might readily occur to either one, not only as to the economic ideas, but as to the prerequisites for their successful operation— prerequisites of which we ourselves are likely to be less than

[3] Martin Bronfenbrenner, "The State of Japanese Economics," *American Economic Review Supplement*, Vol. XLVI (May, 1956), pp. 389–96.

half conscious. The theories are typically models of how the market mechanism would work under specified conditions as to consumer behavior, entrepreneur behavior, etc.; and the specified conditions do not probe deeply enough to explain the extent to which this behavior depends on the presence of a complex set of implementing institutions and pattern-setting institutions and, back of these, the whole body of social mores, all of which converge to make the market behave (approximately) in the ways the models depict, and in ways that are serviceable.

These things are so familiar to us that we tend to take them for granted and forget we are doing so. And this may do no great harm, so long as these preconditions of market behavior go on working in their regular fashion. But it is a different matter when Western market mechanisms are transplanted into civilizations whose preconditions are different. Things may not work as the models indicate; and it seems inherently likely that the departures will be larger than those we always have to allow for even in applying our own theories to our own conditions. I suspect that for successful transplanting there is need for a much more explicit understanding of these underlying preconditions than the formulated theories furnish. We do not succeed too well in explaining to other peoples the bases on which the serviceability of our system rests, largely because we have not formulated them adequately to ourselves. As Dean Courtney C. Brown has expressed it, we have not conceptualized these aspects of our system.[4]

We may leave some things out of our theoretical picture because they are too familiar, others because they are too new. In the latter case, our conscious understanding of our

[4] In a symposium including also articles by Dexter M. Keezer and Leo Cherne, *The Saturday Review*, January 21, 1956; also discussion, *Social Action*, April, 1956.

system has not kept up with the evolving character of the system itself.

To take a very obvious illustration, our formal theory, in most of its models, assumes competition, or at least absence of outright collusion, but it does not tell how this condition is to be maintained. I suspect we have no clear and certain knowledge of the answer for our own country—still less for the countries of the East. Here the first modern establishment in a new industry may have no natural competitors, and the mores of competition in such an industry may have little occasion to develop. In connection with the need for a sufficiently energized body of entrepreneurs willing to risk capital in industrial enterprises, a zeal for profits has been mentioned as one of the qualifications. But if the available entrepreneurs, native or foreign, set out to make the highest possible profit rates in the quickest and easiest way, under Eastern conditions this could too easily mean exorbitant profits and restriction of development.

We Americans are used to a type of industry which, despite imperfect competition, earns profits the hard and constructive way, plowing back earnings, increasing productivity, reducing costs and increasing volume, and diffusing the majority of the resulting gains, so that aggregate net profits are a modest fraction of the whole. We may forget that the conditions that produce this result may not exist in all countries; in fact, as already suggested, we may not know too well what these conditions are. Back of them, in addition to a competitive heritage, are the mores and ethics of corporate loyalty and efficiency, collective bargaining, and social security—each a slow achievement marked by many struggles and abuses. For underdeveloped economies, one observer has suggested the possible usefulness of something we have outgrown ourselves; namely, a paternalistic "welfare capitalism," including company stores and schools, company-sponsored co-operative banks, and even company unions where no other unions exist.[5]

To sum up, it is only natural that the methods devised by the underdeveloped countries for meeting their distinctive problems should lay more stress on nation-wide planning than is typical in the West, rely more on public development of basic facilities, and make up for the absence or uncertainty of the disciplines of competition by subjecting the private sectors of their economies to more direct controls, possibly intended to be temporary transitional measures. Their leaders and scholars are aware of Western economic theories, but find them of limited relevance for their purposes (as do we, of course, in different degree). Their most dynamic thinking consists of inductive study of conditions and a pragmatic search for ways of meeting them.

They have to reckon with Eastern scales of values and to conjecture what alterations in these scales of values will result from the impact of modernization. In the face of such tendencies to change, they must attempt to distinguish essential cultural and community values and preserve them, or at least maintain cultural continuity. Every one of these tasks involves unanswered questions. Needless to say they will not all be answered in the near future, but they should be asked earnestly by anyone carrying responsibility for decisions bearing on historical changes of such far-reaching import.

These countries are engaged in a task of evolutionary adaptation, aiming to direct the productiveness of modern techniques to improving the welfare of the people at large. They conceive this task in the light of democratic ideals and with a large place for voluntary effort. But, if the various essays in the present volume interpret the trend correctly, this is what the Western countries are also doing, with dif-

[5] G. B. Baldwin, *American Economic Review Supplement*, Vol. XLV, No. 2 (May, 1955), p. 187.

ferences of emphasis, of degree, and of specific choice of ways and means, dictated by the material with which they have to work. If the common features of this undertaking are sufficiently understood on both sides, there should be an increased two-sided sense of the kinship of our historical roles—something which at present leaves a good deal to be desired. This should lead, neither to attempted specific prescription on the one side, nor to undiscriminating imitation on the other, but to a readiness for borrowing and for discriminating adaptation wherever such a course seems serviceable. One might hope that the uncommitted countries would become less vulnerable to Communist infiltration. And in such a two-sided interchange, one might hope that the benefit would be mutual—that the West might learn some things to its advantage.

Epilogue

In that garden where Adam lost his primeval innocence there stood, we have been told, two forbidden trees: the tree of the knowledge of good and evil, and the tree of life. Adam ate of the first, and was driven from the garden lest he eat of the second. But between these two stood other trees, of which Adam was not told, and one of which has been found by some of his children.

For Adam taught his children, as he labored to till the soil, that the cure for the ills that come of knowledge is more knowledge. His children did not forget, and in any case they could not have turned back. Some of them came again to the entrance of the garden, where the angel barred the way. Though his flaming sword slew many, some made their way past. But they did not come to the tree of life.

Instead, after many hardships, they came to a great tree which had twin trunks, the branches of which interlaced, and the fruit of the two could not be distinguished. The name of the nearer trunk was the tree of knowledge how worlds are made, and the name of the farther trunk was the tree of knowledge how worlds are destroyed. And Adam's children ate; and they were seized with a great fear, beyond any fear that men had known, which left them no peace nor rest, but drove them on.

The road beyond lies through dark and dangerous chasms; and whether they will win through, it is not given to us to know. If they do, they may come to the tree which bears the knowledge how worlds may be made in which man may safely live. Only then—if their search succeeds thus far—may they be ready to reach out to the tree of life, which stands beyond.

Index

A NOTE ON THE TYPE

The text of this book was set on the Linotype in a face called TIMES ROMAN, *designed by* STANLEY MORISON *for* The Times (*London*), *and first introduced by that newspaper in 1932.*

Among typographers and designers of the twentieth century, Stanley Morison has been a strong forming influence, as typographical adviser to the English Monotype Corporation, as a director of two distinguished English publishing houses, and as a writer of sensibility, erudition, and keen practical sense.

In 1930 Morison wrote: "Type design moves at the pace of the most conservative reader. The good type-designer therefore realises that, for a new fount to be successful, it has to be so good that only very few recognize its novelty. If readers do not notice the consummate reticence and rare discipline of a new type, it is probably a good letter." It is now generally recognized that in the creation of Times Roman *Morison successfully met the qualifications of this theoretical doctrine.*

Composed, printed, and bound by THE PLIMPTON PRESS, *Norwood, Mass. Paper manufactured by* S. D. WARREN COMPANY, *Boston, Mass.*

This book may be kept
FOURTEEN DAYS
A fine of TWO CENTS will be charged
for each day the book is kept overtime.

Demco 291-B5